1ST BATAILLON FUSILIERS MARINS COMMANDO
N° 4 COMMANDO FRANCO - BRITANNIQUE

177 HOMMES LE 6 JUIN 1944 - Aux ordres du C^{dt} P. KIEFFER
SONT TOMBES

SUR LA PLAGE	B^d W.CHURCHILL	FACE AU CASINO
S/M Raymond DUMANOIR	Lieutenant Augustin HUBERT	C^{dt} Docteur Robert LION
Q/M Josephe LETANG	Commando Marcel LABAS	Commando Paul ROLLIN
Commando Raymond FLESCH		Commando Emile RENAULT
Commando Jean ROUSSEAU		Q/M Jean LEMOIGNE

TRENTE TROIS BLESSÉS AYANT ÉTÉ EVACUÉS
Le Bataillon Commando Francais perdit ce jour 1/4 de son effectif.
Leurs Camarades Britanniques de la 1ère Brigade N° 3-4-6 et 45 RM Commando
déplorèrent ce même jour des pertes aussi lourdes.

AVENUE DU 6 JUIN

IN MEMORIAM - CPL TED "HAM & JAM" TAPPENDEN

Near this spot Cpl Ted Tappenden of the Coup de Main Force,
6th Airborne Division, sent the radio message "Ham & Jam"
to signify the successful capture of the Bridges
in the early hours of 6th June 1944
Lest we forget.

Près de cet endroit, le Caporal Ted Tappenden, du groupe de la
6ème Division Aéroportée qui captura le pont, envoya dans les
premières heures du 6 juin 1944 le message radio "Ham & Jam"
qui signalait la réussite de l'opération
Nous n'oublierons pas

In Honour of the
Officers and Kingsmen
of The 5th Battalion
The King's (Liverpool) Regiment
who manned this Beach from
6th June 1944
Nec Aspera Terrent

À la mémoire des hommes
de la 6e Division Aéroportée
qui ont sacrifié leur vie pour la liberté.

*In memory of the men
of the 6th British Airborne Division
who sacrificed their lives
in the pursuit of freedom.*

PEGASUS BRIDGE

ROYAL ARTILLERY

THIS PLAQUE IS DEDICATED TO
THE MEN OF
3RD. RECONNAISSANCE REGIMENT
(8TH Bn. R.N.F.)
WHO PARTICIPATED IN THE LIBERATION
OF HERMANVILLE IN 1944

AVENUE MAJOR JOHN HOWARD

LES PIONNIERS
ALLIÉS
ONT MIS PIED
SUR CETTE PLAGE
LE 5 JUIN 1944
A 23 HEURES

"ON D DAY, JUNE 6TH 1944, ON THIS SECTOR OF "SWORD BEACH", AS THE SCOTS HAVE DONE FOR GENERATIONS, THE BRIGADIER LORD LOVAT, CHIEF OF THE 1ST SPECIAL SERVICE BRIGADE, ALSO A HIGHLANDS CHIEF, ORDERED HIS PERSONAL PIPER, BILL MILLIN, TO PIPE HIS COMMANDOS ASHORE.
ABOVE THE ROAR OF BATTLE CAME THE SKIRL OF LIBERATION WITH A PIPER LEADING THE WAY.
THEY BOTH ENTERED THE LEGEND."

"LE JOUR J, AU MATIN DU 6 JUIN 1944, SUR CE SECTEUR DE "SWORD BEACH", COMME LE FAISAIENT LES ECOSSAIS DEPUIS DES GENERATIONS, LE GENERAL DE BRIGADE LORD LOVAT, CHEF DE LA 1ST SPECIAL SERVICE BRIGADE, MAIS AUSSI CHEF DE CLAN DES HIGHLANDS, ORDONNA A SON "PIPER" PERSONNEL, BILL MILLIN, DE SONNER DE SA CORNEMUSE, TANDIS QUE SES COMMANDOS DEBARQUAIENT.
PAR-DESSUS LE TUMULTE DE LA BATAILLE, LE SON DE LA CORNEMUSE ANNONCA LA LIBERATION, LE "PIPER" OUVRANT LA VOIE.
CE JOUR-LA, ILS ENTRERENT TOUS DEUX DANS LA LEGENDE."

65 YEARS ON FROM D-DAY
In honour of the Normandy Veterans
6th June 2009.

D Day - The Bigger Picture

First Edition 2013
Published in the UK by Red Mist Books
ISBN 978-0955662256

Copyright © Red Mist Books   RedMistBooks@aol.com
All Right Reserved

No part of this book covered by the Copyrights hereon may be reproduced, stored in a database or retrieval system or copied in any manner whatsoever without written permission, except in the case of brief quotations embodied in articles or reviews. For information on this please contact the publishers.

Written by Lorie Coffey
Creative Director : Joanna Cardwell   www.studiojo.co.uk

British Library Cataloguing in Publication Data.
A catalogue record for this book is available from the British Library

Printed and Bound in the UK by Print on Demand - Worldwide

A registered charity dedicated to perpetuate the memory of those who fought to preserve freedom in 1944

Supported by the *New Forest Remembers: Untold Stories of WWII* project. A Heritage Lottery Funded project to record the archaeology, history and living memories of the New Forest during WWII. The project's Interactive Portal, an online archive, is available at www.newforestnpa.gov.uk/wwii *'just follow the Spitfire'*.

D DAY DIARY
THE BIGGER PICTURE

LORIE COFFEY AND THE PROJECT 70 TEAM:-

JOANNA CARDWELL

JAMIE CHESTNUTT

TOM COFFEY

MIKE CRUTCH

STEVE DARLING

BAZ FIRTH

STEVE SHAW

RICHARD SHILVOCK

MANNY TRAINOR

JON WHITWORTH

D Day Diary

The 6th June 1944 and the events leading up to it has been written about many times from many different points of view. The limited amounts of photographs available have been re-produced time and time again and the Normandy landings have been debated and analysed ad infinitum over the past 70 years. Incidentally, the French do not like D Day being referred to as "The Invasion" they had already been invaded…..they prefer the term "debarquement."

The reasons for putting this particular book together were primarily:
- To mark the 70th Anniversary of D Day
- To raise funds for the Normandy Campaign Memorial due to be erected at the National Arboretum.
- To produce a book with never seen before photos, many from private collections, and also previously unpublished accounts from the men and women that were there.
- And finally to produce a book in a slightly different manner to those that have been published over the years, a book that would give the "Bigger Picture" not just an isolated view beach by beach.

To this end, our D Day story is told in the form of a Diary building up from January 1944 to the 6th June 1944. From the conception and planning, training and build up, this account tracks events initially monthly, building up to weekly and daily until the 5th/6th June when we chart the landings virtually minute by minute. Many hours of research through military archives, personal and war diaries and documents have produced an exciting account of the Battle for Normandy. Frequently timings may differ as the reports were written after the event but we have done our best to keep the times as accurate as possible taking into consideration all the different factors. This is by no means an in depth account of Operation Overlord which can be found in many of the other publications available, however, it is specifically designed to give the "Bigger Picture".

The authors have made every effort to ensure that the owners of all photographs not in the public domain and copyright free have been contacted and permission given to re-produce them. If we have mistakenly attributed a photo or have made any errors please accept our apologies and contact us so we can correct any mistakes. We make no apologies however, for the quality of some of the photographs; they were taken at the time and have been stored for 70 years. A few have been cleaned up but overall they are as they were found.

Our appreciation and gratitude goes to everybody who have helped with this project, to the Normandy Veterans who have taken the time to talk to us about their experiences and to the families of those no longer with us for lending us their diaries, sending stories and photos and giving permission to re-produce them. To The Spirit of Normandy Trust and the Normandy Veterans Association who without their help this book could not have been produced. We must also thank the German Bundesarchive and the US National Archives for their help and co-operation in supplying free photos and information for this project.

The reader may disagree with some of the content, it may differ from some other accounts, but please remember when reading that this is how it was remembered by the individual concerned and their perspective at the time. Also there will be conflicting reports between German and Allied accounts for obvious reasons.

A special thank you must go to all our Subscribers, if it was not for your support, generosity and faith in the project it would not have got off the ground.

Finally, the biggest thanks of all go to every single man and woman involved 70 years ago, not only to the brave souls who parachuted in and stormed the beaches, but also to those who packed the parachutes, cooked the food, tended the wounded, said the prayers, manned the guns, stocked the ships and flew the aircraft. The thousands who behind the scenes planned and re planned the landings, the French Resistance, the Special Operations Executive (SOE), the Government, those working on the vital deception plan, to Churchill, Eisenhower, Montgomery, Bradley and Ramsay, this list is enormous. To all of you, we dedicate this book.

Please note that every single penny from the sale of this book will go to The Normandy Campaign Memorial.

Thank you.

Lorie Coffey and the Project 70 Team

CHAPTERS

1 WHY? 9

2 WHERE? 15

3 HOW? 43

4 WHEN? 85

5 WHAT? 227

6 GLOSSARY 250

Porposed Normandy Memorial, Dimensions - Length 900 cm. Centre height 183 cm. End height 61. Width 20 cm. Boulders (from Normandy) represent the five landing beaches Material : Granite.

National Memorial Arboretum, United Kingdom

Proceeds from the sale of this book will go to the Normandy Campaign Memorial

D Day Diary Subscribers, without which this project could not have happened.

Thank you

Luke Bahita
David Bolton
Paul Bottolph
Stephen Brookwell
Lee Carrie
Johnny Carberry-Rogers
Tom Coffey
Lorie Coffey
Caitlin Firth
Clive Ford
Gary Gray
Clint Gurry
Flight Sergeant Andrew L. Halliwell
Elizabeth Hargreaves
Steve Kirby
Geoff Lowe
New Forest Remembers Project
Jacqueline Marshall
Wing Commander Peter Marshall
Charlie Nisbet
Mrs Annette Paton
Rob Rowland-Rouse
Richard Shilvock
Geoff Slee
Paul Stapley
Clare Scherer
Commander Steven Shaw
Peter Vennick
Peter Vickery
Neil Vickery
Elliott Webber
Maj. (Retd) Diana Wilson, Chairman Spirit of Normandy Trust.
Anna and Matthew Wood
David and Margaret Wood
Derek and Karen Wood
Lorraine Wood
Simon Wright

WHY?

*But the past is just the same-
and War's a bloody game...
Have you forgotten yet?...
Look down, and swear by the slain of the
War that you'll never forget.*

Siegfried Sassoon

Introduction

To understand the success of D-Day, one must understand the failures of The Dieppe Raid of 19th August 1942 which highlighted the fact that the Allies could not rely on being able to penetrate the Atlantic Wall to capture a port on the North French coast. The Atlantic Wall being an extensive system of coastal fortifications built by Nazi Germany between 1942 and 1944 along the western coast of Europe as a defence against an anticipated Allied invasion of the mainland continent from Great Britain.

On March 23, 1942 Führer Directive Number 40 called for the official creation of the Atlantic Wall. After the St. Nazaire Raid on April 13, 1942, Adolf Hitler ordered naval and submarine bases to be heavily defended. Fortifications remained concentrated around ports until late in 1943 when defences were increased in other areas.

Fritz Todt created Organisation Todt in 1938 and from 1940 when he became Minister of Arms and munitions he devoted himself to the building of The Atlantic wall. Organisation Todt was a paramilitary group, closely associated to the Nazi Party. It employed volunteers as well as requested workers from occupied countries, in addition to political prisoners and deported people reduced to nothing more than slavery.

Todt died under mysterious circumstances in an aircraft crash on the 8th February 1942 and was replaced by Albert Speer.

Speer was an architect and became the Art Service Director of the Propaganda ministry before taking over from Todt as the Minister of Arms and munitions and then the position of Armament and War production Reich Ministry.

The building of the Atlantic Wall absorbed a huge amount of German resources. The construction used over 17 million cubic metres of concrete and 1.2 million tonnes of steel. In addition six million mines were laid on beaches in Northern France.

By early 1944, victory against Nazi Germany seemed as elusive as ever. In the East the Russians were defeating German troops but, throughout Europe, it was widely accepted that another front would need to sweep towards Berlin from the West if the war was to be won by the allies.

To set up the operation which aimed at opening a new front in Western Europe, the Allies create a new command composed of several combined operations. The combined operations bureau is led by General Frederick Morgan, the Chief of Staff to the Supreme Allied Commander also known as the "COSSAC".

The purposes of the COSSAC are as follows: to choose the exact place of the landing, to collect as much information as possible from the previous combined operations (operations in North Africa: "Sledghammer" and "Torch", and in Northern France : "Jubilee"), and to deal with the troops transport issues. Morgan and his officers began to draft the plans for D-Day.

As the ports were so well-defended, the next best option was to aim for poorly defended beaches – but which ones? It was decided that the best way was to ask for some help from the great British public. In 1942, the BBC issued an appeal for postcards and photographs of the coast of Europe from Norway to the Pyrenees. Millions were sent to the War Office and, together with the aid of the French Resistance and air reconnaissance, Morgan was able to pick his target beach landing spots. All the research pointed to one region – Normandy.

In July 1943, Morgan submitted his plan for the attack, code name - Operation OVERLORD. It was accepted a month later by the US and British Chiefs of Staff meeting in Quebec.

In September 1943 the code name NEPTUNE was chosen for the Naval operations of Overlord.

On the 6th December 1943 Roosevelt named General Dwight D Eisenhower as Supreme Commander for the Operation. Air Chief Marshall Sir Arthur Tedder was nominated as his deputy. He was aided by Britain's hero of the battle of El Alamein, General Sir Bernard Law Montgomery, who was given command of Overlord's allied ground troops. Admiral Sir Bertram Ramsay was appointed Naval Commander in Chief of the Allied Naval Expeditionary Force for the landings.

It was decided that a stronger initial punch was needed than the original plan and it was suggested that The Cotentin Peninsular was added together with the capture of Cherbourg as quickly as possible plus a further eastern sector of the coastline later named as Sword Beach.

A well disguised blockhouse at Batterie Azeville.

Situated on the east coast of the Cotentin Peninsula in Normandy, the German coastal battery - Stützpunkt 133 - had a 170 men garrison, and four blockhouses with 105 mm heavy guns. On 6 June 1944, it was unsuccessful in repulsing the Allied Forces landing on Utah Beach; indeed, the guns were at their maximal range.

Intelligence Gathering

The success of the operation would depend on accurate and detailed topographical information about the beaches and coastal towns along the French coast. Aerial photographs helped identify likely locations but, to obtain more detailed views, the Government appealed once again to the public for holiday photographs and postcards of unspecified coastal areas of France. However much more detailed information on the target beaches and their approaches was required. Local conditions such as the composition of the beaches, hidden underwater banks, German defensive obstacles, depth of water, tidal conditions etc. would all be taken into account in the planning of the project. The stakes were very high - bad intelligence could jeopardise the whole vast project.... there was no room for error.

On New Year's Eve 1943, under the leadership of 24 year old Major Logan Scott Bowden of the Royal Engineers, a unit set out in motor torpedo boats to recce the area around Luc-sur-Mer. They transferred to a hydrographical survey craft and moved closer to shore before Major Logan and Sgt Bruce Ogden-Smith swam to the beaches where they took samples of sand, mud, peat and gravel which they stored in labelled tubes. They were careful not to leave behind any evidence of their visit lest the Germans became alerted to their clandestine activities - much of their lateral movement along the beaches was below the tide mark! Their mission was a total success.

A month or so later, this time using a midget submarine for transport (towed part of the way), the area to the west of Port-en-Bessin and Vierville was visited and a few weeks later the OMAHA beach area.

Two scale models of the landing beaches were prepared using all the information gathered. One was held by the War Department in room 474 of the Great Metropole Hotel in London and a duplicate in the Prime Minister's room in the War Cabinet Offices - two of the most secret rooms in the country.

At Cairnryan, just north of Stranraer in south west Scotland, the information gathered about the beaches was used to construct a "life size" reproduction of the beaches. This would allow the planners to assess the effectiveness of the current landing techniques and the movement of men and machinery over the terrain.

Planning

Two main amphibious forces, an Eastern Naval Task Force (British) under Rear Admiral Sir Philip Vian, and a Western Task Force (American) under Rear Admiral Alan G Kirk USN, were formed.

The Eastern Task Force was to land the British Second Army under Lt General Sir Miles Dempsey on (from east to west) SWORD (UK), JUNO (Canadian) and GOLD (UK) beaches on a thirty mile front west of the River Orne.

The Western Task Force was to land the US First Army under Lt General Omar N Bradley on OMAHA and UTAH beaches, west of the British assault area, UTAH being at the base of the Cotentin peninsula. On the success of the latter would depend the early capture of Cherbourg.

The selection of D-Day was critical and depended on the correct mix of tidal conditions and sunrise. The army wanted a high water landing so as to reduce the depth of beach which the soldiers would have to cross.

The Navy, on the other hand, wanted a low water landing so that the assault craft could beach to seaward of the beach obstacles which Field Marshal Rommel had been so busily building. This would also help with the clearance of the obstacles, which would be dealt with before the tide rose.

Whilst the initial assault forces would approach in darkness (sunrise on 6th June was 0558) the landing would be in daylight in order to avoid pilot errors on the approach to the beaches and to aid fixing to give accurate counter-battery fire by bombarding ships. A further consideration for an early daylight landing was to ensure the army was in good order by nightfall. Airborne troops needed to be dropped by night with sufficient moon if possible for them to identify their targets.

The very sinister looking Batterie Todt.

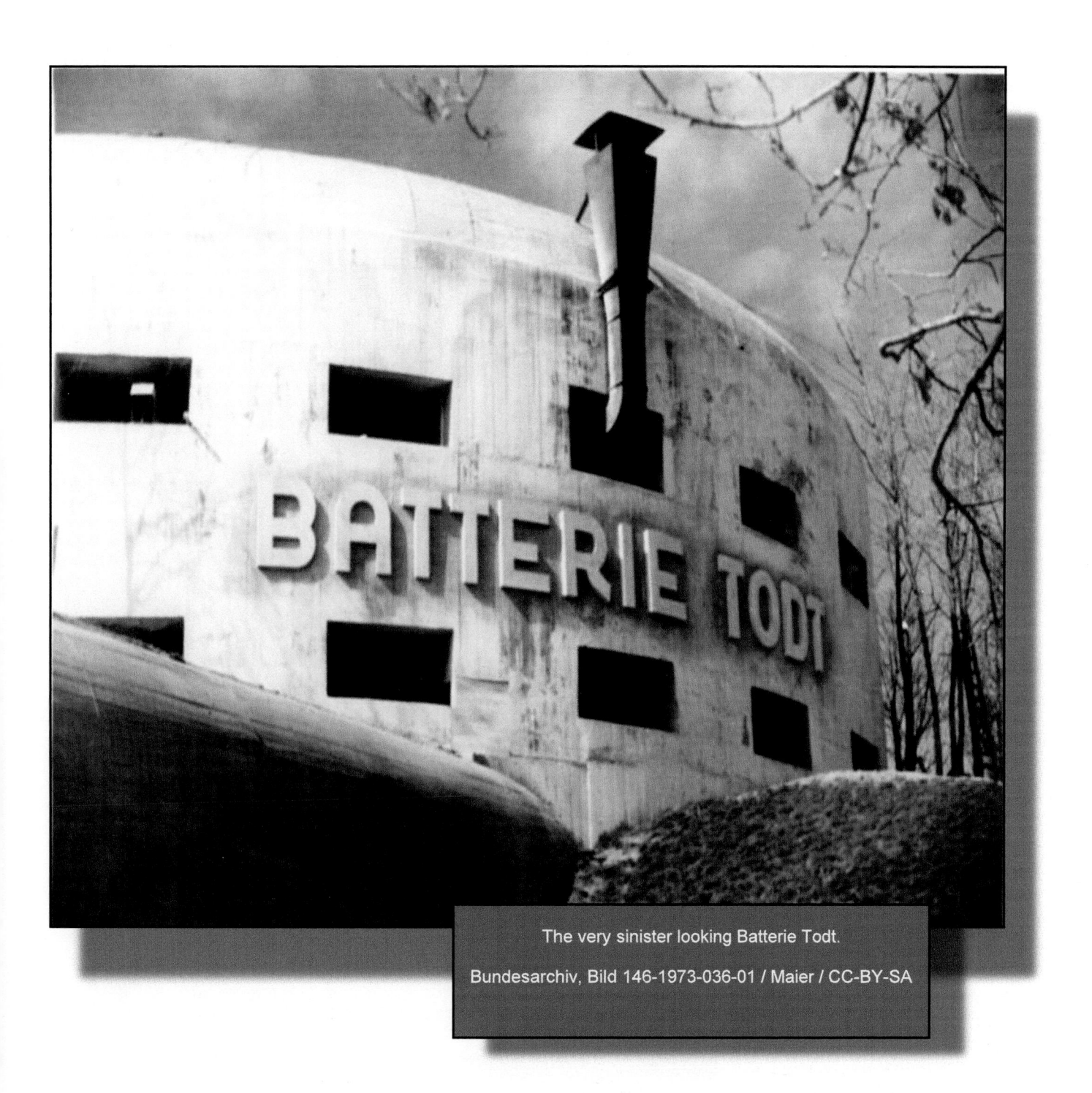

Bundesarchiv, Bild 146-1973-036-01 / Maier / CC-BY-SA

Churchill Memorial in London

Courtesy of www.London-GB.com

WHERE?
NORMANDY

Bankers, butchers, shop-keepers, painters, farmers—men, sway and sweat.
They will fight for the earth, for the increase of the slow, sure roots of peace, for the release of hidden forces.
They jibe at the eagle and his scorching sword.
One! Two!—One! Two!—clump the heavy boots.
The cry hurtles against the sky.
Each man pulls his belt a little tighter, and shifts his gun to make it lighter.
Each man thinks of a woman, and slaps out a curse at the eagle.

Amy Lowell - The Allies

UTAH Beach Memorial
June 2013

UTAH - Force "U"

Code name for the most western beach between Pouppeville and La Madeleine on the east coast of the Cherbourg peninsular. It was divided into zones named Tare Green, Uncle Red and Victor, was 3 miles long and assigned to the US 1st Army, 7th Corps. Of all the landings, casualties here were the lightest - out of 23,000 troops, only 197 men were killed or wounded. More men died (over 700) in Operation Tiger at Slapton Sands in Devon, than died on Utah beach on the 6th June.

Objective: To gain a beachhead, leading in time to the capture of the Cotentin Peninsula and of the port of Cherbourg. The Germans had flooded the area behind the beach. The US advance inland was only possible along a limited number of causeways.

Force "U", Rear Admiral D. P. Moon, USN, had perhaps the most difficult task of all the assault forces as regards its organisation and passage. Not only due to their being a lack of a large port in the West Country necessitating the use of nine different loading ports, but also as Force U was the last force to be formed owing to the change from the original plan that did not included the Cherbourg (Cotentin) Peninsular.

The craft assigned were the last to arrive in England and in many cases they had little if any training. Most of the 12 convoys in which 865 ships were organised contained three of four sections which sailed from different ports and had to rendezvous at sea at a predetermined point. In addition the escorts also had to sail from different ports to the convoys plus the embarkation ports were a further distance from UTAH beach than those of the other assault beaches which resulted in troops being at sea longer entailing greater fatigue.

Cotentin peninsula was in the defence zone of the VIIth German Army. This defence was affiliated to the 709th/243rd static divisions and 91st Luftlanddivision.

Operation Neptune - Organisation of Assault Forces - Utah

Assault Group	Headquarters	Assault Troops	Beach	Remarks
Force "U" (UTAH Beach)				
	USS BAYFIELD		Rear-Admiral D.P.Moon U.S.N. Maj. Gen Collins (VII Corps)	
Green	*L.C.H. 530* Commander A.L.Warburton, U.S.N. (S.O.A.G).	1st Bn. 8th Infy	"Tare" Green	
	L.C.I. (L) 321 Commander J.S. Bresman U.S.C.G (Dep S.O.A.G)			Initial landings by 1 Infantry Battalion on each beach at H + 75 mins, H + 210 mins, H + 240 mins, H + 250 mins leaving 2 Battalions "on call".
Red	*L.C.H. 10* Commander E.W. Wilson U.S.N.R (S.O.A.G)	2nd Bn. 8th Infy.	"Uncle" Red	
	L.C.I. (L) 217 Lt-Com R.G. Newbegin U.S.N.R. (Dep S.O.A.G.)			
	Objective: To gain a beachhead, leading in time to the capture of the Cotentin Peninsula and of the port of Cherbourg.			

Utah Beach, depicting the depth of the beach to be crossed at low tide by invading troops

June 2013

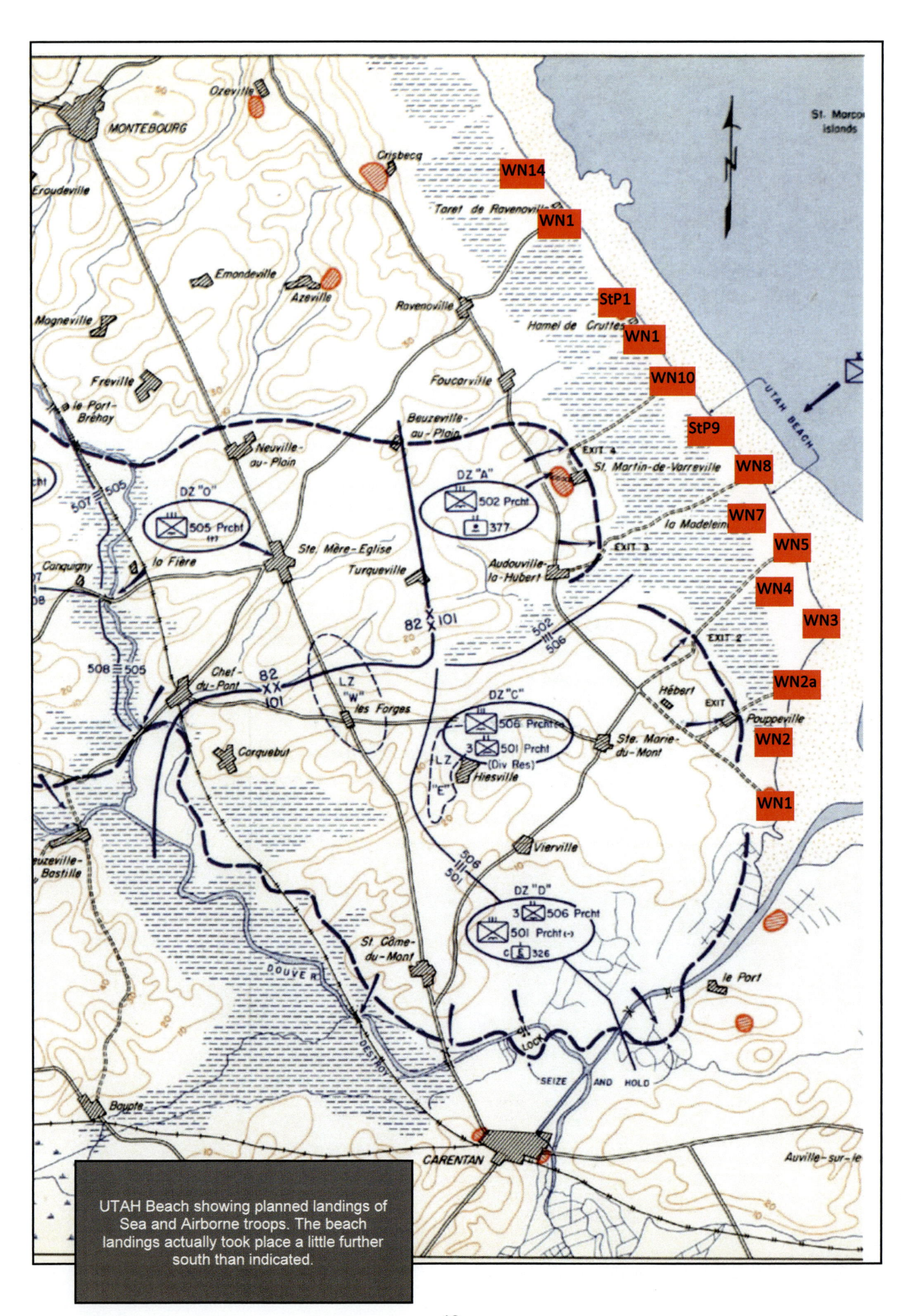

UTAH Beach showing planned landings of Sea and Airborne troops. The beach landings actually took place a little further south than indicated.

Utah Beach Strong points and where possible who attacked them and when they fell.

Strong point	Location	Major Weapons	Defended by	Assaulted by	Fell
WN1 (WN100)	Le Grand Vey	2 x 50mm canon (Pits), 1 x 75mm FK235 b (H612), Panzerstellung R35, 1 50mm mortar	2/IR199 Lt Rohweder.	2/8th Infantry	6th June
WN2a (WN101)	Pouppeville	2 x 50mm canon	2/IR199	2/8th Infantry	6th June About Midday
WN3 (WN102)	Beau Guillot	1 x 50mm, 1 x 47mm	2/IR199, Lt Ritter.	2/8th Infantry	6th June
WN4 (WN103)	Les Dunes	In build, not complete.	2/IR919	Combat Team 8	6th June 9.00 am
WN5 (WN104)	La Madeline	3 x 50mm canon (1x H667)(2xVf600), 1 x75mm FK38 (H612), 1 x panzerstellung, 1 x 50mm mortar, 3 machine guns, 3 ammunition bunkers,	2/IR919 Lt Jahnke	Naval and Air Bombardment-1/8th Infantry, B, C, E and F Coy's plus A and B Coy's 70th Tank Battalion.	Surrendered early morning- around 0700 6th June.
WN6 (WN105)	Hameau du Nord	Command Post,	3/IR919 Lt Matz		6th June About Midday
WN7	La Madeline	Company Command Post	2/IR919	1/8th Infantry	Mid Morning
WN8 (WN106)	Batterie de Quineville	1 x 77mm canon (H612), 2 x 50mm, 1 x 47mm PAK, 1 x 50mm mortar	3/IR919	3/22nd Infantry	6th June
Stp9	Les Dunes de Varreville	2 x 88mm canon Pak (H677), 5 x 37mm KwK 144 (f), 1 x 50mm mortar, 4 machine gun posts,	3/IR919	3/22nd Infantry	6th June
WN10	North of Les Dunes de Varreville	1 x 88mm Pak 43/41 (H677), 1 x 47mm Pak, 3 x 37mm KwK 144 (f), 2 Mortars, 12 Flame throwers, 10 Machine gun posts.	4/IR1919	3/22nd Infantry	D+2
WN11	North of Hamel Cruttes	1 x 50mm KWK L/42, 2 x 37mm KWK (f), 1 mortar, 5 machine gun posts.	4/IR1919	3/22nd Infantry	D+2
WN11a	Utah,	Command post of the 4th Company of the 919th Infantry Regiment.	4/IR1919	3/22nd Infantry	D+2
Stp 12	Chalet Ravenoville	1 x 88mm gun (H612), 1 x 50mm gun, 4 x 37mm, 2 machine gun posts	4/IR1919		Surrendered 7th June

Les Braves
Omaha Beach Memorial
June 2013

OMAHA – Force "O"

Code name for the beach between Sainte-Honorine-des-Pertes and Vierville-sur-Mer, 6 miles long (the largest of all the beaches) and selected as it offered the only break in the 100 foot cliffs. The beach gradient was very gradual. The difference between low and high tide made about 500 yards of dry land.

Objective: The only breaks in the 100-foot high cliffs running between UTAH and GOLD Beaches were at OMAHA Beach. The landings at OMAHA were therefore vital to connect the US troops at UTAH Beach with the British and Canadian beaches to the east.

Taking OMAHA was the responsibility of US 1st Army, 5th Corps, with sea transport provided by the US Navy and elements of the Royal Navy. The 1st Infantry assault experienced the worst ordeal of the D-Day operation; they met heavy resistance from German Troops and were pinned down on the beach for hours
Divided into Charlie, Dog, Easy and Fox zones and where necessary sub divided down further into green, white and red sectors. The beach had strong German defences. The German troops stationed there were in greater numbers, and of higher quality, than the Allies had believed.

The American Assault and Follow up Force convoys were constructed and ordered to fit in with the tides. The convoys, normally larger than the British, was determined largely by the tactical plan, with the underlying idea of not exposing Landing Craft types which were valuable to the build up until it was assured that they could be expeditiously and safely unloaded. E.g. only 15 (Landing Ship Tanks) LST's were permitted to arrive off the US beaches on the first tide. Owing to the variety of ships and craft, and the complex movements involved, the assault convoys were limited to two categories in accordance with speed capabilities.

12 kts – fire support ships, transporters and LCI (L)
5 kts – fire support craft, LST, Landing Craft Tank, (LCT) and Landing Craft Mechanised (LCM) needed for the assault which could not be lifted.

LST's were not put in a separate category as nearly all were engaged in towing rhino ferries and causeway sections during the assault phase that would be needed to create the necessary artificial harbours on the Normandy coast.

Operation Neptune - Organisation of Assault Forces - Omaha

Assault Group	Headquarters	Assault Troops	Beach	Remarks
Force "O" Omaha Beach				
	U.S.S. Ancon	Rear-Admiral J.L. Hall, U.S.N.		
		Maj. Gen. Huebner, U.S.A (1st Div)		
		Col. L.N Tindal, U.S.A. (9th Air Force and 9th Tactical Air Force)		
O1	US Transport Samuel Chase	116th R.C.T.	"Fox"	
	Capt. Fritzsche, U.S.C.G *	(Regimental Combat Team)	Green	
	(S.O.A.G.O.1) (Senior Officer Assault Group Omaha)		"Easy"	
	L.C.I. (L) 87		Red	
	Capt Imlay, U.S.C.G.			
	(Dep. S.O.A.G)			
O2	US Transport Charles Carroll	115th, 116th RCT	"Easy"	* On account of their relative seniority, the transport division Commanders were placed in command of the assault groups, with landing craft officers as their deputies. Rear-Admiral Hall subsequently remarked that this was undesirable because the transports completed their part in the operation at a comparatively early stage ands left the assault area taking with them the Assault Group Commanders while the Deputy Assault Group Commanders remained throughout the assault, and the first three weeks of the build up phase.
	Capt. Bailey, U.S.N*		Green	
	(S.O.A.G.O2)		"Dog"	
	L.C.I. (L) 86		Red	
	Capt. Wright , U.S.N.		White	
	(Dep. S.O.A.G)			
O3	US Transport Anne Arundel	18th R.C.T.	"Fox"	
	Capt. Schulten, U.S.N. *		Green	
	(S.O.A.G.O3)		"Easy"	
	L.C.I. (L) 492		Red	
	Commander Unger, U.S.C.G.			
	(Dep. S.O.A.G)			
O4	H.M.S. Prince Charles	2nd Ranger Bn.	"Charlie"	
	Commander Dennis, R.N.		Pointe du Hoc	

Omaha Beach today, with the tide out it gives some idea of the vast expanse of beach that needed to be crossed whilst under fire. June 2013

OMAHA

CHARLIE | DOG GREEN | DOG WHITE | DOG RED | EASY GREEN

OMAHA

FIRST WAVE LANDINGS - INFANTRY

.... Planned landings

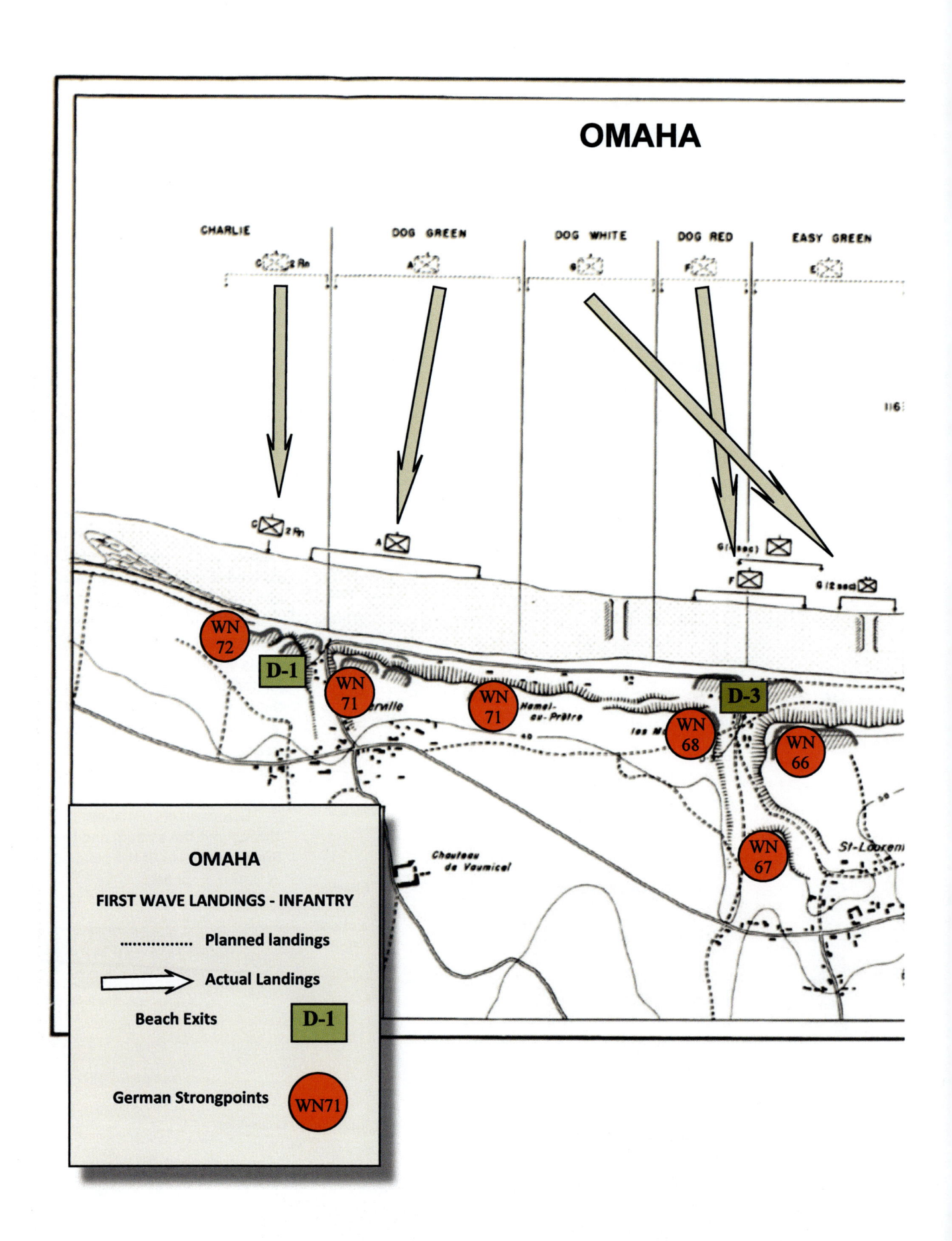

→ Actual Landings

Beach Exits — D-1

German Strongpoints — WN71

22

MAP No. V

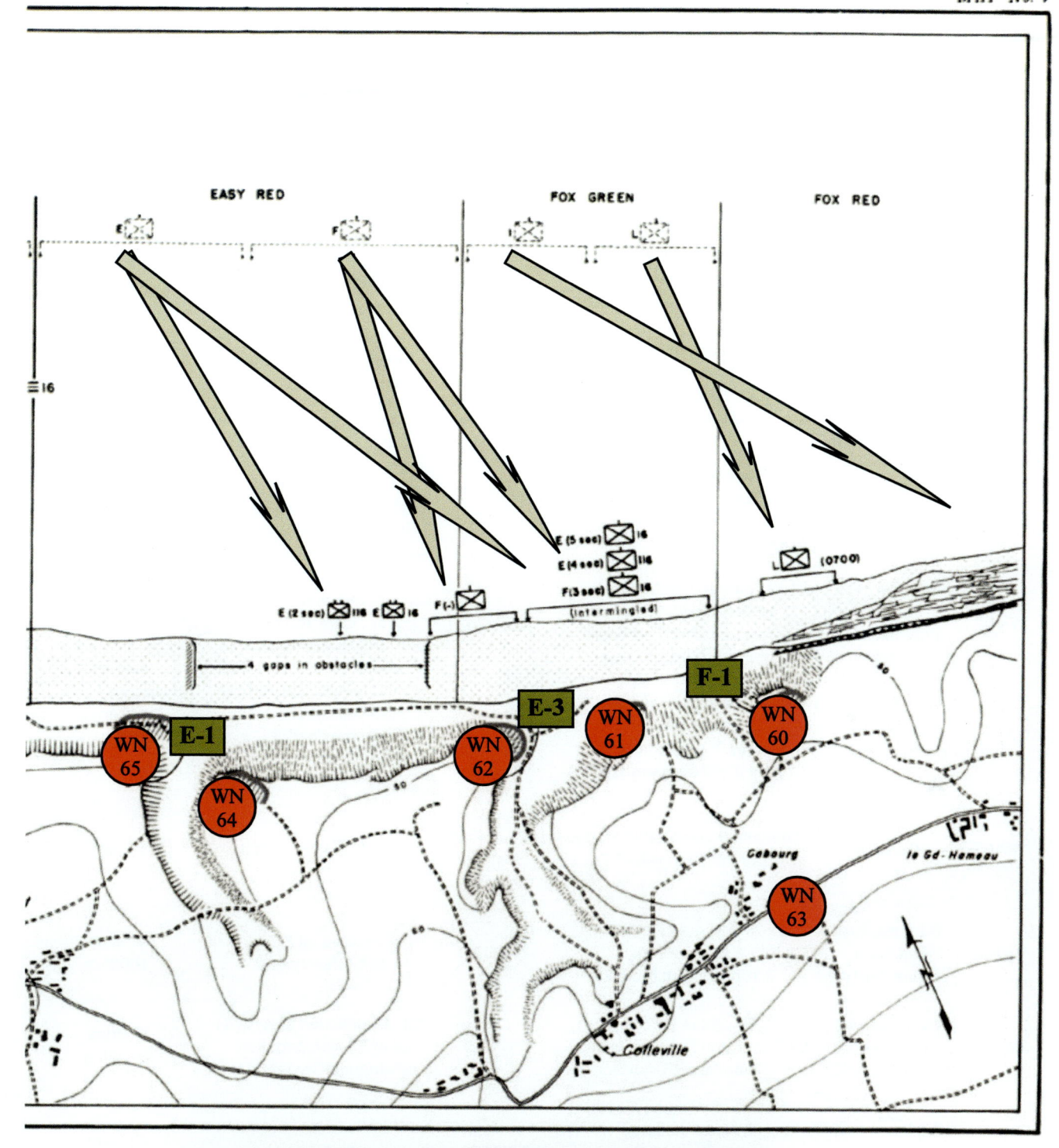

OMAHA - showing the various beaches with planned and actual landings, plus beach exits and approximate positions of German Strongpoints.

Omaha Beach, main Strongpoints.

Strong point	Location	Major Weapons	Defended by	Assaulted by	Fell
WN59	Saint-Honorine-des-Pertes	Observation Post The Strongpoint that served as Major Pluskat (The Longest Day) observation post. In the film he is shown at Longues sur mér battery - he was never there.	1/GR352	Surrendered	D+1
WN60	F-1 Draw * Fox Red, Colleville-sur-Mer	2 x 75m, 3 tobruks with mortars, 1 mortar position, 1 20mm Flak, flamethrowers.	1/GR726	L Company, 16th Infantry	6th June 0900hrs
WN61	E-3 Draw, Fox Green, Colleville-sur-Mer	1 x 88mm gun in H677, 2 x 50mm in VF600, 1 x Panzerstellung, 2 x Tobruks with machine guns, flamethrowers	1/GR726	Taken out by M4A1 tank from B Sqdn 741st Tank battalion, Staff Sgt Sheppard	6th June 0710hrs
WN62	E-3 draw, Fox Green, Colleville-sur-Mer	Two 75 mm cannon (FK235b) housed in H669 casemates 2 x 50mm guns, MG34 and Polish 7.92 machine guns as cover. 2 Tobruks with Motars, 1 artillery observation post (bringing in 352nd artillery-105mm) and flamethrowers. This the largest strongpoint on Omaha and caused the Americans the most problems on the day. It took a huge effort to put it out of commission.	1/GR726,	Between 07:30 and 08:30 WN-62 and the adjacent positions were assaulted by elements of G/16 and E/16 . 16th RCT of the 1st Infantry Division together with E/116 (E Coy. 116th RCT) of the 29th Infantry Division, who landed at 06:29. Later a 25 minute bombardment from USS Arkansas and tanks from the 741st Tank Battalion,	6th June Resistance subsided by mid-late morning, the last MG position was put out of action in the early afternoon (circa 14.30) and abandoned soon after.
WN63	Cabourg	Command Bunker/Radio Station for WN59 to WN63	HQ 3/GR726, Lt Bauch and Major Lohmann.	26th Infantry Regt	6th June
WN64	E-1 draw, Easy Red, Saint-Laurent-sur-Mer	1 x 76.2 Russian Field Gun, 1 x 20mm Flak, 2 Tobruks with motars	7/GR726	Captured by E Coy, 16th Infantry Regt	6th June 1000hrs
WN65	E-1 Draw, Easy Red, Saint-Laurent-sur-Mer	2 x 50mm (H667), 1 x 75mm gun (wooden beams), 2 tobruks with mortars	8/GR726	Put out of action by a AA HT of 467th AAA Battalion, commanded by Sgt Haas.	6th June 10.30hrs
WN66	D-3 Draw, Easy Green, Saint-Laurent-sur-Mer	1 x 50mm, AT gun (VF600), 2 Panzerstellung, 2 heavy mortars in concrete emplacements, 1 double embrasure pillbox	8/GR726	USS Carmick	6th June 0915hrs
WN67	Easy Green, Saint-Laurent-sur-Mer	23 to 40 x 320mm Rocket launcher position - Nebelwerfer	Nebel Abt 84		6th June 0915hrs
WN68	D-3 draw, Dog Red, Saint-Laurent-sur-Mer	1 x 50mm PAK (VF600) , 1 x 47 mm AT gun (open pit), 2 Panzerstellung, 1 double embrasure pillbox	9/GR726	743rd Tank Battalion	6th June 0915hrs

Strong point	Location	Major Weapons	Defended by	Assaulted by	Fell
WN69	Saint-Laurent-sur-Mer, D-3 Draw	1 x 20mm Flak, machine gun positions	9/GR726	Abandoned	7th June
WN70	D1/D3 draw, Vierville-sur-mer	1 x 80mm FK17(t) (H612), 75mm Field Gun in (pit) 1 x 75mm gun, 1 x 75mm in pillbox, 1 x 20mm Flak, 4 tobruks with Machine Guns, 2 mortars in concrete emplacements	10/GR726	116th Infantry	6th June Abandoned during the day.
WN71	D-1 Draw, Dog Green, Vierville-sur-mer	1 x observation post, 1 tobruk with Machine Gun, 1 motar in concrete emplacement, 1 double embrasure pillbox, machine gun positions. Situated on the Bluff to the west of Omaha Beach this position complemented the Beach Defence offered by WN72.	11/GR726	WN71 and WN72 were brought under bombardment by the Navy (Inc USS Texas) around mid day, white flags were seen and dazed defenders exited some of the emplacements. The concrete anti tank wall was blown and exit D1 was open at 14.00hrs. Elements of 116th RCT, 2 Rangers and Engineers of 121st the road to Vierville was finally clear around 1800hrs.	6th June 1400hrs
WN72	Dog Green sector, D-1 Draw, Vierville-sur-mer	1 x 88mm PAK (H667), 1 x 75mm Pak 97/38, 1 x 50mm Pak in double embrasure pillbox, Machine gun positions, 1 tobruk with machine gun, I double embrasure pillbox.	11/GR726	Surrendered	6th June 1300hrs
WN73	D-1 draw. Dog Green Vierville-sur-mer	1 x 75mm FK231, 3 tobruks with mortars, Machine Gun positions, 1 observation post	11/GR726	116th Infantry. USS McCook	6th June Approx 0845
WN74	Pointe-de-Purcee	2 x 75mm guns	9/GR726	B and C Company, 116th Infantry	6th June late afternoon
WN75	STP 75 Pointe du Hoc	6 x 155 mm type K418 guns, 2 x 20 mm Flak 30 guns, various machine gun positions. The guns had been withdrawn into an apple orchard south of the Grandcamp-Vierville road and hidden-due to the heavy allied bombing of the position.	125 men from 726 IR and 85 from 1260th Coastal Artillery Regt.	2nd Ranger Battalion, Colonel Rudder, D,E and F companies	Stars and Stripes hoisted at 1130 on the 8th June.

Arromanches - Gold beach
August 2013

GOLD – Force "G"

GOLD, Code name for beach from Longues-sur-Mer to La Riviere, 5 miles long and included Arromanches where one of the two the *Mulberry Harbours were established. British 2nd Army, 30th Corps landed here and by nightfall, 25,000 troops had landed and pushed the Germans six miles inland. There were just 400 British casualties.

Divided into How, Item, Jig and King zones. Objectives: The troops aimed to capture Bayeux and the Caen-Bayeux road (enabling the Allies to use the east-west road communications), and to join up with the American troops at OMAHA Beach.

GOLD Beach lay in the area assigned to the 50th (Northumbrian) Infantry Division commanded by Major General Douglas Alexander Graham, and the 8th Armoured Brigade, part of Lieutenant General Miles Dempsey's British 2nd Army. GOLD Beach had three main assault sectors – these were designated (from west to east): Item, Jig (split into sections Green and Red), and King (also in two sections named Green and Red). A fourth, named How, was not used as a landing area. The beach was to be assaulted by the 50th Division between Le Hamel and Ver sur Mer. Attached to them were elements of 79th (Armoured) Division. The 231st Infantry Brigade would come ashore on Jig Sector at Le Hamel/Asnelles and the 69th Brigade at King Sector in front of Ver sur Mer. No. 47 (Royal Marine) Commando, attached to the 50th Division for the landing, was assigned to Item sector.

The primary D–Day objectives for the 50th Infantry Division were to establish a beachhead between Arromanches (crucial for the deployment of the artificial Mulberry harbour) and Ver-sur-Mer, then head south towards *Route Nationale* 13 (RN 13), reaching Bayeux and cutting the road to Caen.

The 231st and 69th Infantry Brigades were to be first ashore and establish a beachhead. The follow-up 56th and 151st Infantry Brigades would aim to push south-west towards RN 13 supported by the tanks of the 8th Armoured Brigade.

To the west, 47 Commando's mission was to capture Port-en-Bessin and link-up with American forces landing on OMAHA Beach. 50th Division was also tasked with meeting the Canadian troops coming ashore on JUNO Beach.

---

* (Artificial harbours, see page 48)

Operation Neptune - Organisation of Assault Forces - Gold

Assault Group	Headquarters	Assault Troops	Beach
Force "G" (Gold Beach)			
	H.M.S. Bulolo (Ex Australian Passenger Ship converted to Merchant Cruiser) HQ for Force "G"	Commodore Douglas-Pennant	
		Maj. Gen Graham (50th (N) Div)	
		Gp. Capt. Simonds	
G1	H.M.S. Nith (River Class Frigate) G1 HQ Ship	231st Bde	"Jig" Green
	Capt. J.W. Farquhar, R.N. (S.O.A.G.G. 1).		
	Brig. Sir A. Stanier, Bt (231st Infy. Bde)		
G2	H.M.S. Kingsmill (Destroyer) G2 HQ Ship	69th Bde	"King Green"
	Capt. F.A. Balance, R.N. (S.O.A.G.G. 2).		
	Brig. F.V.C. Knox (69th Infy Bde)		
G3	"H.M.S. Albrighton (HUNT Class Destroyer) G3 Escort Ship	151st Bde	Reserve
	Capt. G.V.M. Dolphin, R.N. (S.O.A.G.G. 3).		
	Brig. R. H. Senior (151st Inf Bde.)		

Gold Beach August 2013 looking east from the top of the Cliffs at Arromanches.

August 2013

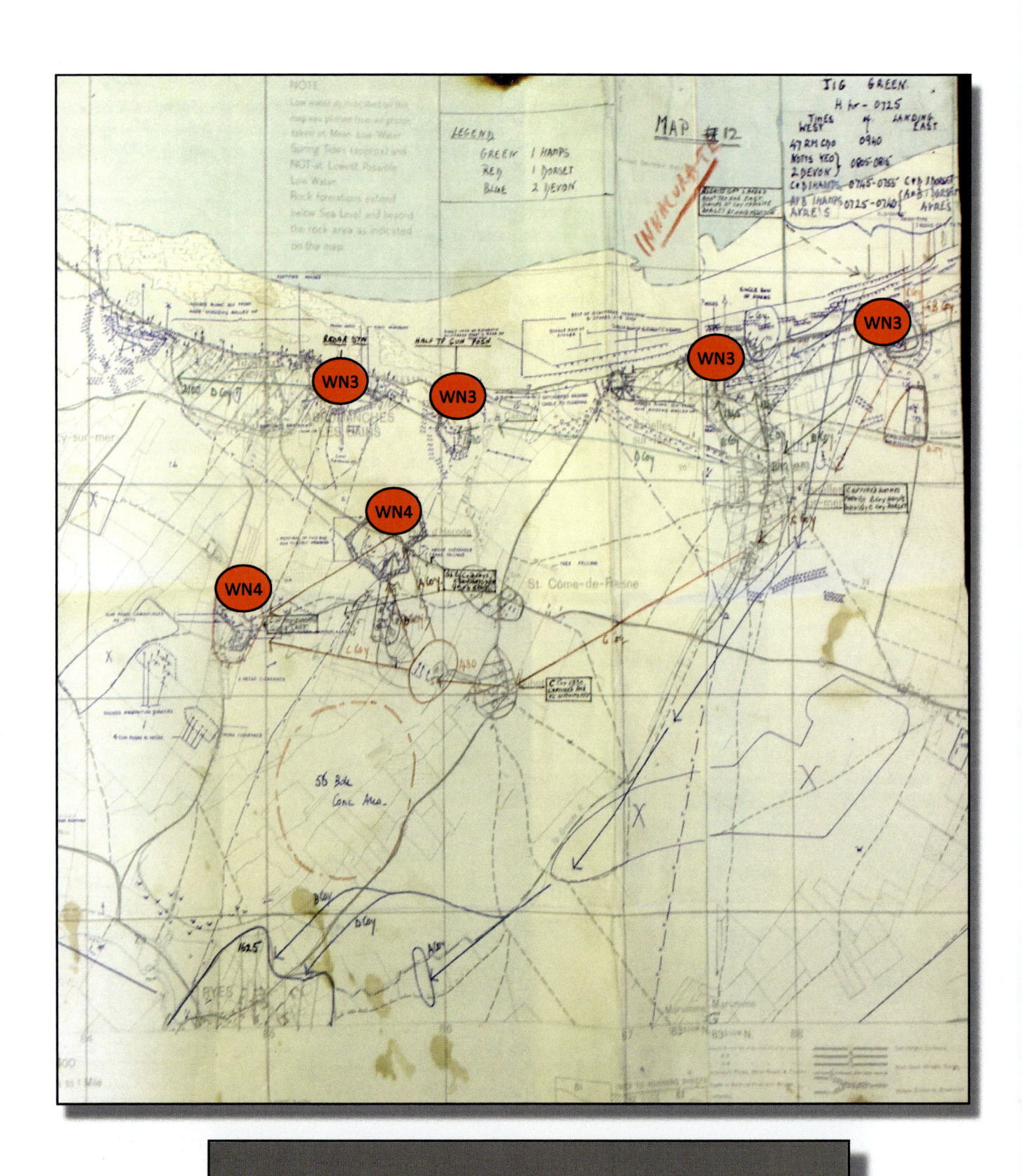

A fascinating map re-produced with the kind permission of the Dorsetshire Regiment Museum in Dorchester. It shows the movements of the Dorset, Hampshire and Devon Regiments upon landing on Gold Beach, Jig Green sector.

Right: Major German Strongpoints on Gold Beach.

Strong point	Location	Major Weapons	Defended by	Assaulted by	Fell
WN32	Mare Fontaine	4 x 100mm Light Field Howitzer (Czech) (H669)	6/AR1716	HMS Belfast/ Green Howards	6th June
WN33	La Riviere, King Red	88mm PaK 43/41 (H677), 1 x 50mm (H667), 1 x 50mm (VF600)	7/GR736	8th Armoured Brigade, 4/7 Dragoon Guards, 5th East Yorkshires and HMS Orion	6th June 0930hrs
WN33a	Graye Sur Mer Breche Le Bisson	1 x 75mm FK	7/GR736	HMS Diadem	6th June
WN34	Ver-sur-Mer, King Red	1 x 50mm (KWK L/42)	7/GR736	5th East Yorkshires	AM 6th June
WN35	Hable de Heurlot, King Green	Six bunkers	3/OST 441	6th Green Howards supported by AVRE tanks from 6th Assault Regiment Royal Engineers	6th June 1600hrs
Wn35a	Chateau de Ver-sur-Mer/Mt Flurey	4 x 122mm K390/I (H649 casemates of which only one was finished with its gun inside)	3/HKAA1260-HK1260 commanded by Major Paul Friedrich-HQ.	HMS Orion and 6th Green Howards	6th June 0930hrs
WN35b	Crepon	4 x 100mm (H669 in process of being finished) Light Field Howitzer	5/AR1716, Lt Theimer	6th Green Howards supported by Churchill AVRE Tanks. It was here than Stan Hollis's actions gained him the Victoria Cross.	6th June
WN36	Asnelles, Cabane des Doyanes, Jig Green	1 x 50mm (KWK L/42) (VF600)	Ost441	1st Hampshires.	6th June
WN37	Asnelles, Le Hamel East, Jig Green/Item	WW1 77mm Field Gun (H612) and supporting 50mm gun.	Ost441	There are different claims by British regiments as to who knocked out the gun, possibly Suffolk Regiment who took it out with a 25lb gun or self propelled 25lb gun armed Sexton under command of Sergeant R.E. Palmer 147th Field Regt (Essex Yeomanry) from a distance of 300 yards.	6th June 1600hrs
WN38	Asnelles Le Hamel West, Item	2 x 50mm, 1 x 50mm mortar	Ost441 plus support from 726IR.	1st Hampshire, 231st Infantry Brigade	6th June
WN39	Sainte-Come-deFresne, near Arromanches, Item	2 x 75mm (H612) Field Guns (Russian),	Ost441	Taken by D Coy 1st Hampshire supported by 5 tanks of B Sqn Sherwood Rangers	6th June 1520hrs
WN40	Arromanches - Puits d'Herode	Observation Bunker, Tobruks	Ost441	Cleared by A Coy 1st Dorsets, supported by C Sqn Sherwood Rangers and 90 Field Regt.	6th June
WN40b	Arromanches Puits d'Herode	Defended Wood, 81mm Mortars, MG's and AT guns.	Ost441	D Company 1st Dorsets	6th June
WN41	Arromanches Petie Fontaine	4 x 105mm Gun Emplacement	352 Art Regt Battery	Shelled by HMS Emerald with seven 6" guns. Position was attacked by A and C Co's 1st Dorset, supported by Sherwood Rangers tanks and 90 Field Regt. The Germans had however fled after using all their ammo.	6th June around 1600hrs
WN42 (Stp42)	Arromanches	3 x 20mm, 1 x 75mm, German Navy radar Station.	Luftwaffe and Kriegsmarine personnel.	Naval and Artillery bombardment by 147 Field Regt prepared the way for D Company 1st Hampshires assault around 1900.	6th June 1900hrs
WN48	Batterie de Longues-sur-Mer	4 x 150mm gun (M272), 2 x 75mm FK, 1 x 122mm K390/1(Soviet), 3 x 20mm Flak	4/HKAA1260	HMS Ajax/ HMS Argonaut bombarded WN48 until it ceased firing at 0845hrs after two guns were knocked out. The remaining two guns commenced firing again at Omaha Beach in the afternoon. The French Cruiser Georges Leygues then bombarded the position and silenced it.	6th June 0845hrs and again finally in the afternoon.

Canadian Memorial
Juno Beach August 2013

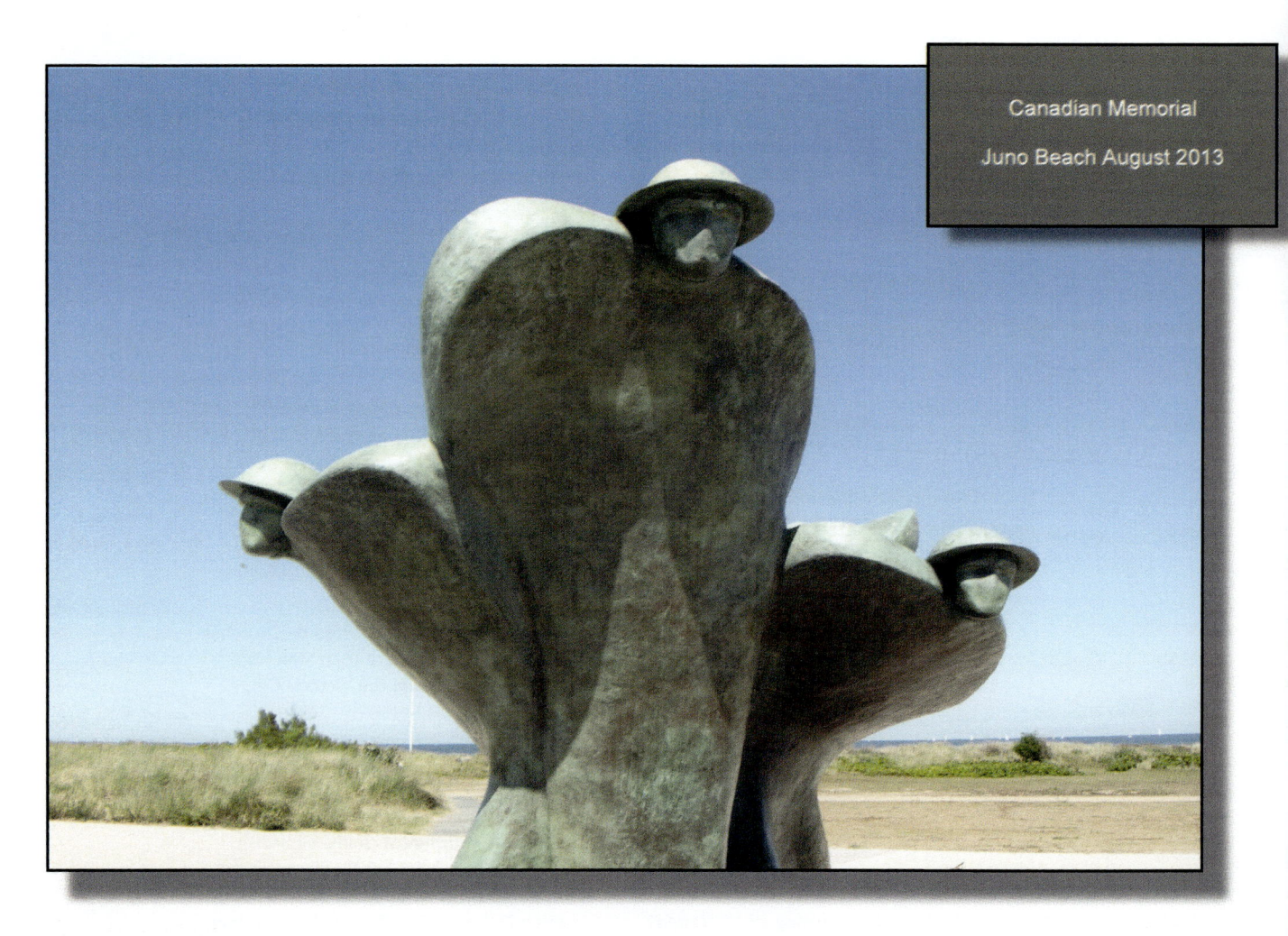

JUNO – Force "J"

Juno beach was five miles wide and stretched on either side of Courseulles-sur-Mer.

The JUNO landings were judged necessary to provide flanking support to the British drive on Caen from SWORD, as well as to capture the German airfield at Carpiquet west of Caen. Taking JUNO was the responsibility of the 3rd Canadian Infantry Division and commandos of the Royal Marines.

The beach was defended by two battalions of the German 716th Infantry Division, with elements of the 21st Panzer Division held in reserve near Caen.

The 3rd Canadian Infantry Division with the 2nd Canadian Armoured Brigade under command landed in two brigade groups, the 7th Canadian Infantry Brigade and the 8th Canadian Infantry Brigade, each Brigade had three Infantry Battalions and an armoured regiment in support, 2 artillery field regiments, combat engineer companies and extra units from the 79th Armoured Division. The Fort Garry Horse tanks (10th Armoured Regiment) supported the 7th brigade landing on the left and the tanks of the 1st Hussars (6th Armoured Regiment) supported the landing on the right.

The 9th Canadian Infantry Brigade was kept in reserve and landed later that day and advanced through the lead brigades. The Sherbrooke Fusiliers tanks (27th Armoured Regiment) provided tank support.

The initial assault was carried out by:
- North Shore Regiment on the left at St. Aubin (Nan Red beach)
- Queen's Own Rifles in the centre at Bernières (Nan White beach)
- Regina Rifles at Courseulles (Nan Green beach)
- Royal Winnipeg Rifles on the western edge of Courseulles (Mike Red and Mike Green beaches)

Objectives: To reach the Caen-Bayeux road, capture the Carpiquet airfield west of Caen and link-up with the British coming from Gold and Sword.

Operation Neptune - Organisation of Assault Forces - Juno

Assault Group	Headquarters	Assault Troops	Beach
Force "J" (Juno Beach)			
	"H.M.S. Hilary (Converted Passenger Liner) Force J HQ Ship"	Commodore G.N. Oliver	
		Lt-Gen C.J. Crocker (1st Corps)	
		Maj-Gen Keller (3rd Can. Div.)	
		Gp. Capt. R. Cleland	
J1	"H.M.S. Lawford Captain Class Frigate J.1. HQ Ship"	7th Can. Bde	
	Capt. A.F. Pugsley, R.N.		"Mike" Green
	R.N. (S.O.A.G.J. 1)		"Red"
	Brig H.W. Foster		Nan
	(7th Can Infy. Bde.)		Green
J2	H.M.S. Waveny River Class Frigate J.2. HQ Ship	8th Can. Bde	
	Capt. R.J.O. Otway-Ruthven		
	R.N. (S.O.A.G.J. 2)		
	Brig. K.D. Blackader		"Nan"
	(8th Can. Infy. Bde.)		White
J3 Reserve	"H.M.S. Royal Ulsterman Passenge Ship Converted for reserve Troop Transport J.3. HQ Ship	9th Can. Bde.	
	Capt A.B. Fanshawe, R.N.		"Nan"
	Brig. D.G. Cunningham		White
	(9th Can.Infy.Bde.)		Red

Landing craft memorial

JUNO Beach August 2013

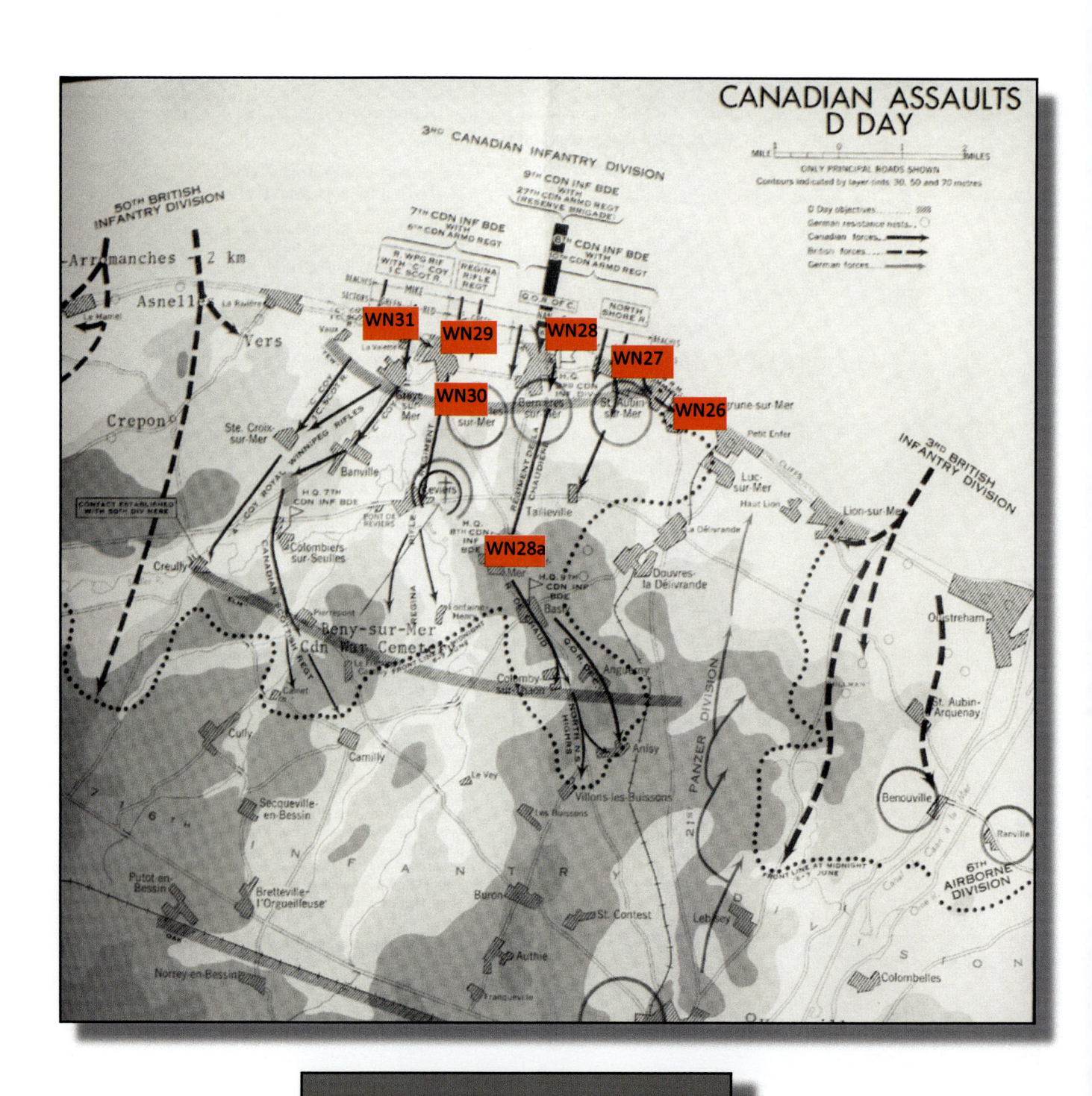

Map showing Sword, Juno and Gold Beaches with emphasis on the Canadian landings.

Major strongpoints on Juno

Strongpoint	Location	Major Weapons	Defended by	Assaulted by	Fell
WN26	Langrune-sur-Mer	1 x 75mm Field Gun, Field Entrenchment	9/GR736	48 RM Commando	7th June
WN27	Nan Red, St Aubin-sur-Mer.	1 x 50mm (VF600)	5/GR736, Lt Gustav Pfloksch	Canadian North Shore Regiment	6th June 1115hrs
WN28	Nan White, Bernières-la-Rive	1 x 75mm (H604) ,Mortar, machine guns, plus 50mm in Timber emplacement and 1 Panzerstellung FT	5/GR736 HQ	Queens Own Rifles of Canada	6th June 08.15 approx, 2 hours after landing.
WN28a	Moulin a Beny-sur-Mer	4 x 100mm Light Field Howitzer (H669) Capt Franke	7/AR1716	La Regiment de la Chaudiere (the only French/Canadian regiment to participate in Operation Overlord, and the only French speaking unit that day along with the Free-French Commando Kieffer.	6th June
WN29	Nan Green, Courseulles-sur-Mer	1 x 88mm (H677), 2 x 75mm (H612), 1 x 50mm guarding the Harbour (open pit), mortars and machine guns	6/GR736	Reginas commenced landing 08.09 hours, it took around 2 hours to fight through WN29. Centaur Tanks and DD tanks from the 1st Hussars assisted. WN 29 became active again through the morning by Germans who had been missed in the labyrinth of trenches, finally cleared later on D-day	6th June
WN30	Mike Red, Courseulles-sur-Mer	Reinforced Houses	6/GR736	Regina Rifles	6th June Around Noon
WN31	Mike Red, Courseulles-sur-Mer	1 x 75mm (H612), 2 x 50mm, mortars and machine guns	6/GR736	B Coy, Royal Winnipeg Rifles supported later by A Squadron 1st Hussars in DD Tanks.	6th June Landed 07.49, approx 2 hours to clear, 09.50

Sword beach, Memorial to the Free French.

May 2013

SWORD – Force "S"

Code name for the beach stretching 5 miles from Saint-Aubin-sur-Mer to Ouistreham at the mouth of the River Orne, the beach was the eastern most landing site and was divided into several sectors, with each sector divided into beaches; thus the British 3rd Infantry Division, under the Command of Major General T G Rennie, assigned to land on SWORD, assaulted a two mile (3 km) stretch named Queen Sector - Queen Red, White and Green beaches.

Objectives: SWORD Beach was at the eastern end of the Allied landings. The troops' objectives were: to advance inland and capture the city of Caen as soon as possible; to link up with the 6th Airborne Division, who had landed by parachute and glider and were protecting the eastern flank of landings against German counter-attack. The first landings on SWORD were made by the British 3rd Infantry Division, 27th Armoured Brigade and Royal Marine and Army Commando units. By nightfall the British had 28,850 men ashore and the Orne Bridge had been seized.

SWORD is around 15 km from Caen, the ultimate goal of the 3rd Infantry Division. The initial landings were achieved with low casualties but the advance from the beach encountered traffic congestion, heavily defended areas behind the beachhead and was met by the only armoured counterattack of the day, mounted by the 21st Panzer Division that halted further Allied progress towards Caen.

For the passage, each British Assault Force was organised in 16 or 18 convoys or groups, the composition and numbering of the groups being based on their arrival in Normandy. A detailed programme was planned in minute detail, the timings of the departure of the various convoys being adjusted to the wide variety of speeds and seagoing capabilities of the diverse collection of vessels transporting the assault forces. The situation was not helped by the weather in the channel which added further complications.

Operation Neptune - Organisation of Assault Forces - Sword beach

Assault Group	Headquarters	Assault Troops	Beach
Force S (Sword beach)	**H.M.S. Largs** **Combined Operations Headquarters ship**	Rear-Admiral A.G. Talbot	
		Maj-Gen R.G. Rennie (3rd Div.)	
		Gp. Capt. W.G. Tailyour	
S1	**H.M.S. Locust** **(River Gun Boat)** **S.1. HQ Ship**	9th Bde	Reserve
	Capt. W.R.C. Leggatt, R.N.		
	(S.O.A.G.S,1 and N.O.I.C. "Sword")		
	Brig. J.C. Cunningham		
	(9th Infy. Bde.)		
S2	**H.M.S. Dacres** **(Captain Class Frigate)** **S.2. HQ Ship**	185th Bde	Intermediate Group
	Capt. R. Gotto, R.N.		
	(S.O.A.G.S. 2)		
	Brig. K.P. Smith		
	(185th Infy. Bde.)		
S3	**H.M.S. Goathland** **(Hunt Class Destroyer)** **S.3. HQ Ship**	8th Bde	Assault Group
	Capt. E.W. Bush, R.N.		
	(S.O.A.G.S. 3)		"Queen"
	Brig. E.E. Cass		White
	(8th Infy Bde.)		Red

Sword beach with the tide fully out.

June 2013

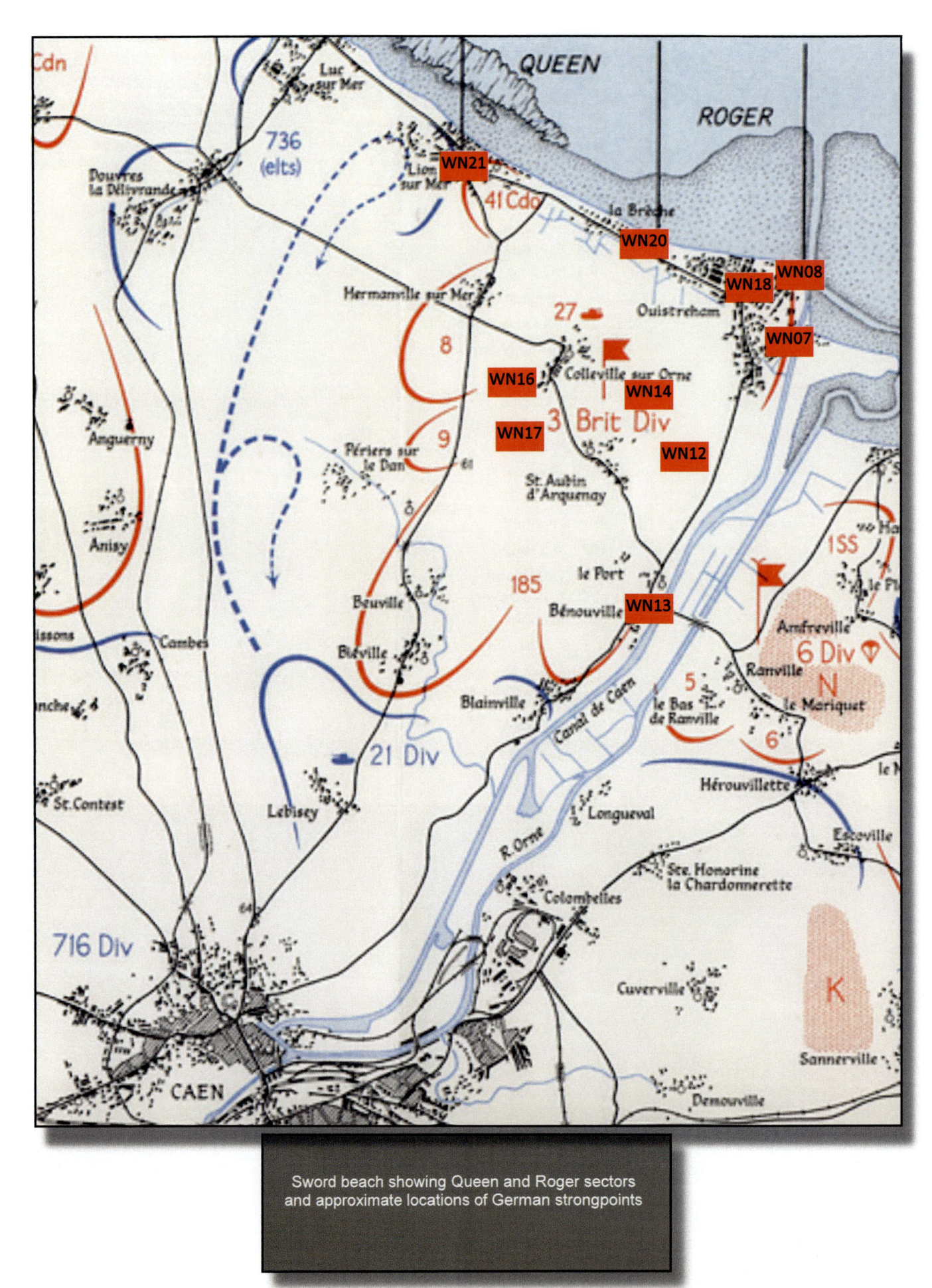

Sword beach showing Queen and Roger sectors
and approximate locations of German strongpoints

Major strongpoints on Sword

Strong point	Location	Major Weapons	Defended by	Assaulted by	Fell
WN01	Merville Battery	4 x 100mm Skoda LFH 14/19 (t) (H669, H611, H612)	1/AR1716	6th Airborne Division, 3rd Parachute Brigade, 9th Parachute Battalion commanded by Lt-Colonel Terence Otway.	6th June 0530hrs
WN08	Riva Bella, STP (Stutzpunkt) 08	4 x 155mm, 1 x Panzerstellung, 1 x machine gun	2nd Co, 2/GR736	91st Field Company Royal Engineers	6th June
WN09	Ouisterham (STP09)	Centre of Ouisterham, no fixed defences.	2/GR736		6th June
WN10(B)	Riva Bella, Roger	1 x 75mm Howitzer (H626), 1 x 50mm	2/GR736	No 4 Commando with attached Capt Kieffer's Free French Commandos and 8th Brigade DD tanks	6th June
WN12	South of Ouisterham, Chateau D'eau (Daimler)	4 x 155mm FH414 (f) (3 in H607), 1 x 50mm mortar, 2 x 20mm FLAK, 6 machine guns.	4/AR1716	2nd East Yorks, 8th Brigade	6th June
WN13	Pont de Benouville (Pegasus Bridge)	1 x 50mm		6th Airborne, D Company, 2nd Ox and Bucks Light Infantry	6th June 0024hrs
WN14	Ouisterham, Chateau D'eau (Sole)	Company HQ position.	HQ i/GR736	2nd East Yorks, 8th Brigade	6th June
WN15	St Aubin d-Arquenay	Billets	GR736	1st Kings Own Scottish Borderers, 9th Brigade	6th June
WN15a	St Aubin d-Arquenay	6 x 155mm	1/HKAA1260	1st Kings Own Scottish Borderers, 9th Brigade	6th June
WN16	Colleville sur Orne (Morris)	Artillery Battery, 4 x 100mm FH (H669- but not fully completed by the time of the invasion)	2/AR1716	1st Suffolks	6th June 1300hrs
WN17	South West of Colleville sur Orne (Hillman)	Grenadier Regiment 736 HQ, Colonel Krug, 1 x 75mm, 2 x AT guns (H605)	HQ /GR736	1st Suffolks	6th June 2015hrs
WN18	Riva Bella, Queen Red	1 x 88mm (H677), 3 x 50mm (2x50mm Casemates, 1 x VF600)	10th Co 356th Regt of 10/GR736	Capt Phillippe Kieffer's and his two Free French troops from 10 Commando (attached to 4 Commando)	6th June
WN19	Colleville sur Orne			1st Battalion of the Suffolk Regiment	Morning 6th June
WN20	Hermanville- La Breche, (Cod), Queen Red	1 x 88mm (H677), 3 x 50mm Pedestal Guns	10/GR736	Taken by 1st South Lancs, 2nd East Yorks supported by tanks from 13th/18th Hussars.	6th June About 1000hrs
WN21	Lion-sur,Mer, (Trout), Queen Green.	1 x 75mm, 2 x 50mm (VF600)	9th Co,356th Regt, 10/GR736	41 RM Commando	Deserted

Pointe du Hoc Memorial
Looking towards Utah Beach
August 2013

Pointe du Hoc (often referred to as Pointe du Hoe by the Americans due to a typing error).

Located on the coast to the west of Omaha beach was the home of six 155 mm cannon with a range of 25,000 yards and had a commanding view of both Omaha and Utah beaches. The area had been bombed since May and then grew in intensity during the three days and nights before D-Day.

The point stands on 100 feet high cliffs with a rocky beach below with little or no protection. Because the guns were positioned on near impregnable cliffs, the Germans felt sure that they would only be attacked from the ground at the rear. However, they had not banked on the US Rangers.

The site was a mass of heavily fortified concrete casements interlaced with tunnels, trenches, and machine-gun positions around the perimeter. Approximately 200 German troops of the 716th Infantry Division(125 infantry and 85 artillery men) were garrisoned in or around the point. The task fell to Lt. Col. James Earl Rudder's 2nd Ranger Battalion and called for 3 Companies (D, E, and F) of the battalion to scale the heights. Company D was to approach the heights on the west, while E and F were to attack on the east.

The main Ranger force 5th Battalion and Companies A and B of the 2nd, were to wait off shore for signal of success and then land at the Point. In addition to destroying the guns, the Rangers were to move inland and cut the coastal highway that connected Grandcamp and Vierville. They were then to wait for the arrival of the US 116th Infantry from Omaha Beach to the east - scheduled to relieve them at noon on the 6th. Once linking up with the main force, they were then to move on *Grandcamp and Maisy to the west in order to attempt to link up with the forces that were to land at Utah beach.

---

* In 1944 Grandcamp les Bains and Maisy were two separate towns, they amalgamated to form Grandcamp-Maisy in 1972.

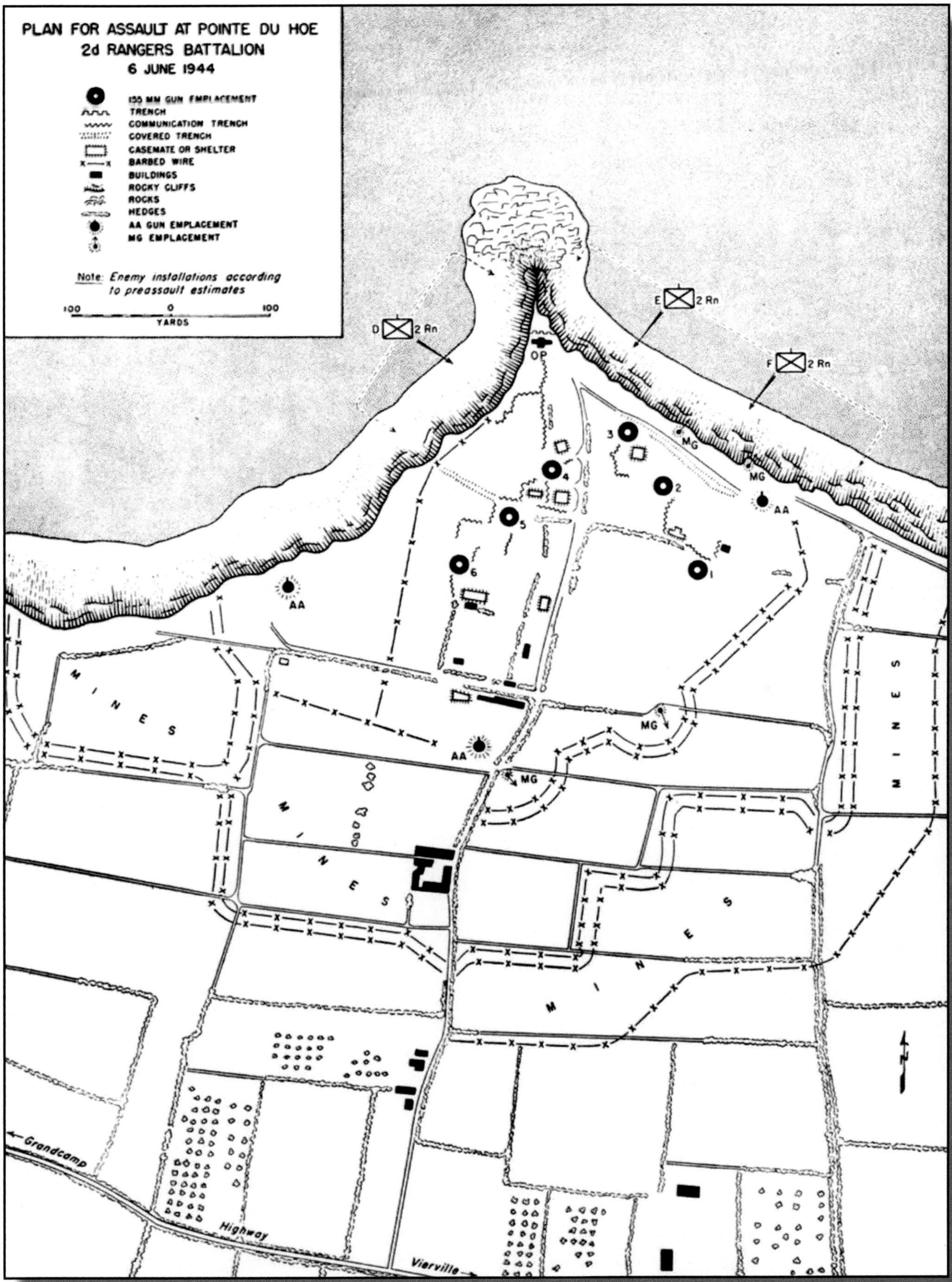

PLAN FOR ASSAULT AT POINTE DU HOE
2d RANGERS BATTALION
6 JUNE 1944
155 MM GUN EMPLACEMENT
TRENCH
COMMUNICATION TRENCH
COVERED TRENCH
CASEMATE OR SHELTER
BARBED WIRE
BUILDINGS
ROCKY CLIFFS
ROCKS
HEDGES
AA GUN EMPLACEMENT
MG EMPLACEMENT
Note: Enemy installations according to preassault estimates
100 0 100
YARDS
D 2 Rn
E 2 Rn
F 2 Rn
OP
MG
AA
MINES
Grandcamp
Highway
Vierville

GOLD BEACH LANDING DIAGRAM

Follow Up Formations		XXX Corps 33 Armoured Brigade 49 Division 7 Armoured Division		
Assault Divisions		50 Division Group		
		HQ 8 Armoured Bde		
Reserve Brigades	56 Brigade Group		151 Brigade Group	
Assault Brigades	231 Brigade Group		69 Brigade Group	
Self propelled artillery	90 & 147 Fd Regt RA		86 Fd Regt RA	
Commandos	47 RM Cdo			
Reserve Battalions	2 Devon		7 Green Howards	
Assault Battalion Groups Underwater obstacle clarance teams	RN & RE		RN & RE	
Breaching Teams AVRE's Flail Tanks	Sqn 6 Assault Regiment Royal Engineers Sqn W Dgns		Sqn 6 Assault Regiment Royal Engineers Sqn W Dgns	
Assault Battalions	1 Dorset	1 Hamps	6 Green Howards	5 East Yorks
Close support Tanks - Centaurs	Bty 1 RM Armoured Support Regiment		Bty 1 RM Armoured Support Regiment	
DD Tanks - Shermans	Notts Yeomanry		4/7 Dragoons	
Landing Beaches	Jig	Jig	King	King
Assault Area		GOLD		

This diagram of Gold Beach gives an idea of how the landings took place, it was much the same on all five beaches.

This table summarises the relationships and relative sizes of the military units involved.

Of particular note is the fact that exact details could vary from country to country in relation to names and sizes. Variation will also occur naturally depending on role and circumstance.

The numbers given for men in each unit is more representative of infantry units than armoured units.

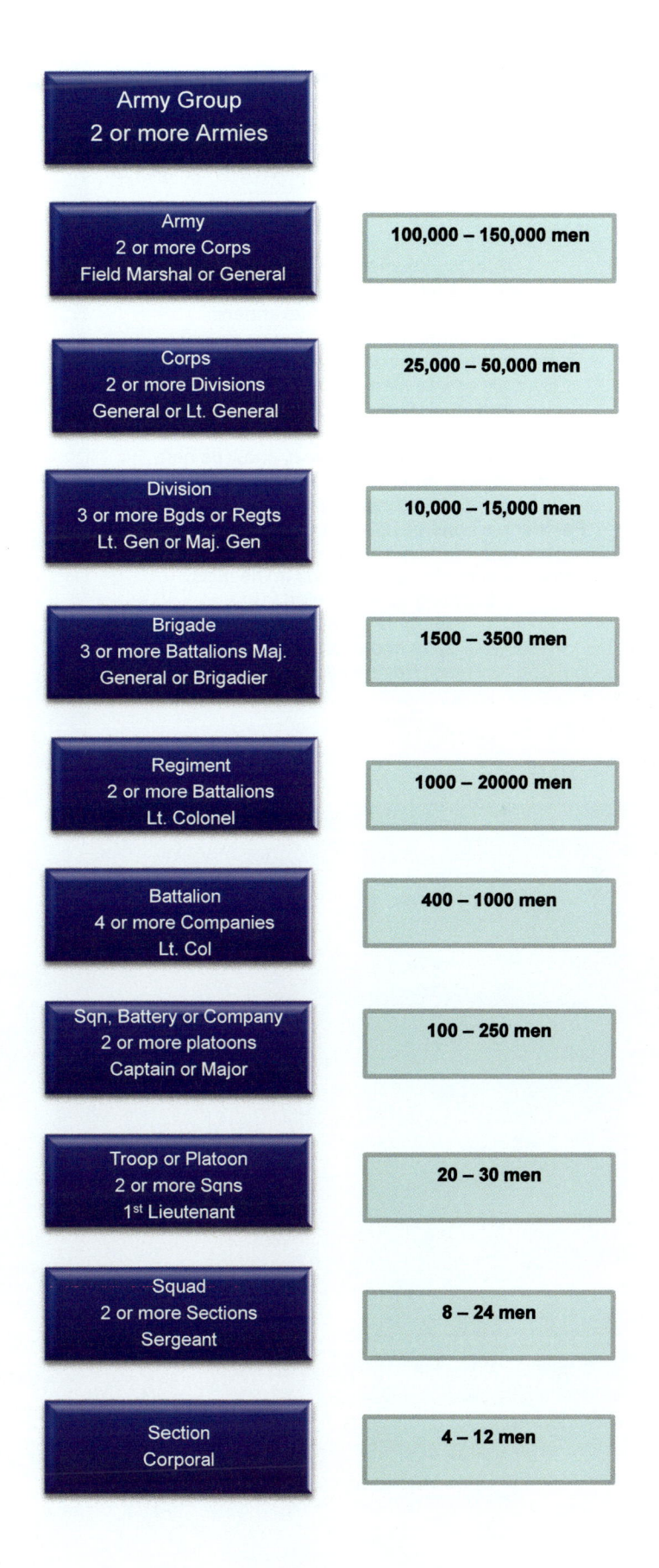

Army Group — 2 or more Armies	
Army — 2 or more Corps — Field Marshal or General	100,000 – 150,000 men
Corps — 2 or more Divisions — General or Lt. General	25,000 – 50,000 men
Division — 3 or more Bgds or Regts — Lt. Gen or Maj. Gen	10,000 – 15,000 men
Brigade — 3 or more Battalions Maj. General or Brigadier	1500 – 3500 men
Regiment — 2 or more Battalions — Lt. Colonel	1000 – 20000 men
Battalion — 4 or more Companies — Lt. Col	400 – 1000 men
Sqn, Battery or Company — 2 or more platoons — Captain or Major	100 – 250 men
Troop or Platoon — 2 or more Sqns — 1st Lieutenant	20 – 30 men
Squad — 2 or more Sections — Sergeant	8 – 24 men
Section — Corporal	4 – 12 men

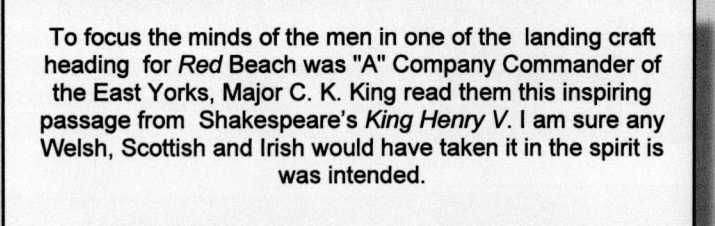

To focus the minds of the men in one of the landing craft heading for *Red* Beach was "A" Company Commander of the East Yorks, Major C. K. King read them this inspiring passage from Shakespeare's *King Henry V*. I am sure any Welsh, Scottish and Irish would have taken it in the spirit is was intended.

"On, on, you noble English!
Whose blood is fet from fathers of war-proof,
Fathers that, like so many Alexanders,
Have in these parts from mom till even fought,
And sheath'd their swords for lack of argument:
Be copy now to men of grosser blood
And teach them how to war!
And you, good yeoman,
Whose limbs were made in England, show us here
The mettle of your pasture; let us swear
That you are worth your breeding; which I doubt not;
For there is none of you so mean and base,
That hath not noble lustre in your eyes.
I see you stand like greyhounds in the slips,
Straining upon the start.
The game's afoot:
Follow your spirit and upon this charge,
cry God for Harry, England and St George. "

Henry V

HOW?

"O God of battles! Steel my soldiers' hearts. Possess them not with fear."

William Shakespeare, Henry V

Training sites

D-Day training sites were created in Britain in order to practice for Operation Overlord. In 1943, in an area of Hankley Common in Elstead, Surrey, known as the Lion's Mouth, Canadian troops built a replica of a section of the Atlantic Wall. It is constructed from reinforced concrete and was used as a major training aid to develop and practise techniques to breach the defences of the French coast prior to the D-Day landings. The wall is divided into two sections between which there were originally huge steel gates. Nearby are other obstacles such as dragon's teeth, huge reinforced concrete blocks and lengths of railway track set in concrete and wire entanglements.

Beach training took place along the South Coast of the UK. The Americans using Devon primarily and the British and Canadians using areas such as Hayling Island near Portsmouth.

Much of the North Devon coast was used for military training due to its similarity to the coast of Normandy. The Assault Training Centre moved its headquarters from Grosvenor Square to Woolacombe and many thousands of US troops with landing barges and tanks moved into the area. There were occasional casualties, but the rigorous training which the troops underwent prepared them for the landings in Normandy.

On Baggy Point, dummy pillboxes were built to represent enemy gun emplacements and some show evidence of having been subjected to heavy fire and repair. There was also an observation house at the western end of the promontory and temporary roads which are still visible as earthworks. The 146th Engineer Combat Battalion of the US Army which trained on Baggy, was among the first troops to land on Omaha Beach.

Lt. Col. Terrence Otway, 9th Parachute Battalion, used farmland a few miles away from Newbury in Berkshire at a place called Wallbury Hill where he had a full size replica of the Merville Battery built. He devised a plan and took his men through it nine times before he was happy.

The New Forest and its part in D Day.

The New Forest, played a huge part in the planning and logistics of the Normandy landings and changes to the area appeared to happen almost over night. The British Government realised that it would be possible to not only hide armies because of its sheer size and location within the forest but to also have fighter and bomber bases as close to the front line as possible. So, the New Forest became a prime preparation area for D Day.

A vast army lived, planned, trained and assembled for the D Day Landings and the impact on the people of the New Forest was tremendous. At that period in time it was not a wealthy area and it was a struggle for the Commoners to survive.

As the armies moved in and needed more and more land to live and train on, so the Commoners were offered money for their land. Initially 2 shillings an acre which is 10p in today's money. The average annual earnings in 1943 being around £350. This appallingly low amount of money was offered to Commoners around Beaulieu and Holmsley South.

After some discussion and a number of negotiations this was put up to 4 shillings per acre being offered around the Stoney Cross area, which was needed as an airfield, but this was reduced to 2/6 (2 shillings and 6 pence) as the Air Ministry decided Commoners were not entitled to compensation under the Defence Act of 1939.

As roads were widened and slabs of concrete appeared some people even awoke to find a large swathe of their front garden had disappeared, and it was not just the Commoners that had to give up their land for the war effort. The beautiful Rothschild family estate was used by Naval Intelligence and over 1000 Nissen huts were erected to house the personnel who were collecting vital intelligence data. At nearby Inchmery House, Free French and Polish Commandos were also involved in intelligence training.

Exbury was renamed Her Majesty's Stone frigate "Mastodon". And the owner Mr de Rothschild was given 48 hours to clear the house in readiness for the Intelligence Service occupation. Exbury became one of the centres for the D Day planning being responsible for the administration of victualing, arming and training of crews for the landing craft that were used as part of Operation Neptune, the Naval aspect of the Normandy landings. King George VI visited Exbury on Wednesday May 24th 1944 for a brief visit and Royal Salute shortly before D-Day.

The Beaulieu river runs along the bottom of the garden and landing craft were regularly tested there ready for the Normandy landings - there is still a small naval craft left in the mud today. In fact all the areas of the New Forest coastline were

Braunton Burrows, Devon - There are four concrete mock-ups of beach landing craft on which US troops rehearsed the disembarkation procedure.

Lt. Col. Otway had a full sized replica of the Merville Battery fabricated in the valley and repeatedly attacked it, in the final practice live ammunition was used and the mock up destroyed.

packed full of crafts of all shapes and sizes awaiting instructions.

The build up to D-Day was not just about the build up of forces and the collection of men, armaments, Mulberry Harbours, and landing craft in the Forest and along the coast. An essential part was the work required to keep the roads open and in useable condition for local residents as well as essential troop and supply movement.

The damage to roads and bridges was a huge issue for the New Forest roads originally constructed to carry only light traffic, but were now receiving continuous use by heavy traffic. This heavy use also hindered running repairs to the roads and led to regular complaints from the county surveyor, who also had to contend with a diminished workforce following regular competition from other military contracts.

During early 1944 a large undertaking of road widening, junction improvements and bridge strengthening was commenced as essential preparations for the movement of men and equipment to their marshalling areas, which were located short distances from the embarkation points. Lepe and Lymington came under marshalling area B.

The work necessary on the south coast of Hampshire before D-Day can be summarised as follows:

- 59 miles of road widened to 22 feet (for two way traffic)
- 17 miles of road widened to 16 feet (for one way traffic)
- 16 bridges widened or strengthened
- 337 passing places or laybys (for breakdowns) constructed
- 118 road junctions or sharp bends reconstructed in concrete or asphalt for tracked vehicles.[*1]

Elements of the Mulberry Harbours [*2] were constructed at various points along the New Forest coast.

Some parts called Beetles, which supported the floating roadways, still survive today and lie along the foreshore between Hythe and Marchwood. These units were surplus to requirement and were not towed over to the Normandy Beaches, but were recycled firstly as breakwaters and then as coastal defence to protect reclamation areas.

In November 1943 a new military port was built at Marchwood to specifically assist with Mulberry Harbour construction in the build up to D Day and to give extra docking space for the ever increasing number of vessels waiting in Southampton Water for the Normandy landings. It became the base for the newly formed No. 1 Port and Inland Water Transport Repair Depot, Royal Engineers. The unit's responsibilities included the construction of Mulberry Harbour components; particularly the floating spans made up of the 'Whales' roadways and 'Beetles' support pontoons

Wates Group Ltd. construction firm, who had been employed to build elements of Mulberry, also built a slipway and other facilities. Part of the waterfront was also roofed over so that Mulberry construction could continue in bad weather.

Marchwood, the Beaulieu River and nearby Lepe played very important roles in the construction of temporary Mulberry Harbours, which consisted of 'Spuds' (pier heads), 'Whales' (roads) and 'Beetles' (pontoons). These experimental units were towed across the English Channel to successfully disembark troops, machinery and supplies on the Normandy beaches, circumnavigating the heavily defended French harbours.

Today at Lepe you can still see plenty of evidence of wartime activity. If you walk along the beach or track, about half a mile east of the car parks you will come across the extensive concrete and brick structures were used for three different tasks: construction of the 'Mulberry Harbours' (caissons), caisson launching, and for embarkation of men, vehicles and supplies. Including:

- The concrete floor remains of the site buildings used by construction workers and the military. They are dotted about in the Country Park area.
- Water Tower Base used for water purification, required because so little fresh water was available on site.
- Construction Platforms where the caissons were constructed. Today, although parts are storm damaged, the platforms run for 374 metres and are 11m wide and 1.3m high. The platforms were large enough to construct all six caissons simultaneously, reflecting the urgency of the work.
- Beach Hardening Mats which resemble huge bars of chocolate, were held in place by a series of iron hooks. They were laid out to strengthen the beach enough to take the

---

[*1] Based on extracts from an article: *Hampshire's Highways Under Military Occupation* by Malcolm Walford in Hampshire Studies 2012 (11): Proceedings of the Hampshire Field Club & Archaeological Society.

[*2] A portable temporary harbour developed by the British in World War II to facilitate rapid offloading of cargo onto the beaches during the Allied invasion of Normandy.

Stan Grayland recalls... *"For four days our Landing Craft Flack, (LCF 30), sat tied to a buoy off Whale Island, the Royal Navy Gunnery School at Portsmouth, on the South Coast of England. LCF 30 was sealed, meaning no one could leave the craft, and was readied for what everyone knew was inevitable... the invasion of France, considered to be the beginning of the end of World War 2... D DAY. "*

D-Day embarkation remains at Lepe looking south west from one of the concrete platforms at the bollards and dolphins that formed part of the pier head

The beach hardening mats (giant chocolate blocks) being washed by the waves. These covered the beach to prevent tanks sinking into the sand during loading

(Photos taken 2012 Courtesy of New Forest Remembers)

weight of the tanks and other vehicles being driven onto landing craft.
- Dolphins forming part of the pier head used to load ships departing for Normandy.
- Bollards used to tie up the ships that were being loaded for the landings.
- Concrete Slipways run from the rolling track walls to the sea. These were used to launch the caissons at high tide.

New Forest Airfields

The New Forest was also host to 12 airfield, nine were built for the Second World War with many of them directly or indirectly being involved in the D Day operations.

1. **East Boldre:** Also known as Beaulieu airfield, Beaulieu aerodrome and USAAF Station AAF 408. It is located next to the village of East Boldre, about 2 miles west of the village of Beaulieu and 5 miles east-northeast of Lymington. Opened on 8 August 1942, it was used by both the Royal Air Force and then later United States Army Air Forces. During the war it was used as a bomber and fighter airfield.

2. **Calshot:** RAF Calshot was located at the end of Calshot Spit in Southampton Water, Hampshire. It was the main seaplane/flying boat development and training unit in the UK.

3. **Christchurch:** In 1943, RAF And USAAF engineers built a wire-mesh runway for use by P47 Thunderbolt fighter-bombers of the 9th Air Force supporting D-Day, 1944.

4. **Ibsley:** Operating RAF Hurricanes and Spitfires flown by British, Polish, Czech and Australian pilots, and joined by USAAF P-38 Lightnings, P-47 Thunderbolts and P-51 Mustangs after 1942, supporting Allied forces up to and beyond D-day

5. **Hurn:** In 1944, RAF Typhoons flown by British and Canadian pilots, and United Stated Army Air Force (USAAF) B-26 Marauder bombers supported D-day operations; RAF Mosquitos and USAAF Black Widows provided night-fighter defence.

6. **Beaulieu:** In 1944 RAF Typhoons and Bostons were joined by USAAF P-47 and B-26 aircraft to support D-day.

7. **Holmsley South:** The three-runway airfield north of New Milton opened in October 1942 operating RAF Wellington and Halifax bombers and the USAAF B-17 Fortress on anti-U-boat patrols. Up to and beyond D-day RAF Typhoons and Mustangs, RCAF Spitfires, supported by USAAF B-26s and RCAF Night-Intruder Mosquitos, flew missions over occupied France.

8. **Stoney Cross:** Opened in November 1942, west of Cadnam. The airfields three runways operated RAF Hurricanes and Mustangs of the Army Cooperation Command, then Stirlings, Whitleys and Albermares training Horsa glider pilots. D-day support given by USAAF P-38 and B-26s was superceded by RAF

9. **Bisterne Advanced Landing Ground:** Built south of Ringwood in 1943, this two-runway base constructed of Sommerfield Steel Tracking, operated three squadrons of P-47's for D-day, moving to France on the 17th June 1944; Bisterne closed later that year.

10. **Lymington Advanced Landing Ground:** Constructed East of Lymington Ferry Terminal, the two steel-tracking runways were used by three squadrons of P-47s supporting D-day operations, moving to France on the 24th June 1944.

11. **Needs Oar Point Advanced Landing Ground:** Like Bisterne and Lymington, this simple 1943-built steel -track two-runway base supported D-day operations but with four squadrons of RAF Typhoons.

12. **Winkton Advanced Landing Ground:** Built just west of Bransgore in 1943, the two-runway, steel-tracking base used three squadrons of P-47's to cover D-day forces.

Secrecy, at all times, during the planning of the D Day Landings was crucial to its success, and to protect as many Allied personnel as possible from losing their lives during this manoeuvre.

Although by living in such close proximity to all the troops and equipment during the past months, it was inconceivable to the people of the New Forest, just what a massive operation was going on a few miles away from them.

Camps which had been on high security very recently, were suddenly virtually "open house". They were deserted and many of the children were given rations, which were very welcome. After living for so long with troops and camps all over the New Forest: conducting training manoeuvres, planning and practising sorties, and generally living amongst the people, suddenly the New Forest would have become eerily quiet once the approach of the Normandy Landings had begun. At this time, the Solent has been described as being so full of craft, awaiting the decision to attack, that it looked as though you could walk across to the Isle of Wight.

Memorial to the 12 New Forest Airfields, most of which were involved in D Day.

Below: Remains of MkII Churchill Tank on a hill near Storrington on the South Downs as used by the 14th Canadian Army Tank Battalion as target practice during their rehearsals for the Normandy landings. Photos taken 2012

Keeping D-Day Secret

Security was always going to be a problem, from its conception in July 1943 right up until D-Day itself 11 months later. In September 1943, all personnel who had access to the top secret documents regarding Operation Overlord were given an ID card stamped with the word, BIGOT. An inspired idea which assumed that no sane person was likely to brag about such a classification. All relevant secret documents were also stamped BIGOT and marked with a red cross.

There was real concern however, that the vast amount of men and resources that would be required for the attack, could potentially be discovered by enemy reconnaissance aircraft.

This again got Morgan thinking, who came up with a very elaborate deception plan – code named Operation Fortitude which would run alongside the real assault plan. This would attempt to disguise where the real attack would take place and dupe the Germans into believing it was in fact going to take place further up the coast.

A Spanish-born agent, Joan Pujol Garcia – code named Garbo and the German codename Arabel – became the Allies' top double agent, providing the Germans with misinformation on troop force and movement in the run-up to D-Day. He managed to encourage the Germans to over-estimate the number of Allied Divisions by an incredible 50 per cent. The trust the Germans placed in him was wholly genuine and totally misplaced. This included the fictitious First US Army Group (FUSAG), Commanded by US General George S. Patton, the existence of which led the Germans to hold back seven of their Divisions in the Pas de Calais uselessly for two weeks after D-Day. Pujol had done a good job in convincing the enemy that FUSAG did exist, but had been disbanded and attached to the forces at Normandy because the "diversion" had been so successful that the Calais landing had become unnecessary.

Pujol had the distinction of being one of the few people – if there were any others – during World War II to receive decorations from both sides, gaining both an Iron Cross from the Germans and an MBE from the British. The FUSAG only ever existed on paper.

THE BBC

The BBC played a crucial part in the war not only reporting events as they happened, but also encouraging hope in occupied territories.

In June 1944, the BBC occupied the tower of the Chateau at Cruelly near Bayeux as its base for broadcasting reports of the D-Day landings back to the UK. Using the BBC-designed 'Midget' portable recorder for recording in the field, war correspondents such as Frank Gillard filed reports using a low-powered transmitter which was delivered precariously on 18 June. These reports came via one of the BBC's receiving stations in the South of England where they were passed by landline up to Broadcasting House for editing and inclusion in War Report and news bulletins.

The BBC used these premises until the end of July when more powerful transmitters were brought over to France, which could follow the Allies' advance.

The Royal Army Medical Corps

In September 1941 the 1st Parachute Brigade comprising of three parachute infantry battalions began forming after Winston Churchill, directed the War Office to investigate the possibility of creating a corps of 5,000 parachute troops. Airborne supporting arms were also created, including the Royal Army Medical Corps volunteers. Of the seven airborne field ambulances formed during the Second World War, the 181st and the 195th were glider borne and the other five, the 16th, 127th, 133rd, 224th and the 225th were parachute trained.

224 Parachute Field Ambulance was converted from 224 Field Ambulance to an Airborne parachute unit in 1942. Lt Col D.H. Thompson assumed command in 1943, and would remain CO until the eventual disbandment of the unit after the war. 224 Para Field Ambulance was attached to the new 6th Airborne Division, and formed part of the 3rd Parachute Brigade, undertaking numerous training exercises.

On 5-6 June 1944, D-Day, most of 224 Para Field Ambulance landed near Varaville, Normandy in the early morning of 6 June. An H.Q. contingent were dropped as the Main Dressing Station (MDS), whilst three further sections were attached to 1st (Canadian) Parachute Battalion and 8th (Midlands) and 9th (Essex) Parachute Battalions. The drop itself did not go to plan however. Some, including

Chateau Cruelly from where the BBC broadcast reports of the D-Day landings from the tower, now re-named the "BBC Tower."

August 2013

that of the C.O . Lt Col Thompson, were dropped several miles from their DZ.

225 Parachute Field Ambulance was formed in June 1943, taking its name from 225 Light Field Ambulance, of Guards Armoured Division which had been disbanded earlier that year. The 225 Para Field Ambulance was attached to 5th Parachute Brigade, of the new 6th Airborne Division who had been tasked with seizing, and holding the bridges over the River Orne and Caen Canal near Ranville and Benouville, and to then secure and hold the area around these two villages and that of Le Bas de Ranville, where 225 would establish their MDS.

SOE and the French Resistance

The Allies needed the help of the French Resistance networks during and after the preparation of the Invasion which is then given the codename: Operation Overlord.

Through a London-based headquarters the British Special Operations Executive (SOE) orchestrated a massive campaign of sabotage. The Allies developed four plans for the French Resistance to execute on D-Day and the following days:

- Plan VERT was a fifteen day operation involving sabotage against the rail system.
- Plan BLEU dealt with destroying electrical facilities.
- Plan TORTUE was a delaying operation aimed at the enemy forces that would potentially reinforce Axis forces at Normandy.
- Plan VIOLET dealt with the cutting of underground telephone and teleprinter cables.

The resistance was alerted to carry out these tasks by means of the *messages personnels*, transmitted by the BBC in its French service from London. In 1940, the BBC opened its studio to the first members of the Resistance who fled occupied France. Radio Londres was born and would become the daily appointment of the French people for four years. It opened its transmission with : "*Ici Londres ! Les Français parlent aux Français.*".. ("This is London! The French speaking to the French."..) Broadcasts would start with "*Before we begin, please listen to some personal messages.*"

Georges Begue an operative with the SOE had the idea of sending seemingly obscure personal messages to SOE agents out in France to reduce radio traffic to and from agents.

Several hundred of these often strange messages, were regularly transmitted, it was pretty much clear to all that they were coded messages, often amusing, and completely without context. For example "*Jean has a long moustache*" and "*There is a fire at the insurance agency,*" each one having meaning to a specific Resistance Group.

Because of the sheer number of messages broadcast and the limited number of Germans available to decipher them, the Nazis were frequently behind the curve. Often by the time they were able to decipher a message, the operation would have already been carried out.

In the weeks preceding D Day, lists of "A" and "B" messages were distributed, usually by courier, to the resistance groups giving them instructions as to what to do when the message was broadcast.

The "A" message would then be read out on the radio and upon hearing it the groups were to make preparations to carry out a particular operation, this could be by retrieving arms or explosives from where they had been secretly stashed or moving resistance fighters to the vicinity of the target. On hearing the "B" message, they were to mount the operation immediately.

The most famous pair of these messages is often mistakenly stated to be a general call to arms by the Resistance.

A few days before D-Day, the (slightly misquoted) first line of Verlaine's poem, *Chanson d'Automne*, was transmitted. "*Les sanglots longs des violons de l'automne*" (*Long sobs of autumn violins*) this was an "A" message which alerted the resistance fighters of the Ventriliquist network in the Orléans region, to attack pre-specified railway targets within the next few days once they get the next part of the message.

The second line, and the "B" message "*Bercent mon coeur d'une langueur monotone*" ("soothe my heart with a monotonous languor"), was transmitted late on 5th June, informed the Resistance that the attacks previously mentioned were to be mounted immediately. This in turn would have been interpreted as "The invasion will commence tomorrow."

"Les sanglots longs des violons de l'automne"

From conception to reality, the frame designed to fit on a jeep to transport three stretchers.

RAMC/PE/1/WALL/4

3 STRETCHER FRAME FITTED TO JEEP
BACK SEAT REMOVED
SPARE WHEEL
WINDSCREEN LOWERED

COUNTDOWN TO D DAY

NOVEMBER 1943

In the name of 'national interest', notice is given to the villagers of Tyneham in Dorset that they would be required to leave within 28 days as the area was needed for troops training for the invasion.

The letter explained that a special office would be set up in Wareham for residents' questions, and that: "The Government appreciate that this is no small sacrifice which you are asked to make, but they are sure that you will give this further help towards winning the war with a good heart".

DECEMBER 1943

The last villagers in Tyneham leave on the 17th December believing that one day they would be able to return. Sadly this was never to happen. 252 people were displaced, the last person leaving a notice on the church door:

Please treat the church and houses with care; we have given up our homes where many of us lived for generations to help win the war to keep men free. We shall return one day and thank you for treating the village kindly

JANUARY 1944

The plans for the invasion are revised after the Allied Commanders decided that a far larger force of troops is required than originally thought. To enable this to happen additional aircraft and equipment needed to be found to support the troops and to allow sufficient time for these preparations the date for the invasion slipped a month from the 1st May to the 31st.

Midget submarines of the Combined Operations Pilotage Parties (COPP) are sent to the Normandy beaches in a secret operation to take sand samples. These are needed to confirm that the sand on certain beaches will support the weight of the tanks that the Allies plan to land on D-Day.

British and US aircraft begin to drop weapons and supplies to the Resistance in France thus enabling them to take part in any pre – invasion manoeuvres that will be sent to them via coded messages from the BBC. Back in the UK, the first amphibious exercise for American troops takes place at Slapton Sands, Devon. The exercise involves 16,000 assault troops, and is a rehearsal of the techniques that will be used on D-Day. Slapton Sands was chosen due to its similarity to the beach on the eastern side of the Cotentin Peninsular that will become known as UTAH.

FEBRUARY 1944

In the UK the training and planning for the invasion intensifies. Over a long period of time, The Allied Air Forces of RAF Bomber Command, and the United States Army Air Force's 8th Air Force make a series of bombing raids against key German cities. German fighter aircraft defend against the attacks, resulting in heavy casualties on both sides. However, the Germans feel the impact of these losses more heavily than the Allies and struggle to replace the losses. As a result, by June 1944 the Luftwaffe is not strong enough to oppose any invasion.

27th February:
Sea trials started in the Clyde estuary for the Fighter Direction Tenders (FDT's) these were floating command and control centres which bristled with antenna and aerials for radar, communications and intelligence gathering purposes. Below deck there were various rooms to receive, interpret and communicate data including a radar room, a control room and a filter room. This was in effect a very sophisticated command and control centre. Little wonder secrecy was paramount and remained so for decades. The normal ships complement was about 250 - 7 RN Officers, 53 Seamen, 174 RAF radar & communication personnel plus other specialists.

There were 3 Fighter Direction Tenders designated FDT 13, 216 & 217 which were to become the eyes and ears for the invasion forces. For the trials aircraft were provided by 29 Squadron RAF, 409 Sqn. RCAF and 516 Combined Operations Sqn. RAF all flying from RAF Dundonald the home base of No. 516 Sqn. *

MARCH 1944

After outgrowing its premises, Supreme Allied Commander (General Dwight D. Eisenhower) felt that Supreme Headquarters Allied Expeditionary Force (SHAEF) would be better away from the distractions of London so moves from Norfolk House in central London to Bushy Park, on the western outskirts of the capital.

6th March:
In an attempt to stop the Germans using the French railway network, the Allied Air Forces start the first of many bombing raids.

---

* With thanks to www.combinedops.com

8470. Tyneham, nr. Corfe Castle.

Post Office Row, Tyneham c1930

The same place August 2013

APRIL 1944

3rd April:
Southwick House just North of Portsmouth is earmarked for SHAEF and the Navigational Schools begins to move out.

In early April, much of Britain's coastline becomes a restricted zone. Civilians living outside the ten mile zone cannot enter it, and those inside are unable to leave.

The Royal Navy begins laying mines along the Channel coast to prevent E-Boats (Fast German motor torpedo boats) from attacking Allied shipping.

The Allied Commanders complete the planning for the Invasion, now code named Operation Overlord. Now, the officers in charge of the actual units that will land on the beaches early on D-Day are briefed and begin to draw up their own plans. The troops themselves still have no idea where or when it will happen and continue training.

4th April:
Exercise Smash 1 was held at STUDLAND BAY with the 4th/7th Royal Dragoon Guards and their DD Valentine tanks. Shortly after launching the weather underwent a change, the wind increased and the waves grew bigger. As a result six tanks sank with the loss of six crew members. A valuable lesson was learnt that the tanks were not seaworthy in rough weather.

10th April:
The Allied Naval Officers are now briefed on a landing in Normandy. The operation, code named Neptune, will be supervised by Admiral Bertram Ramsay, the Commander in Chief of the Allied Fleet.

18th April:
Prime Minister Winston Churchill, King George VI and General Dwight D. Eisenhower meet at Fort Henry on Redend Point at Studland to watch the Allied Forces training for D-Day. The VIPs were kept safe in Fort Henry. Built in the previous year it was a specially constructed concrete bunker and observation post, 90 feet long with three feet thick walls, floor and ceiling and was considered a safe place for such VIPs to witness the rehearsal of the Normandy landings.

21st April: Eisenhower has dinner at the Ship Hotel in Chichester, part of a three day visit to troops training in the area. They dined upon, Oysters, Salmon, Filet de Beouf a la Americane, Pomme de Terre Bataille, Pudding Noel and Truffles. The dinner was also attended by nine Air Chief Marshals, Air Marshals or Air vice Marshals and 52 other senior officers. Air Chief Marshal Sir Trafford Leigh-Mallory presided with Wing Commander D Walker as Mr Vice.

Besides Eisenhower and Leigh-Mallory other well known officers included: Sir Arthur Tedder, (Deputy Supreme Commander at SHAEF), 'Sailor' Malan, (Commander of the 145 - Free French - Fighter Wing), Sir Arthur Coningham, (Commander of the tactical air forces for the Normandy campaign) Air Chief Marshal Sir Harry Broadhurst, Roly Beaumont and John Cunningham.

Eisenhower gave an after-dinner speech and flew back to his Headquarters at Bushy Park the next day. He and Air Chief Marshal Leigh-Mallory sent to the officers mess at RAF Tangmere a couple of boxes of cigars which they hoped would be found acceptable.

26th April:
Admiral Sir Bertram Ramsay, moves his headquarters to Southwick House.

27th April.
Exercise Tiger, under the command of Admiral Don P Moon United States (US) Navy, was one of many Invasion rehearsals conducted at Slapton Sands on the South Devon coast. The exercise was so important that Commanders ordered the use of live ammunition to make the exercise as authentic as possible. The first assault landings by LST were made on the morning of the 27th April, following the "bombardment" by the Navy which was to continue throughout the day. A follow up convoy of eight LST were expected later that night and it was this convoy that met with tragedy following a series of blunders.

2145:
LST Group 32, (Plymouth Convoy T-4 section) left Plymouth heading towards Brixham, it consisted of LST 515, 496, 511, 531 and 58 and was joined by the escort vessel, HMS *Azela* near the Eddystone Rocks where it was joined by the Brixham section of the Convoy T-4 composed of LST 499, 289 and 507.

2200+:
Lyme Bay: a group of nine German E-Boats set out on a normal reconnaissance mission from their base in Cherbourg. Following their regular route they head towards the Lyme Bay area and spotted the LST convoy. Since they could not see any

Fort Henry at Studland
2013

Southwick House, near Portsmouth
2013

Naval escorts, they positioned themselves for a torpedo attack. As the convoy approached Lyme Bay it was turning to head back towards the shore. It was around here that the E-Boats attacked.

German E-Boats, regularly patrolled the English Channel at night, following the same route. The Commander in Chief at Plymouth who was overall responsible for the safety of the exercise placed extra patrols across the mouth of Lyme Bay, consisting of two destroyers from the Royal Navy, three motor torpedo boats (MTB) and two motor gunboats. Another MTB patrol was sent to watch Cherbourg, where the German E-Boats were based.

28th April. 0200:
LST 507 was hit in the auxiliary engine room cutting all electrical power. The ship then burst into flames and due to the lack of power the crew were unable to contain the fire.

0245:
All those left on LST 507 were ordered to abandon ship. LST 531 was hit by two torpedoes causing her to burst into flames and sink inside of six minutes. Several minutes later LST 289 was also torpedoed, however, she managed to limp back to port with many dead and wounded on board. Many soldiers and sailors went down with their ships after being trapped below deck. Some leapt into the sea and drowned, weighed down by the waterlogged coats and others who had mistakenly put their life belts around their waists rather than under their armpits. In all 749 American soldiers and sailors died that evening during Exercise Tiger. Recent investigations state that this may well have been more. This exercise turned out to be one of the great tragedies of World War II. More American soldiers and sailors died needlessly on the exercise than did on Utah beach on D Day.

In addition to the above the bombing of the beaches by the destroyers had been put back an hour, this message, due to the wrong frequency being given out, did not reach the troops scheduled to land on the beach when the bombing stopped. This resulted in the troops landing as the firing was still going on and as live ammunition was used this resulted in men being shelled as they arrived on the beach. Hundreds of men died needlessly.

Investigations revealed two main reasons for the tragedy, firstly lack of naval escort vessels and secondly an error in radio frequencies which were issued with serious typographical errors which resulted in the LST's being on different radio frequencies to the Corvette and the commanding officers on shore. The convoy was supposed to be accompanied by a Royal Navy Corvette and a World War I destroyer. The Corvette was there but the Destroyer was in for repair, with a replacement not being available.

When the news reached the Allied Commanders, not only were they saddened about the great loss of life, but also that 10 BIGOT cleared officers who held the Invasion Plans were also missing. If this information fell into German hands it would reveal all the details of the Normandy landings. This was so serious the Allied Commanders considered changing the details of Operation Overlord presuming that the plans were in enemy hands. Incredibly every one of the missing bodies were found thus ensuring that the safety of the D Day secrets.

Meanwhile the incident was kept at top secret level. All survivors were given strict orders not to discuss it with anybody. Even medical staff at the military hospitals who treated the wounded were sworn to secrecy under pain of court martial; they could not even ask the injured how they acquired their wounds. What happened at Lyme Bay was just seen as a wartime incident.

"After leave we sailed for Plymouth and while we were there took part in 'Operation Tiger', a full scale rehearsal for the invasion of France. HMS Hawkins, HMS Enterprise and 3 'O' class Destroyers had to bombard the beach at Slapton sands. Although 'H' hour had been retarded by 1 hour some of the LCT's and LST's had landed gear and troops. After about 10 minutes of high explosive shoot we were stopped and told that the Americans on the beach had about 200 casualties. We steamed back to Devonport dockyard and later that night an 'E' Boat flotilla from Cherbourg attacked the convoy of Landing Ships, sinking two and badly damaging a third with a combined loss of over 1100 troops. Some of the Americans drowned because they wore their life belts around their waists and when they dived in the water they floated upside down. Their belts were instantly inflated by a little compressed air cylinder in the belt. Royal Naval life belts were worn under the arms with a loop around the neck and tied with tapes and were inflated by mouth through a rubber teat. We were taught to go over the side feet first.. This disaster, at the time, had to be kept under wraps because we were so near the '2nd Front' and knowledge in America of the 'incident' would have caused an outcry among American public." *Royal Marine WCS Hiscock, PO/X112968 - HQ192 Squad

---

* Extract from Marine Hiscocks diary with the kind permission of his family.

Rommel observes the fall of shot at Riva-Bella, just north of Caen in the area that would become Sword Beach in Normandy.

Bundesarchiv, Bild 101I-300-1863-29 / Speck / CC-BY-SA

May 1944

Eisenhower and Montgomery move into Southwick House, just north of Portsmouth which for the next four months becomes the Headquarters for Operation Overlord. An order was placed with Chad Valley Toys, of Birmingham, to produce a map covering the area from Northern Norway down to Spain. When the map was completed it was packed into cases and was taken to Southwick House under the escort of a Naval Lieutenant and 2 carpenters from Chad Valley. On arrival the map was put up on the east wall of the Drawing Room by the carpenters, the packing cases were then destroyed. To maintain secrecy the 2 carpenters were retained at Southwick House for several weeks doing odd jobs until after D Day.

Admiral Ramsay the Allied Naval Commander wrote over 3000 orders for OPERATION NEPTUNE and the House visitors list shows some 300 senior Naval and Royal Marine Officers from many nations that came to be briefed in the days leading up to the 6th June.

Around this time a Royal Navy CPO and his family moved from Portsmouth to Porchester to be a bit safer and away from the bombs. The CPO was based at Southwick House as a wireless operator. His job was to drive up and down the south coast in an Austin Tilly packed with radio equipment and transmit "dummy" messages as part of the effort to fool the enemy into believing that second front would be arriving at Calais. Whilst all this was going on his 12 year old son was digging bullets out of the chalk pit the local "Dads Army" were using as target practice whilst his 18 year old daughter was amusing herself with the troops based in the area. Apparently, there were many American visitors at the house for tea!

2nd May:
The date for D-Day is delayed from 31 May. Two windows in the following month are identified based on the tides and moonlight: 5-7 June and 18-20 June.

Exercise Fabius commences at several sites along the south coast of England. This is the last and largest exercise before D-Day. In total, 25,000 troops are involved in practice landings at a number of different beaches: the British 50th Division at Hayling Island; the Canadian 3rd Division at Bracklesham Bay; the British 3rd Division at Littlehampton. The exercises last until 8 May.

4th May 0337:
Whilst taking part in Exercise Fabius, HMS *Offa*, an O-Class Destroyer, was attacked by aircraft off St Catherine's Point. One bomb hit the upper deck and caused splinter holes in the hull. Structure damage was light, unfortunately three were killed and four wounded.

0352:
2 MTB's, (Motor torpedo boat) 708 and 720 were attacked by Beaufighters. 708 was set alight and subsequently sank, four officers and seven ratings wounded.

"In the Bristol Channel all day long, waiting to be called. Weather very rough, felt rather sea sick."
Signalman John Emrys, HMS Diadem

15th May:
The final briefing for Allied Senior Officers takes place at St Paul's School, London. It is attended by King George VI and Prime Minister Winston Churchill.

*A Personal Account of the days leading up to D Day by Patrick L. Payne.

Patrick was assigned a Landing Craft Assault (LCA) that had been adapted to fire spigot bombs over a landing beach. Over 20 were released as a salvo with a spread and range designed to cover a large area of the beach. The bombs were designed to explode before they hit the beach so that the pressure wave they created would set off any land mines designed to destroy vehicles or men.

"By now we were in the second week of May 1944 and the pace of the preparations for the long awaited invasion visibly intensified. There was a sense of purpose and urgency in the air, as the years of planning and training came to fruition. Many taking part in the invasion experienced a perplexing mixture of emotions from excitement to anxiety but overriding all, amongst my group at least, there was a strong sense that we had a job to do. My actual diary entries invite you to share my experiences and thoughts during what turned out to be the Countdown to D-Day.

9th May:
This forenoon I went out on speed trials on Southampton Water. The fairway was crowded with landing craft of all types and sizes. The preparations for the invasion must be ready and

---
* Taken from "Flat Bottoms and Square Ends" by Geoffrey Slee due out 2014 - with thanks.

C-47s with CG-4 Waco Gliders just before D-Day, 1944, 316th Troop Carrier Group, 37th TCS. United States Army Air Force from National Archives.

Resolute faces of paratroopers just before they took off for the initial assault of D-Day. Paratrooper in foreground has just read Gen. Eisenhower's message of good luck and clasps his bazooka in grim determination. USNA *now we all wait for our orders and commands, the nights are still frosty but the days are sunny and hot.*

12th May:
It is all very well to say that invasion fever is not gripping the nation (as a Swedish newspaper says) but there is tension in the air. Yesterday houses in London are said to have been shaken by the explosions in France from our bombing, and today the air here has vibrated all the time with the sound of aircraft engines. Today 12 white sacks arrived for the flotilla. They are marked 'Not to be opened till signal, 'Open on One' and obviously contain invasion orders, charts and plans, - or at least that's what we think. Each bag is locked and sealed and I have the custody of the keys.

14th May:
I went over to Northney with Paddy Martin to do a shoot in his craft in company with two other craft. We loaded twelve bombs and set course down the Hamble at 0924. In the Solent we had a strong NE wind on our beam and off Southsea we turned head to it and much spray came on board. We had our bag luncheon at Sandy Point near the entrance to Chichester Harbour and finally did the shoot out to sea, as the beach was being used. When fired, the bombs shoot high into the air and always remind me of large black dots. They curve over and land about 250 yards away, bursting on impact and making a huge explosion and blast and columns of black smoke and water were shot high up into the air. Having successfully done our shoot, we returned to Cricket by 1630.

The papers certainly have 'invasionitis' and every day there are maps and comments. In Italy, the great offensive is going well and the 8th and 5th Armies have reached the Gustav Line, a heavily fortified German defensive line. The barrage put down before the infantry went in was the heaviest yet, with 2000 guns firing. The Russians, having captured Sebastopol, are now fairly quiet but I think they are preparing another offensive along the whole of their front. The Japs in Burma are taking a drubbing and are being pushed back by the 14th Army. In New Guinea things are quiet except for heavy bombing. America has invasion and election fever, the former seemingly stronger than the latter.

A Mosquito has just flown the Atlantic in five and a half hours, an average speed of 325 m.p.h. How we progress! The King having completed the Empire Conference has been with the Home Fleet. He saw the 'human torpedo', one of which recently sank an Italian cruiser in Palermo Harbour and also the X class midget sub, three of which attacked and hard hit 'Tirpitz' in Alten Fiord recently. Barracuda aircraft gave him a demonstration of how they smashed Tirpitz at a later date. In fact we might say that apart from E and U boats, the enemy fleet is no more.

16th May:
I am duty officer today and all the others have gone off to Southampton for an inspection by Commander Force J, who happens to be my old skipper, G, M Oliver from Hermione days. I am sorry not to be there.

For the last two nights the air and ground have been shaking due to German planes blitzing our troops and ships. The raid last night was complete with flares, cannon fire, night fighters, AA fire and German planes. Hello, - there go the sirens again so I suppose a Hun has returned to have a look at the results of last night. Actually there were not many bombs and I think the main reason was recce. On Sunday night (or Monday morning) there was very heavy flak and searchlights but few bombs. In all, 15 German planes were shot down, 14 over here and 1 over France. I turned out as usual to watch the raid and saw a JU-88 caught in a cone of searchlights and held there for several moments. Tracer, Bofors, 3.7", 4.5" were all having a go at it, and when I last saw the plane, it seemed to be going down.

Last night the gunfire was more intense and the planes seemed more numerous. The air seemed to break and then reform with the noise varying from the sharp 'crack, crack, crack' of the Bofors to the thunder of the long-barrelled 3.5" guns. I ventured outside to watch but was driven back for shelter as debris came down, - pieces of shell or perhaps bullets. Planes roared and dived overhead and bursts of machine gun and cannon fire indicated that battles were going on up there between the German planes and our night fighters. One Jerry came roaring down towards Brixie at full throttle and I thought for a moment he might drop an egg. I get quite a nervous thrill at these times for one never knows what is going to happen and the anticipation of 'something' is quite stimulating.

19th May:
At last I have a craft! I went over to Hayling Island yesterday to store her up and today I brought her round to the Base. She is LCA (HR) 1071 and, though rather dirty and knocked about, yet I think with a bit of hard work, some paint and a few hours with the chippies, she'll be shipshape. I think I shall call her Hitler's Hearse, but I'll have to consult the

Rommel and his officers inspecting the Atlantic Wall April 1944
Bundesarchiv, Bild 101I-719-0243-33 / Jesse / CC-BY-SA

Anti Tank ditch at Riva Bella. Capt. G Lugg personal collection *crew. Anyway it's something to get on with and I feel quite proud of her, as proud perhaps as if she was my own 35,000 ton battleship.*

Yesterday at long last I had a letter from Alan who appears to be in Empire Cutlass somewhere near here. This is the first time I've heard from him since I left Inverary. More shipping in the Solent.
Yesterday, the 8th Army captured Cassino and the Gustav Line has been bust wide open. Today I saw a JU-88 and a FW-190. They were part of a circus of captured German planes, which is being used for aircraft recognition purposes.

20th May:
Yesterday spent the whole time in 1071 and the same today, painting and tidying her up. We've now painted the whole of the upper deck, the upper works, and the letters on her hull and quite a bit of the interior. I've got my machine guns and the 2" mortars and tomorrow I'm taking in my 24 HR bombs. In fact, apart from storing up and fuelling, we shall be ready to go. There is one thing, which worries me, - we are only using 16 craft, 8 to a Division and we've got 18 craft. That means that two will be spares and I only hope that mine is not to be one of those. I wouldn't miss the coming show for anything. The great offensive in Italy goes on and makes progress.

Last night we had a noisy half hour when the Huns came over for a 'look/see' again. The flak was heavy and concentrated and I saw one plane caught in the searchlights with shells bursting all round it. The Germans dropped 'staircases' of green flares over the Solent and the Bofors had a good time shooting these out.

24th May:
Am just about to go down to the craft for another day's work. We had a signal that HM The King will be in the Hamble for a short time this morning, so I wonder if he'll come up as far as Cricket. A quiet night and no noise to be heard except for tanks moving on the main road.

25th May:
Troops are no longer permitted to send or receive mail.

26th May:
The weather has reverted to the proper type for this time of the year and it's been quite warm. The work on the craft is nearly finished and she's trim from stem to stern.

27th May:
A really scorching day with no cloud and a blazing summer sun. I'm sunbathing in a jock strap but now have to go down to Cleaver's Yard to put the craft on the slip. It's annoying but can't be helped. Tomorrow I take her to Tormentor to get work started on her towing gear. When that's done, I shall really be ready except for bombing up again.

29th May:
Whit Monday. The weather is exceeding its usual summer nature for May and yesterday was the hottest Whit Sunday for 10 years and the temperature exceeded 87F in the shade!

England at Whitsun is a happy place and war does not alter that. Rail travel has been cut down, food and drink are short and of course there are no cars. However, the English have amused themselves with a stay at home holiday and all places of entertainment have been full. At Lords an English XI is playing an Australian XI before 40,000 spectators. Hampstead has its Fun Fair and the Zoo and Kew Gardens have been packed, whilst all the available seaside resorts have had their quota. Of course the South Coast is a banned area now and it is empty.

At Easter I went over to Torquay with Alan and Joan and it was practically deserted. Here, we've been lying on the grass practically naked and spraying one another using a stirrup pump. Last night it was so hot that I took my bedding outside and slept by the hut. The sirens went just after I had gone to sleep but the alert did not last long. I shall sleep outside again tonight. One thing, which might cause Nelson to show surprise, - the sight of the Waterhens, the Wrens who crew the despatch boats down at Tormentor. They are a very comely lot and certainly care for their craft. They wear white flannels and blue matlot trousers and either go bare foot or wear gym shoes.

30th May:
Have just finished breakfast and am about to go down to Tormentor. Slept outside again last night and was joined by Harper and Watts. The sirens went as usual but no guns or bombs, and the 'Raiders Passed' sounded. Later there was another alert and this time plenty of gunfire. A Jerry came over and there was a red flash in the sky, as if it had dropped a large flare. It only lasted for a few seconds and then went out to be followed by much cracklings and pops, which I could not understand. However, the noise went on and on and I suddenly realised that a bomb must have hit an ammunition dump.

"*On the afternoon of 5 June our officers walked amongst us, giving the lads confidence, but there was always the boy who didn't give a damn. They cleared the air a lot with their wisecracks and later on made Jerry sit up. They were the tough lads of nineteen, some of whom were awarded the Military Medal for their exploits. Then another request, not an order as such - the Padre, Captain Lovegrove, wanted to say a few words to us. Padres were always very kind and understanding and would always have something to say about their beliefs. We were given a short sermon and I will tell you, everybody listened. It gave us food for thought. After the Padre was finished, our battalion commander gave us a message from Monty, saying what he was expecting of us, knowing he could rely on our ability to put up a good show." Bill Cheall - Green Howards

* Reproduced with the kind permission of his family.

France -. German soldiers (pioneers) in mining of a bridge of 815 N Calvados, Le Canal ... adives. Inscription on bridge "Caution mine chamber"; KBZ Whether West

Bundesarchiv, Bild 101I-721-0382-31A / Vennemann, Wolfgang / CC BY-SA

Later, back from Tormentor, heard that the noises last night resulted from a Hun crashing on to a Canadian tank ammunition dump at Sarisbury Green and that 30 people were killed. I have not heard this is confirmed. At Tormentor put craft on the slip and worked on her. She'll be finished tomorrow and I'll bring her back here and then we only have to store up again and we shall be ready.

1800:
Have spent the afternoon on my bunk, in a cold bath and having my hair cut. After all that, I repaired to the office where we had a meeting to discuss the coming operation. We still don't know where or when. The SECRET plan of action is as follows: - and is not to be read by any spy...!

a) There are two beaches, one shallow, one steep-to. Our division goes to the shallow one and beaches to fire. The other division goes to the steep one and does not beach.

We are all towed over by LCG (Landing Craft Gun,) a converted LCT mounting a 4" Quick Firing gun. or LCF [Landing Craft Flak, an LCT with AA weapons) to within 5000 yards of the beaches. We then slip and proceed towards the beaches taking up position ahead of our respective LCT. We fire our bombs when about 500 yards from the beach entrances, which could be gullies, ravines or gaps. Our bombs will cause a noise and blow up any booby traps, etc. We shall then come quietly out and rush off to our LSI, which will hoist us and bring us back to dear old Angleterre; there to await further orders. That is the plan and we now wait for the order 'Open on One'

By now, the troops that will land in Normandy on D-Day and immediately afterwards are in camps all along the south coast of England. Before the end of May, the troops are sealed in the camps, to guard the secret that the landings are imminent. Vehicles and other equipment are waterproofed, to ensure that they can wade through deep water when landing on the beaches. In the last days of May, the troops are briefed on their tasks for D-Day.

31st May:
The first troops begin to load onto the ships and landing craft that will take them to Normandy. The size of the landing force means that the embarkation process is spread over five days. The majority still do not know exactly where the landings will take place."

THURSDAY 1st June

In the evening, the first part of a poem by Paul Verlaine is broadcast by the BBC: "Les sanglots lourds/Des violons de l'automne..." ("The heavy sobs of autumn's violins..."). This is a coded warning message for the French Resistance relating to the preparations for railway sabotage (not a general message to the Resistance, as is often stated) and means that the invasion will take place within one month. The second part of the poem will be broadcast on the night preceding the invasion. The Abwehr (German military intelligence) intercepts the message and is aware of its significance.

At midday on 1st June Admiral Sir Bertram Ramsay assumed operational command of "Neptune" Forces and general control of Operations in the channel.

FRIDAY 2ND June

All across the South of England, huge military conveys make their way from the camps they have been waiting in for some time towards the embarkation ports.

In each port, special vehicle slipways (hards) were built, and the existing piers were converted into ammunition dumps. Hundreds of silver barrage balloons attached to the landing-craft filled the skies.

A special train was sent to Droxford in Hampshire. It was shunted into the long siding, where it stayed under armed guard for 2 days. On board is Winston Churchill, General Eisenhower, William Mackenzie King, Jan Smuts and other Allied leaders. During their stay they make crucial decisions regarding the final planning and execution of the invasion of Europe. General D'Gaulle is also briefed here but due to the location of the train he has to walk up the track from the station. The location is chosen as there is a tunnel nearby that the train can be pulled into in case the Luftwaffe strike in the area.

Today a wooden plaque on the post box outside the Station commemorates the event.

SATURDAY 3rd June

Early in the morning, the chief weather forecaster, Group Captain James Stagg, predicts bad weather in the channel and South of England (at this point, the chosen date is the 5 June). Churchill visits Southampton, Portsmouth and Southwick House. US airborne troops are briefed, they now know

The Atlantic Wall Pas de Calais

Bundesarchiv, Bild 101I-719-0240-05 / Jesse / CC-BY-SA

where they are going. Most other troops are still in the dark.

*"*Everybody was wondering when we were going to get cracking; it was becoming a bit boring. Sometimes, we would lie on our bunks thinking and some lad would start talking about what he would do when it was all over and wondering if his girl would be waiting for him. Sadly, some of these lads would never see their girls again if fate played a tragic part. Then, after three days of almost claustrophobic conditions, the tannoy system came to life, telling us to pay utmost attention. Our commanding officer then proceeded to speak. You could have heard a pin drop; no longer were we going to be kept in the dark.*

"It was to be France. That moment made the deepest impression in my mind. Our battalion would be landing on a three-mile stretch of beach between Le Hamel and La Riviere, having the code name King on the coast of Normandy, on a sixty mile front. Then we knew we would be the first and it all began to come together; what we had been training for. The invasion was so vast and complex that it was beyond our capacity to absorb it all. "he talk put us in the picture and we all knew how very important it was to go into the battle with the determination and grit which had been drilled into us for months. I don't know how the two hundred or so newcomers to the battalion coped with the news, because this would be their first confrontation with the enemy. Most of us had faced the enemy several times but gave no hint to the new lads about what could happen in the battle. We gave them every means of support and when the critical time came, found they were made of good stuff and soon learned the vital lessons of conflict." Bill Cheall - Green Howards

SUNDAY 4th June.

Erwin Rommel travels to Germany for his wife's birthday. He plans to return on 8th June and believes that the weather is too bad for the Allies to land in the meantime. In the afternoon, an Associated Press report announces that the invasion has begun! Apparently a teletype operator was practising and didn't realise the machine was live. The news is then broadcast around the world, until Associated Press issues a hastily prepared correction five minutes later.

Major-General Gale visits the Airborne Troops and wishes them God speed and good hunting.

1100:
Christ Church, Portsdown. Allied headquarters staff held a church service. It was afterwards that the news arrived that D Day had been postponed for 24 hours due to bad weather. London Road that ran outside the church was one of the main routes into Portsmouth (the A3) for the various troops and vehicles, it was also the limit at which locals could enter without a pass. Those present at the service returned in 1948 to present two stained glass windows to the church to commemorate the vigil.

MONDAY 5TH June.

0500:
Southwick House, near Portsmouth. It is a relaxed gathering of the Chiefs of Staff that meet on the morning of the 5th June. Mallory is smoking his pipe sitting in an arm chair chatting to Major General Bedel Smith, other Chiefs of Staff sit around a table, Monty strutted about in a slightly less relaxed manner. Eisenhower enters the room in battledress and smiles.
Group Captain Stagg who heads up the British weather team knows the British climate well. He has been correct so far and has now discovered a brief "window" between the bad weather of the 5th and another impending low, there is a small break sufficient to get the vital part of the invasion underway. After briefing everybody Stagg is bombarded with questions from every angle. There is then silence for about 30 seconds with all eyes on Eisenhower, then very quietly he said...."*OK. We'll Go!*" Eisenhower had come to the decision that despite the weather not being perfect, the invasion would have to take place the next day, 6th June 1944. Any further postponement for days or even several weeks until tide and moon were favourable would be most harmful to the morale of the troops and would also lose the benefit of surprise.

H Hour would therefore be 0630 for the American sector and 0725 to 0745 in the British Sector.

Admiral Ramsay subsequently remarked that although the terrible weather caused difficulties and damage to craft off the beaches, the advantage gained by surprise were so striking that the decision of the Supreme Commander to go despite the weather was justified. *"A postponement of more than one day would, in the event, have proved disastrous owing to conditions of sea off the beaches. The problems arising out of postponement of 12 to 14 days to the next suitable period are too appalling to contemplate."*

* Reproduced with the kind permission of his family.

Christ Church, Portsdown and the two stained glass window panels. July 2013

Marshalling Area Certificate for the Emsworth area in Hampshire.

RM Museum, Southsea. 7/19/5

Nº 02459

MARSHALLING AREA CERTIFICATE

This card certifies that the holder described as under is on essential duty and requires to enter Marshalling Camps and Embarkation Areas. It is NOT VALID unless produced with an official Identity document.

Name......C. F. Phillips..........

Rank......Lt. Col. RM..........

No. of Identity document......03719..........

Formation or Unit......47 (RM) Cdo..........

Signature of holder......C.F. Phillips..........

Signature of issuing authority...... H.Q. 50 (N) DIVISION

Date...... 2 MAY 1944

(B44/301)   G.S. BRANCH

It was now all go. Allied Junior Officers open their sealed orders to find out the exact location of the landings. Black and white stripes are painted on all Allied aircraft, for recognition purposes. Not the nice masked off straight lines you see on aircraft today but hastily painted by hand and with floor brushes.

In case the operation failed, Eisenhower prepared a statement that read: *"Our landings in the Cherbourg-La Harve area have failed to gain a satisfactory foothold and I have withdrawn the troops. My decision to attack at this time and place was based on the best information available. If any blame or fault attaches to this attempt, it is mine alone."* It is wrongly dated as 5th July 1944

The second half of Verlaine's poem is broadcast by the BBC as a coded message to the French Resistance. *Blessent mon cœur d'une langueur monotone* (wound my heart with a monotonous languor) was the specific call to action and meant that the Invasion would take place in the next 48 hours and that the resistance should begin to sabotage the railways and communication lines.
The German Military Intelligence Service (The Abwehr) intercepted the message and knew exactly what it meant. They immediately pass an invasion alert on to various headquarters, including that of the German 15th Army (based in Northern France). However, the German 7th Army in Normandy is not alerted as German Commanders had received a number of invasion alerts over recent months and consider this to be another incident of The Abwehr crying wolf.

6th Green Howard War Diaries: *Today should have been D Day with H Hour at 0635 hrs, but owing to the adverse weather conditions, the landing has been postponed 24 hours.*

1815:
LSI's with 6th Green Howard's aboard move down the Solent towards the open sea.

1900:
LCT's with Carriers, Anti Tank and specialist platoons move down the Solent in one huge array - flotilla following flotilla! Weather moderate to fair but the sea still is "choppy."

"It was Monday June 5th 1944 and our craft, together with some 4000 other forms of shipping with thousands of fully trained men. lifted themselves, took up their stations and, with a last wave to onlookers on the shore, headed slowly out into the English Channel to assemble on the southern side of the Isle of Wight. In the early evening, with high winds and rough seas, the journey to France was about to begin.

Large passenger vessels crammed with troops, minesweepers, escort ships scurrying about, large warships and landing craft took up their places ready to move off and the men entrusted with the initial assault looked, thought and wondered, where would they be tomorrow. Barrage balloons floated above at the end of steel ropes to deter low flying aircraft from attacking the invasion force. They were blown from side to side in the strong winds and the men watched the choppy seas and knew it would be a very uncomfortable trip ending with disembarkation onto heavily defended enemy held beaches. Sadly the journey for some would end all too soon.

"Action Stations" for the men of LCF.30 required the manning of small Pom-Pom and Oerlikon anti aircraft guns throughout the night, not knowing what the morning would bring. For most of those 18 and 19 year olds, this was to be their first big adventure. Hundreds of planes flew overhead, some to drop bombs on the beach defences, some to slow down the deployment of enemy reinforcements and some troop carrying planes towing gliders packed full with troops with the task of landing silently to capture strategic positions before the main assault force had landed.

At sea the invading armada kept steadily on, no lights were visible. "Maintain your station" was the order, a very difficult thing to achieve with flat bottomed craft with no hull. Collisions at sea at this crucial time would be disastrous and could not be allowed to happen. During the night, the coast of France came into view. As far as the eye could see along the 80 kilometre of landing beaches, they were lit by fires caused by bombing and shelling. At this early stage there was no indication that the enemy knew we were coming." *Stan Grayland

0900:
5th June, the first groups of landing craft sail from the Portsmouth area and from then on there was a constant stream of ships passing the Needles and the Nab Tower. Force "G" proceeds through the Needles Channel, Force "J" and those portions of Force "S" in this area – Assault Groups S1 and S3 use the Spithead and Lumps Fort entrances. As the first convoy leaves Spithead the signal *"Good Luck: Drive on"* was hoisted on the Largs, Rear Admiral Talbots Flagship, which was anchored at the eastern end of the Force "S" line of LST, and kept flying until her own departure at 2145.

---
* Reproduced with the kind permission of his family.

The weather in the Channel was the worst for twenty years and, to our cost, we soon found out for ourselves."

Bill Cheall - Green Howards

The USS TIDE a Navy minesweeper that preceded the invasion armada to the coast of Normandy, dies in the waters off France. This striking picture, made from a Coast Guard Fighting ship, shows the stricken vessel burning as two other ships stand by to pick up survivors. A few moments later the TIDE sank to the bottom. As a photo that would have been printed at the time, you will notice that the equipment on the masts have been painted out.

USNA

The weather conditions were unexpectedly severe and tested the landing craft crews. The wind was west, force 5, easing to force 3 and 4 and veering to the North West later in the evening. Apparently, the German Meteorological Officer informed the German Command that the invasion would not be possible on the 5th or 6th June on account of the terrible weather which was expected to last for a few days, thus enforcing the element of surprise which was firmly in the favour of the allies.

Men of the 3rd Canadian Infantry Division and the 2nd Canadian Armoured Brigade have already boarded the ships. LCA slung from the davits, the ships sail at dawn, followed by the large landing crafts for infantry and tanks. On the way, Subaltern Officers and later troops were briefed. They broke open the seals and took out the maps where the actual targets were shown. This was no exercise…

1100:
Keevil, 225th Parachute Field Ambulance attached to the 5th Parachute Brigade. The unit, less No 2 + 3 Sections paraded and marched to the airfield, for final fitting of parachutes, and for stowing kit in the aircraft.

1700:
The French Commandos board two LCI (Landing Craft Infantry): No 527 LCI for Troop 1 and 528 for Troop 8 and learn the destination of the invasion. Specifically, they must land near the town of Ouistreham, in front of a place called La Breche (Sword Beach).

1745:
"We set sail with the armada to the coast of France. With the number of ships around us, we could barely see the water at all. The ship's engines began to throb. This was the big battle, and we were going to give the enemy something to contemplate. Altogether, 160,000 men would take part in the first landing.

"We were prepared even more than the Germans were in the early years of the war. Hitler was going to be beaten; no longer would he think he had the God given right to be victorious. These thoughts were going through our heads as we sang, 'Will I Live to See another Day'. Sadly, many of us would not see another sunrise. But for those of us who survived, the memories would be everlasting.

It was getting dusk as we put to sea and we were all below decks. It would have been good to see England from the sea but perhaps it was just as well that we couldn't as it might have made us think of home and this was not the time to let our concentration wander to things sentimental. I believe that any soldier, no matter what control he has over his feelings, would feel a little thoughtful about the outcome of what we were about to undertake. Beneath the surface, I am certain that he is aware of the fact that he might be killed. If so, how would he die? But once the attack goes in, that strange, natural feeling changes to one of grim determination. Fear does not come into the equation as he is alongside thousands of boys just like him and will not let them down no matter what."
Bill Cheall - Green Howards

1830:
Churchill held the last meeting before D Day in the war cabinet. The meeting was missing a key player, that of General De Gaulle who was still in his hotel room in the Connaught fuming that in the pre-arranged BBC broadcast to the French for the following day, he was last behind various Heads of State and Eisenhower. This together with the wording of Eisenhower's declaration and the part the Free French would play in the invasion seriously irritated him. He also refused to send liaison officers out with the invasion fleet resulting in the situation between the Free French leader and Churchill being very strained. In fact he upset Churchill so much that he suggested that the General should be deported.

1900:
Garbo's radio operator sends a message to Germany stating that the Invasion was imminent and that it would be in Normandy but that it was a diversion and the real landings would be taking place in Pas de Calais. If the Germans took the bait, when the troops did arrive in Normandy they would assume that Garbo was telling the truth and would believe the deception that the "real" raid would be in Calais. And take it they did, hook line and sinker.

225th Parachute Field Ambulance were given a hot meal. Following this the unit paraded and messages from C-in-C 21 Army Group and Allied Supreme HQ were read out. Rev Briscoe said a few short prayers.

1930:
1st Canadian Parachute Battalion paraded in full kit. All ranks checked and inspected to see if escape kits were well hidden and that no incriminating documents were being carried. C Company left for their airfield. Remainder of Battalion proceed to Down Ampney where each stick reports to its aircraft.

2030: The pilots of the three Czech squadrons based at the makeshift airfield of Appledram just

"[1] The call has come at last. We are on our way to the greatest invasion ever. Feeling very cool and collected. I pray to be given the strength to go through this like a man and not lose my nerve, and hope that I may return to my little family who are so dear to me.

Tomorrow morning at 3 o'clock we fire the first shot. There are hundreds of invasion barges with us how hard it is to be away from my family in such a place as this I went on duty at midnight till 4 o'clock."

Signalman John Emrys, HMS Diadem.

[1] Reproduced with the kind permission of his family.

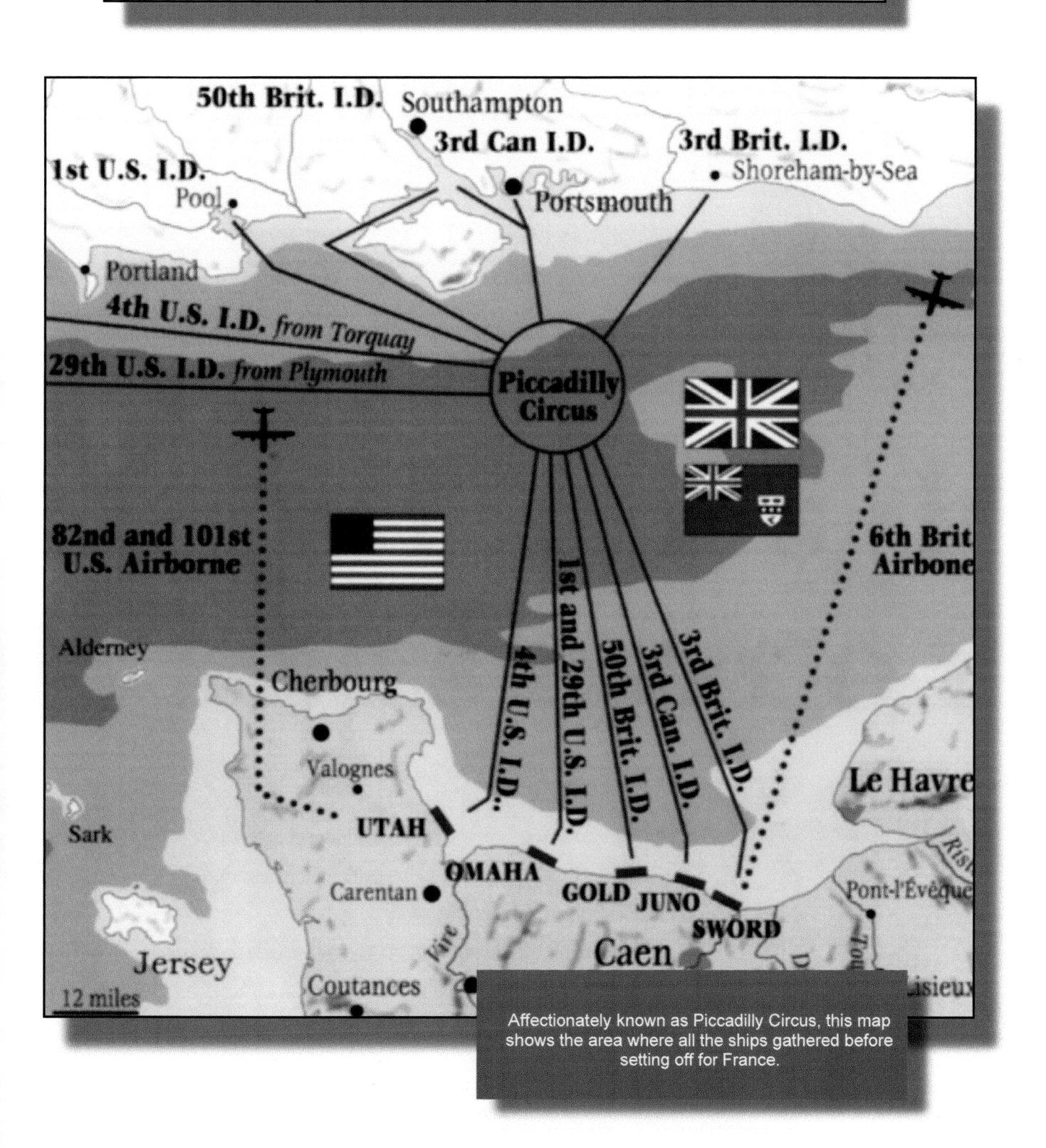

Affectionately known as Piccadilly Circus, this map shows the area where all the ships gathered before setting off for France.

BIGOT — ~~TOP~~ SECRET — Col LEE — BIGOT

~~SECRET~~

SCAEF 21st MEETING

2nd June, 1944

SUPREME HEADQUARTERS
ALLIED EXPEDITIONARY FORCE
Office of AC of S, G-3

Minutes of Meeting held in the ANXF Conference Room
at SOUTHWICK HOUSE at 1000 hours, 2nd June, 1944

PRESENT

General Dwight D. Eisenhower
Air Chief Marshal Sir A. Tedder
Admiral Sir B.H. Ramsay
General Sir B.L. Montgomery
Air Chief Marshal Sir T.L. Leigh-Mallory
Lieutenant General W.B. Smith
Lieutenant General Sir H.M. Gale
Rear Admiral J.E. Creasy
Major General H.R. Bull
Major General K.V. Strong
Major General F.W. de Guingand
Air Vice Marshal H.E.P. Wigglesworth
Air Vice Marshal J.M. Robb
Brigadier General A.S. Nevins

I. WEATHER FORECAST

The agreed weather forecast was presented orally by Group Captain Stagg. Admiral Ramsay and Air Chief Marshal Leigh-Mallory stated the effect of the predicted weather conditions from the Naval and Air Force viewpoints, respectively. General discussion followed.

The Supreme Commander directed that the sailing of Bombarding Squadrons and other preparations necessary at this time should proceed. The next SCAEF meeting for further critical examination of the weather forecast is to be held at 2130 hours, 2nd June, in the ANXF Conference Room at SOUTHWICK HOUSE.

II. BOMBING ON D DAY AND SUBSEQUENT DAYS

Air Chief Marshal Leigh-Mallory discussed the plan for bombing, on D day and subsequent days, designated to establish a belt of bombed routes through towns and villages thereby preventing or impeding the movement of enemy formations toward the areas seized by our troops. He inquired as to his freedom to proceed with the execution of this plan in view of the civilian casualties which would result. Air Chief Marshal Tedder stated the necessity of being certain of the efficacy of this line of action.

The Supreme Commander announced his approval of the planned bombing as an operational necessity to assist the Army in landing and in securing a firm foothold.

III. WARNING THE FRENCH

Air Chief Marshal Leigh-Mallory inquired if any additional methods could be adopted to warn the FRENCH inhabitants of the bombing. Air Chief Marshal Tedder advocated the dropping of warning leaflets on D day and subsequent days to minimize civilian casualties.

DECLASSIFIED
Authority _Guidelines for Con Hdqr 7/5/72_
By _ARK_ NLE DATE _11/5/73_

Downgraded to SECRET per
DoD dir 5200.9, 9-27-58.
WGL 7-18-67

~~TOP~~ SECRET — BIGOT

The AC of S, G-3, was directed to arrange with the PW Division for the provision of appropriate leaflets to be dropped by the Air Forces within the lodgement and cover areas on D day and subsequent days.

IV. NEXT SCAEF MEETING

It was announced that the next SCAEF meeting would be held in the ANXF Conference Room at Southwick House at 2130 hours, 2nd June, 1944.

DISTRIBUTION

    One copy each officer present
    One extra copy to Air Chief Marshal Sir A. Tedder
    One copy each to Lieutenant General F. E. Morgan
        and Major General Hoyt Vandenburg
    One copy AG Records

Minutes of the SHAEF 21st Meeting, June 2, 1944 held at Southwick House.

[DDE's Pre-Presidential Papers, Box 136, Conferences Supreme Commanders (Jan-June 1944)]

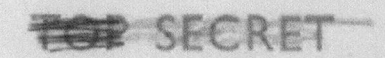

south of Chichester, were briefed on their role for D-Day. Early the following day, they were placed on 30 minutes notice, their allotted task being to cover the British and Canadian landing forces on the Eastern sector of the beaches. Throughout the day they flew 50 minute patrols and it is claimed that Apuldram's Czech squadrons carried out more operational sorties on 6 June than any other unit.

2100:
224th Parachute Field Ambulance attached to the third Parachute Brigade. Brigade H.Q. & Main Dressing Station parties parade in parachute order & move off to Down Ampney airfield.

2130:
225th Parachute Field Ambulance embussed for airfield.

2200:
82nd Airborne ordered to "chute up" followed by "load up" and a short prayer was offered for success of the mission. The men filed onto the aircraft and took up their jump positions on hard wooded benches on either side of the aircraft. All over England 13,000 British, Canadian and American paratroops were doing exactly the same thing in 800 aircraft.

2215:
432 C-47's began taking off from 7 departure airdromes in England, with 6,600 paratroops of the 101st Airborne Division. At dawn (H minus 2 hours) they were to be reinforced by approximately 150 glider troops from 51 gliders, and at dusk (H plus 15 hours) by an additional 165 in 32 gliders. Preceding the main echelons of paratroops by half an hour were 20 pathfinder aircraft which had the mission of marking six drop zones (for both divisions) and one landing zone. Marking of the zones was not entirely successful, but all of the pathfinder teams carried out at least part of their missions.

2230:
225th Parachute Field Ambulance emplaned.

Brigadier The Lord Lovat, addresses the entire Brigade.

Ten Serials (formations containing 36, 45, or 54, C-47s), and 432 aircraft assemble into formations and star to fly southwest over the channel at 500 feet to stay below German Radar. Whilst flying over all the lights were extinguished except for the formation lights which were kept at the lowest possible intensity. They flew towards a marker boat called Hoboken with a Eureka beacon (The Rebecca/Eureka transponding radar was a short-range radio navigation system used for the dropping of airborne forces and their supplies. It consisted of two parts, the Rebecca airborne transceiver and antenna system, and the Eureka ground-based transponder. Rebecca calculated the range to the Eureka based on the timing of the return signals, and its relative position using a highly directional antenna) which told them to turn left and head for the Channel Islands where they then found their next point on the Cotentin coast. Up until that point all was going well until they encountered very heavy cloud, fog and intense flak scattering many of the formations, the ensuing confusion resulted in them missing their drop zones completely and in some cases ending up as far away as Cherbourg.

Whitehall: Churchill made a last ditch attempt to get DeGaulle on side before D Day but the General was not for turning. This angered Churchill to the point of him dictating a letter ordering him to leave the country forthwith.

2245:
225th Parachute Field Ambulance take off.

2256:
A force of 181 men, led by Major John Howard, took off from RAF Tarrant Rushton in Dorset, Southern England in six Horsa gliders towed by the mighty Halifax. Their mission was to capture the Bénouville and Ranville Bridges, now more familiarly known as the Pegasus and Horsa Bridges, and hold them until relieved. The object of this action was to prevent German armour from crossing the bridges and attacking the eastern flank of the landings at SWORD Beach.

Howard was prone to airsickness and had vomited on just about every training flight he had been involved in. However, this time was different; the prospect of going into battle gave him something else to think about. For good luck, he had packed a red shoe belonging to his two year old son. Before they left he tried to give his men a bit of a pep talk. "*I am a sentimental man at heart, for which reason I don't think I am a good soldier. I found offering my thanks to these chaps a devil of a job. My voice just wasn't my own.*"

Before they left they were given a meal by the Air Force WAAFs as Corporal A. Darlington of 6th Airborne Reconnaissance Regiment remembers. "*We even had sugar in bowls and the best meal we'd had in years. WAAF refilled our water bottles for us, and gave us what turned out to be a useless object called Soap! This we termed the "Last Supper" and for many of us it was. We had been issued with a 48 hour emergency ration, which*

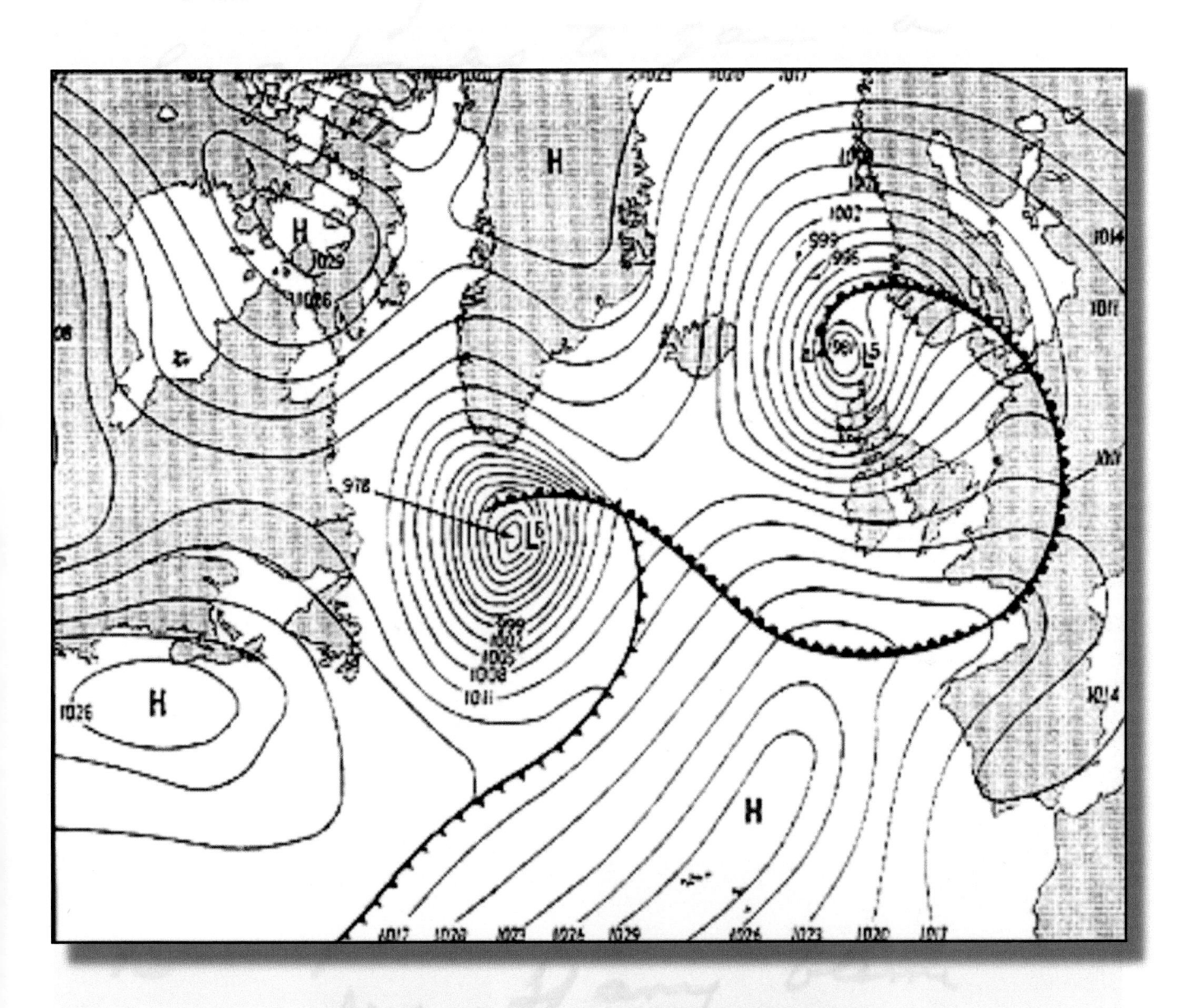

The weather map for the 5th June 1944 showing the worse weather in the channel for 20 years with a further front coming in and a small window between the two.

looked more like a child's compendium of games when opened. Creamy coloured dominoes turned out to be porridge with milk and sugar, if reconstituted, the dice were tea, milk and sugar cubes. Chocolate was so hard it could only be gnawed with the front teeth, and there were boiled sweets and a couple of 'pink pills' to keep us awake if necessary. Two pieces of tin plate could be slotted together to become a cooker with solidified methylated spirits, and another useless component was 6 pieces of brown bumph! This 48 hour emergency pack, however, lasted me 10 days, and there was no opportunity to cook them, nor had we any room in the overladen Jeep for anything else but our equipment, weapons and ammo, so our food was nibbled with sips of water from our bottles. What other vehicles carried I do not know as we were supposed to be relieved before our rations ran out."

2330:

Men from the 3rd Parachute Squadron, RE. were paraded, fully equipped and "tooled up" on the airfield near Bulford. The Dakota aircraft were lined up ready to transport them to France.

2340:

224th Parachute Field Ambulance take off for Normandy.

2350:

3rd Parachute Squadron is airborne. The mood was almost jovial but as they approached the French coastline and heard the noise of the bombings the chain smoking started.

"No smoking till we were airborne; so to ease the tension we sang para songs to the tune of 'Knees up Mother Brown', the end of the chorus going "I'll always keep my trousers on when jumping through the hole." I wondered if that might be true that night." Sgt Edgar Gurney, 5th Parachute Brigade

"Few of us slept on the night of 5 June. Most of the boys were very quiet, keeping their thoughts to themselves as we were well aware that a good number of us would be killed and the suspense was awful. Many lads wrote letters to be posted after the invasion had started. Many went to their hammocks early and turned their backs to others, to be with their thoughts – alone – thinking about the loved ones they had back home, saying a silent prayer that God would keep them safe.

The weather in the Channel was the worst for twenty years and, to our cost, we soon found out for ourselves." Bill Cheall - Green Howards

*"We came back from a dive bombing trip and later we went out again from Tangmere where we'd landed to search for Squadron Leader Ross of 193 Squadron who had bailed out over the Channel just south of the Isle of Wight. We could not find him but we were flying across in a long line, searching the sea, when we suddenly became aware of all these boats, hundreds and hundreds of boats, as far as the eye could see, It was an incredible picture and our Wing Leader, Reg Baker, called up and ordered R/T silence '…not another word until you land.' So when we got back he said, 'Well obviously you know tomorrow is D Day - and that was it."
Flying Officer S J Eaton (267 Squadron)

---

* With thanks to http://www.eregbaker.info/ww2_1944.htm

Pvt. Clarence C. Ware, 438 W. 15th St., San Pedro, Calif., gives a last second touch to Pvt. Charles R. Plaudo, 210 N. James, Minneapolis, Minn., make-up patterned after the American Indians. Somewhere in England. The black and white paint was taken from the freshly painted invasion stripes on the aircraft.

USNA 111-SC-193551

Squadrons Controlled by Signals Complex, Bishop Otter College, Chichester, Order of Battle 6th June 1944

Airfield	Squadron	Aircraft	Info
Funtingdon	19, 65, 122	Mustang III	
Coolham	129, 306, 315	Mustang III	
Ford	132, 453, 602, 441, 442, 443	Spitfire IX	
Tangmere	401, 411, 412, 402, 416, 421	Spitfire IX	
Bognor	66, 331, 332	Spitfire IX	
Chailey	308, 302, 317,	Spitfire IX	
Apuldram	310, 312, 313	Spitfire IX	
Selsey	222, 349, 485	Spitfire IX	
Merston	329, 340, 341,	Spitfire IX	
Horne	130, 303, 402	Spitfire Vb	11 Group, Fighter Command Squadrons
Deanland	64, 234, 611	Spitfire Vb	11 Group, Fighter Command Squadrons
Friston	350, 501,	Spitfire Vb	11 Group, Fighter Command Squadrons
Shoreham	345	Spitfire Vb	11 Group, Fighter Command Squadrons
Westhampnett	184	Typhoon RB 1b	
Northolt	16,	Spitfire PR XI	
	140,	Mosquito PR9	
	69	Wellington XIII	Special duties - illuminating targets for Naval bombardment
Odiham	168, 414, 430,	Mustang I	
	400	Spitfire PR, XI	
Lee on Solent	26, 63	Spitfire Vb Vc	Air Spotting Pool
	808, 885, 886, 897	Seafire III	Special duties - illuminating targets for Naval bombardment
Ford	456	Mosquito NF30	
Hartford Bridge (Blackbushe)	264	Mosquito XIII	
Shoreham	277 ASR	Spitfire Vb	
		Walrun	11 Group, Fighter Command Squadrons
		Sea Otter	

Heaviest German coastal battery on standby.

Bundesarchiv, Bild 146-1986-104-10A / Maier / CC BY-SA

RAMC Regimental Aid Post on one of the beaches.

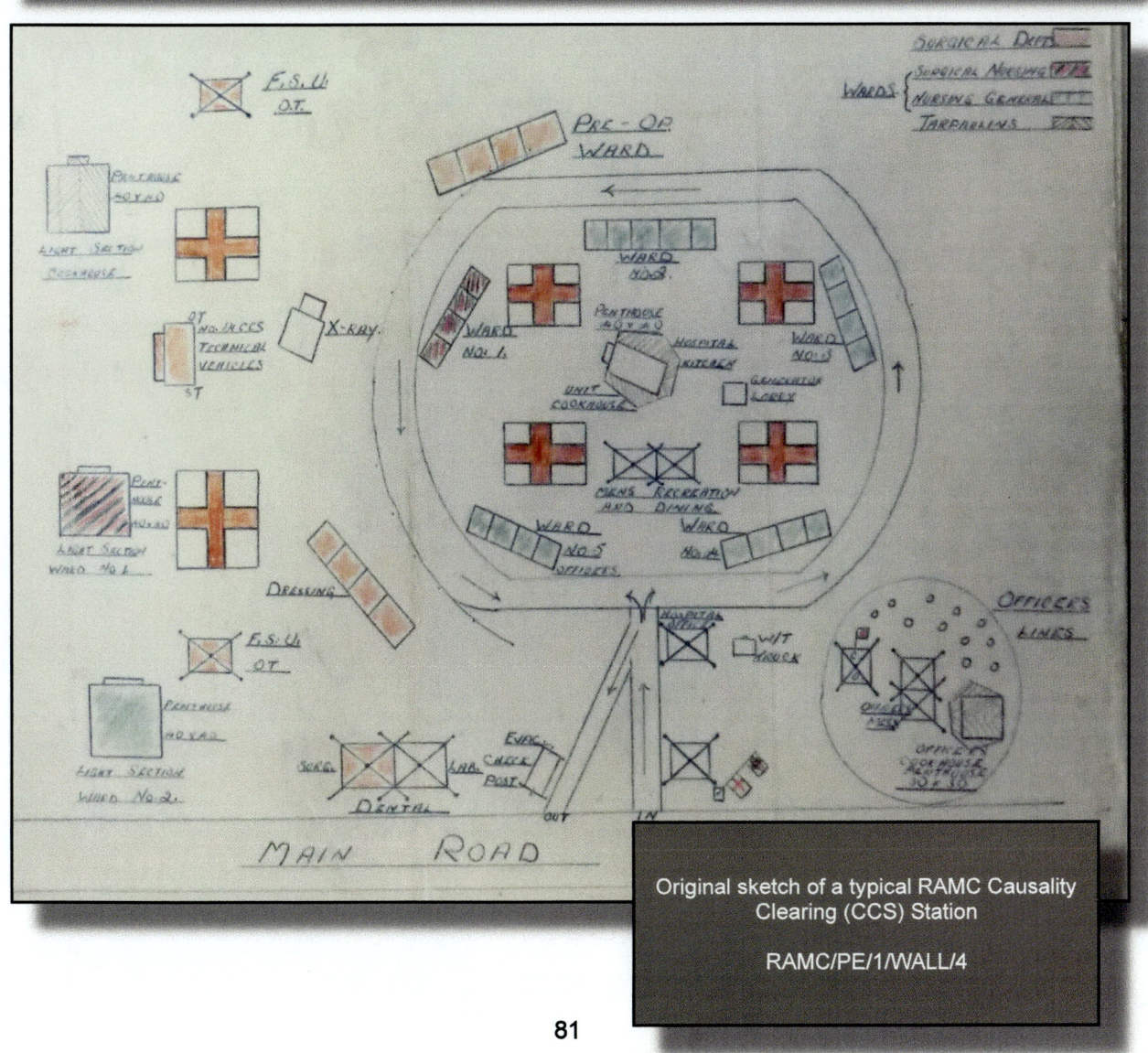

R.A.M.C./PE/1/WALL/4

Original sketch of a typical RAMC Causality Clearing (CCS) Station

RAMC/PE/1/WALL/4

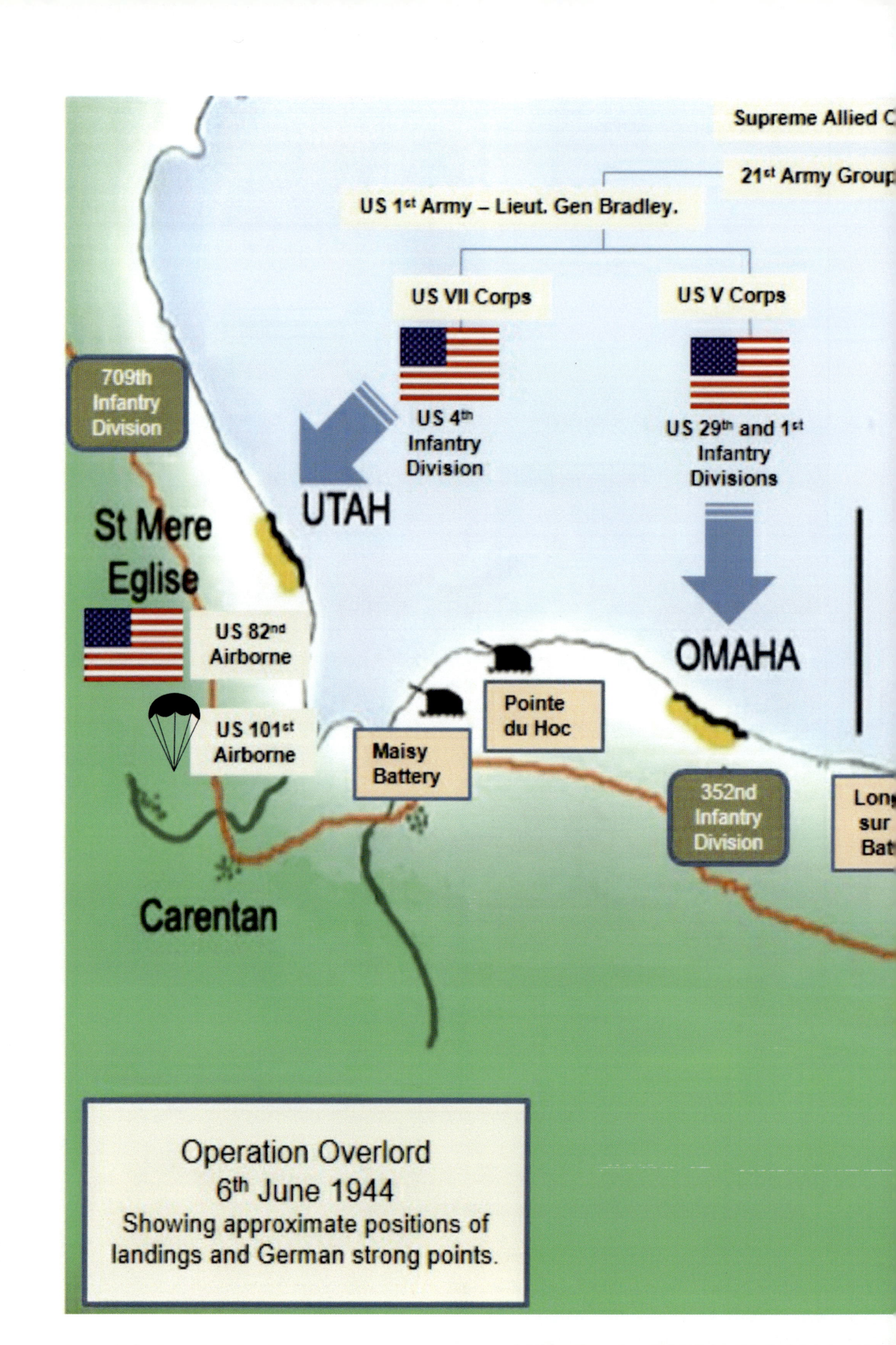

Operation Overlord
6th June 1944
Showing approximate positions of landings and German strong points.

Supreme Allied C
21st Army Group
US 1st Army – Lieut. Gen Bradley.

- **US VII Corps** — US 4th Infantry Division → UTAH
- **US V Corps** — US 29th and 1st Infantry Divisions → OMAHA

709th Infantry Division

St Mere Eglise
- US 82nd Airborne
- US 101st Airborne

Maisy Battery
Pointe du Hoc
352nd Infantry Division
Long sur Bat
Carentan

Allied Commander – General Eisenhower

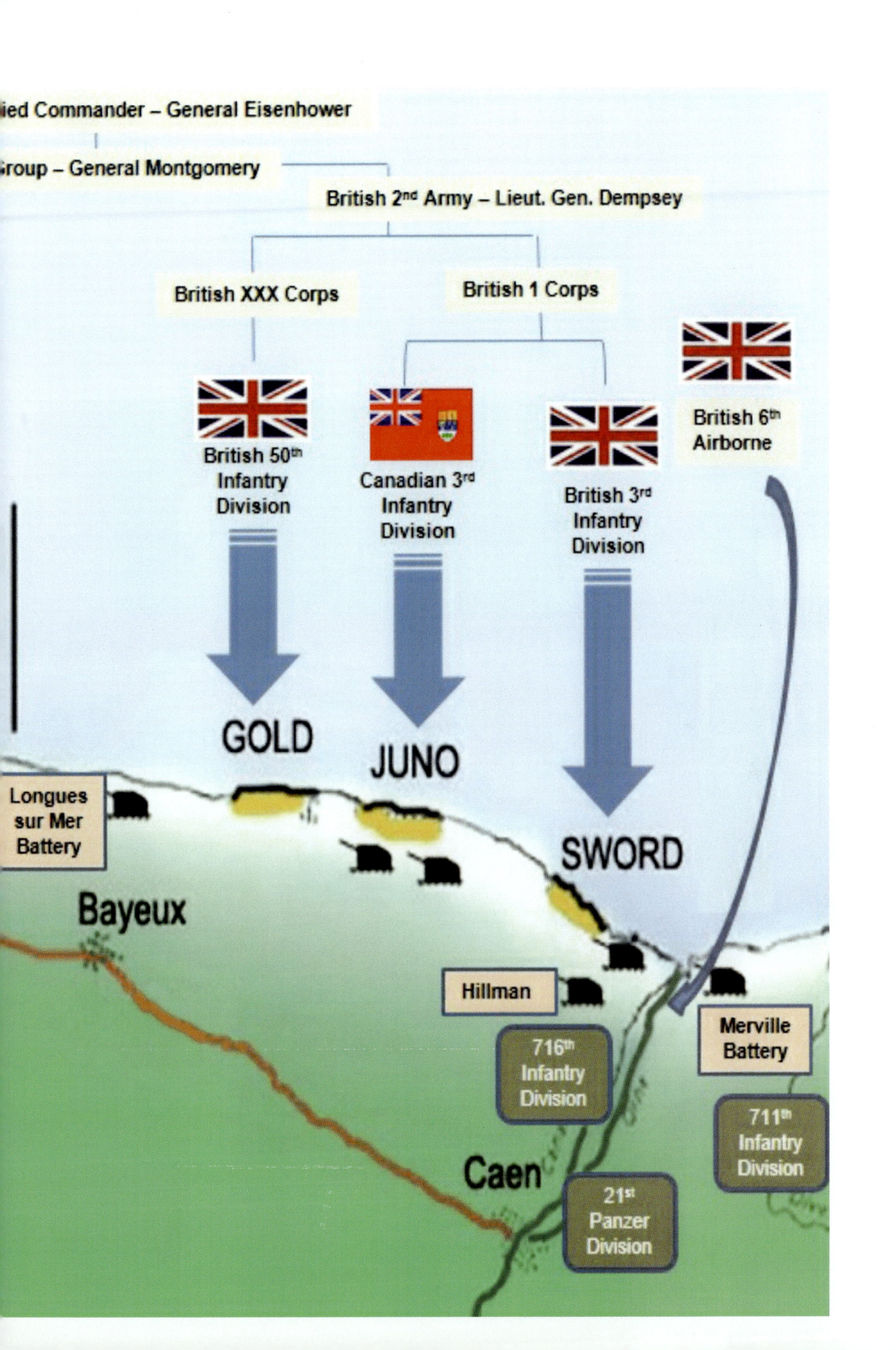

...Group – General Montgomery

British 2nd Army – Lieut. Gen. Dempsey

British XXX Corps — British 1 Corps

- British 50th Infantry Division → **GOLD**
- Canadian 3rd Infantry Division → **JUNO**
- British 3rd Infantry Division → **SWORD**
- British 6th Airborne

Longues sur Mer Battery

Bayeux

Hillman

Merville Battery

716th Infantry Division

711th Infantry Division

Caen

21st Panzer Division

Invasion equipment taken onboard an LST for the channel crossing to Normandy.
Someone told him that when the jeep breaks down, you hop on the bicycle.

USNA

WHEN?

6TH JUNE 1944

From this day to the ending of the world,
But we in it shall be remembered-
We few, we happy few, we band of brothers;
For he to-day that sheds his blood with me
Shall be my brother; be he ne'er so vile,
This day shall gentle his condition;
And gentlemen in England now-a-bed
Shall think themselves accurs'd they were not here.

William Shakespeare, Henry V

D DAY

All timings are in British Double Summer Time (BDST) which is two hours ahead of Greenwich Mean Time (GMT).

The text is colour coded so the reader can either follow the story of a Force/Country or read the whole thing for the bigger picture.

Entries are extracts from personal diaries, Regimental War Diaries and radio messages.

British - Blue
Canadian - Red
US - Green
French - Claret
Others: Dark Blue
German - Black

The decision was made that the seaborne assault would start 40 minutes after Nautical Twilight (which begins when the sun is 12 degrees below the horizon) and between three and four hours before high water.

Tuesday 6th June 1944

0010:

Operation Titanic - The first Titanic team made of 3 SAS men jump from a Stirling and land in a field 8km west of Saint-Lô. Lieutenant Norman Harry Poole becomes the first man to jump over Normandy. A few minutes later, a second team under Captain Frederick James 'Chick' Fowles lands in the same area. In order to simulate a large scale assault, other Stirling Aircraft drop 200 decoy paratrooper dummies – named Rupert - which, upon landing, fire up flares and play rifles and machine guns recordings. The Ruperts' were not life size – about three foot tall - they were made from sack cloth and stuffed with straw and sand and fitted to scaled down parachutes. Rupert was portrayed in the film The Longest Day as a three foot dummy fully dressed in a replica uniform with insignia etc, this was not the case they were far more basic, but against the night sky were good enough to divert the Germans attention away from the real airborne landings. The men also install amplifiers to play combat noises, mortar explosions and the sound of soldiers cursing. 30 minutes later, quietness returns to the countryside and the men disappeared in the night.
The amount of Rupert's dropped are
200 around Yvetot
50 around Lisieux
50 around Caen
200 Rupert's and 6 SAS Paratroopers around Lessay.

The first American pathfinders jump over the Cotentin Peninsular, in order to mark out the drop zones for the C-47 pilots who arrive in the minutes which follow.

COUP DE MAIN RAID

(Operation Deadstick) Capture of the bridges over the Caen Canal and River Orne. (Code name Rugger and Cricket.)

At the Eastern end of the Normandy Beaches are three waterways. The Caen Canal, the River Orne and the River Dives. The role of the British 6th Airborne is to drop between the two rivers and protect the invading seaborne forces from a counter attack by the Germans who were in the area east of Caen. Seven bridges cross these waterways. Five over the Dives, one over the Orne and one over the canal. If the bridges over the Dives can be destroyed and the two over the Orne and and the canal captured, then attack from the east would be impossible.

The gliders are released at 6000 feet above Cabourg, just after crossing the coast line. The force was composed of "D" Company (reinforced with two platoons of "B" company), 2nd Battalion, Oxfordshire and Buckinghamshire (Ox and Bucks) Light Infantry; and Royal Engineers from the 249th (Airborne) Field Company commanded by Captain Jock Neilson plus men of the Glider Pilot Regiment

0016:

Ox and Bucks's gliders land close to the Bénouville (Pegasus) bridge. *"We were coming in at 90 mph on touchdown. I suppose that really was the most exhilarating moment of my life. I could see the bridge tower 50 yards away from where I was standing. Above all, the tremendous thing was there was no firing at all. We had complete surprise; we had caught old Jerry with his pants down."* Major John Howard

Jim Wallwork in Glider No 1 not only had to get the aircraft and its contents down safely he also was instructed to try and break through the barbed wire upon landing. He had to try and miss the anti glider poles and also deploy the drag chute if he was going too fast, which was an untried procedure. However, he could not slow down too quickly for fear of the following Horsa hitting them from behind. His glider was also heavily overloaded which didn't help matters. He landed heavily and with such force that it threw him and his co-pilot through the windscreen of the aircraft and on to

"I could see the bridge and the whites of their eyes, I knew bloody well we were going to make it, and we did, I was delighted."

Jim Wallwork, pilot of the first glider to land within 50 yards of the Benouville Bridge

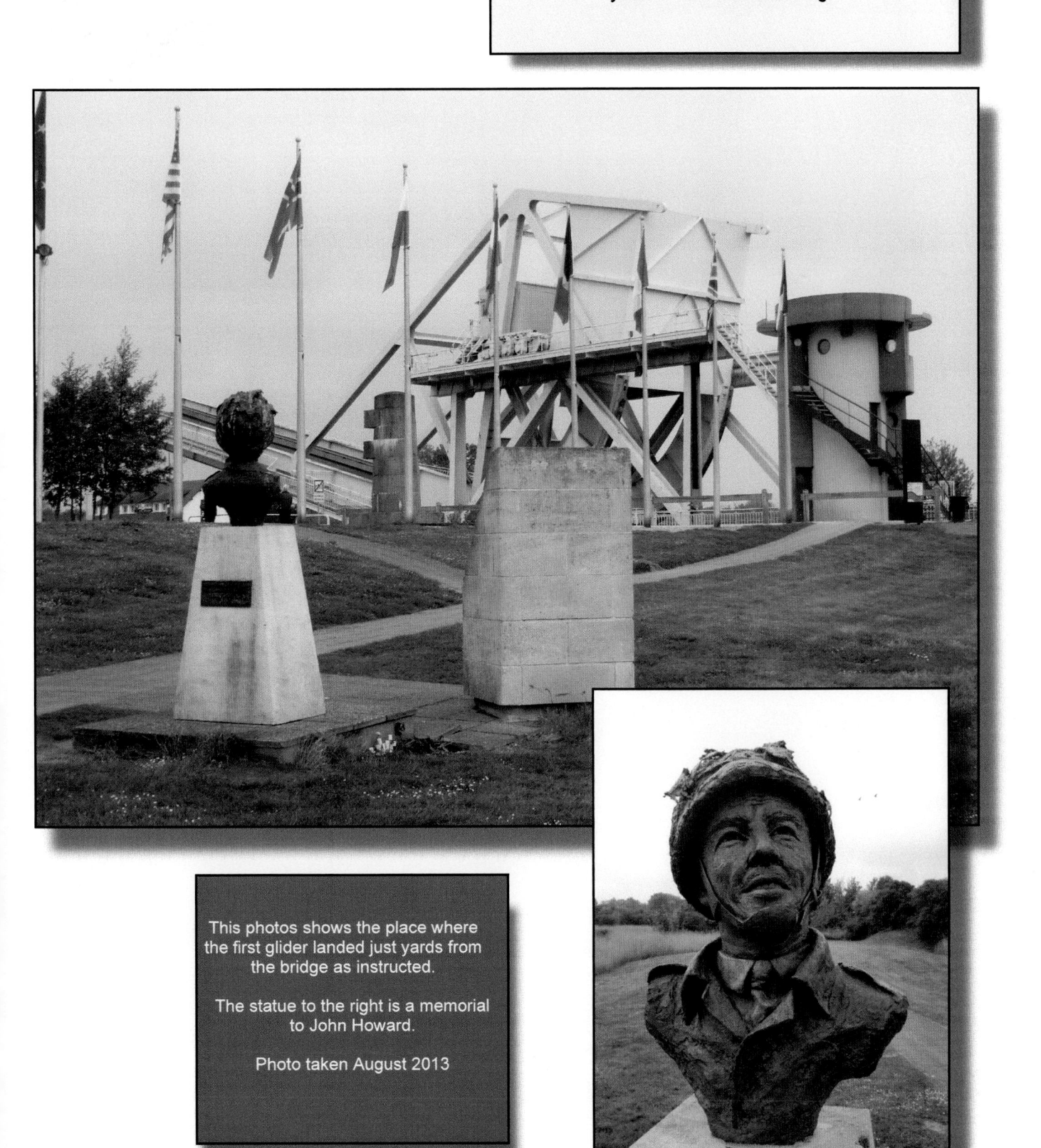

This photos shows the place where the first glider landed just yards from the bridge as instructed.

The statue to the right is a memorial to John Howard.

Photo taken August 2013

the ground, still strapped into their seats. The rest of the passengers were also briefly knocked unconscious, the force so great that it stopped Howards watch at 1216. Incredibly the glider came to a halt 47 yards from the bridge with the nose just breaking through the barbed wire as requested.

The other two gliders put down a few yards behind. To land so closely without power and within yards of the target was an incredible feat of flying. So often the pilots are not recognised for their achievements. Below are a list of names of the Halifax pilots who towed them across the channel and the pilots of the Horsa Gliders.

Bénouville/Pegasus Bridge

Glider No. 1 towed by a Halifax tug piloted by Wing Commander Duder. Light Infantry.
Staff-Sergeant Jim Wallwork (Glider Pilot Regiment)
Staff-Sergeant John Ainsworth (Glider Pilot Regiment)

Glider No. 2 towed by a Halifax tug piloted by Warrant Officer Berry. Light Infantry.
Staff-Sergeant Boland (Glider Pilot Regiment)
Staff-Sergeant Hobbs (Glider Pilot Regiment)

Glider No. 3 towed by a Halifax tug piloted by Warrant Officer Herman.
Staff-Sergeant Barkway (Glider Pilot Regiment)
Staff-Sergeant Boyle (Glider Pilot Regiment)

Ranville / Horsa Bridge

Glider No. 4 towed by a Halifax tug piloted by Flying Officer Clapperton.
Staff-Sergeant Lawrence (Glider Pilot Regiment)
Staff-Sergeant Shorter (Glider Pilot Regiment)

Glider No. 5 towed by a Halifax tug piloted by Warrant Officer Bain.
Staff-Sergeant Pearson (Glider Pilot Regiment)
Staff-Sergeant Guthrie (Glider Pilot Regiment)

Glider No. 6 towed by a Halifax tug piloted by Flying Officer Archibald.
Staff-Sergeant Howard (Glider Pilot Regiment)
Staff-Sergeant Baacke (Glider Pilot Regiment)

One of the gliders landed some 7 miles off by mistake. Most of the troops in this glider moved through German lines towards the village of Ranville where they eventually re-joined the British forces.

Both bridges are captured in less than 15 minutes and Corporal Tappenden ("D" Company Headquarters, Wireless Operator) sends the "Ham & Jam" victory message. He was unable to get an acknowledgement from from Brigade H.Q. so sits at the side of the road for thirty minutes repeating the signal. They now have to sit and await Col. Pine-Coffin's 7th Parachute Battalion reinforcements and later link up with the beach landing forces of Lord Lovat's Commandos. One of the members of the 7th Battalion reinforcements was actor Richard Todd who would, nearly two decades later, play Major Howard in the film *The Longest Day*. They lost two men in the process, Lieutenant Den Brotheridge and Lance-Corporal Fred Greenhalgh. Lieutenant Brotheridge was killed crossing the bridge when he was shot in the neck in the first minutes of the assault and died thirty minutes later, he is widely recognised as the first British causality in Normandy, however this was not the case. He was posthumously awarded the DSO.

His citation reads: *Lieutenant Denham Brotheridge, 6th Airborne Division - 6th Air landing Brigade - 2nd Ox & Bucks - D Company, part of the coup de main assault by glider to seize the bridge over the Caen Canal at Bénouville on 6th June 1944. His glider crash landed close to strong enemy defences and some of the men were too stunned to get out quickly. Lieutenant Brotheridge, however, rallied the remainder and led them over the bridge in the face of superior numbers of enemy who were entrenched on the far bank with machine guns sited to fire on the bridge itself. Lieutenant Brotheridge showed the highest qualities of leadership and bravery and his outstanding example and dash was responsible for getting his men across and seizing the bridge intact - a vital factor in the success of the airborne plan.*

The news that Brotheridge had been killed hit Howard hard, "*It really shook me, because it was Denham and how much of a friend he was, and because my leading platoon was now without an officer. At the top of my mind was the fact that I knew Margaret, his wife, was expecting a baby almost any time.*"

Lance-Corporal Fred Greenhalgh, was thrown out of the Horsa as it came to a halt and broke in two and drowned in a nearby pond, becoming the first British Casualty and the only one of the landing.

The glider pilots assist the troops on the ground and as soon as released from their duties they are evacuated back to the UK according to plan.

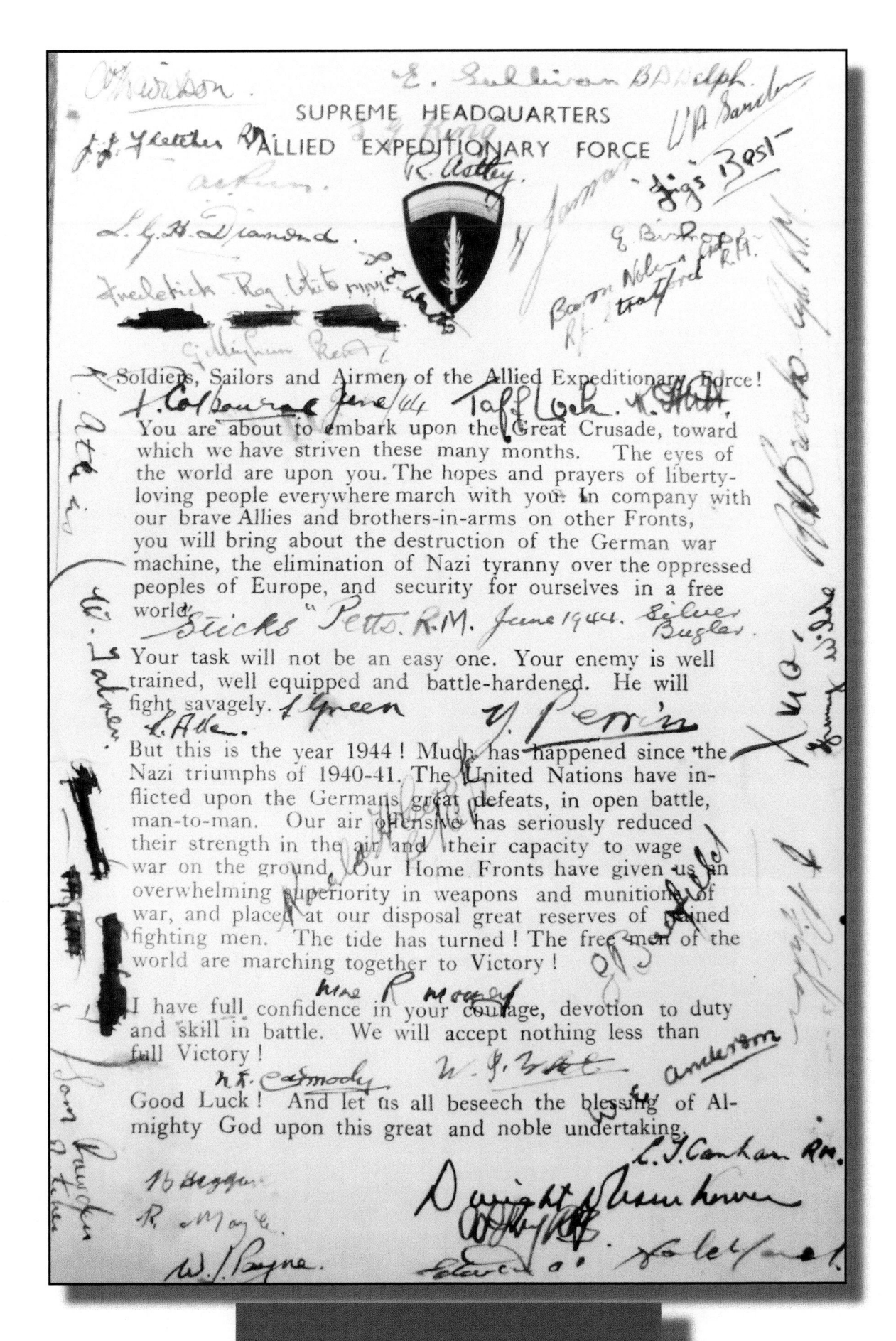

SUPREME HEADQUARTERS
ALLIED EXPEDITIONARY FORCE

Soldiers, Sailors and Airmen of the Allied Expeditionary Force!

You are about to embark upon the Great Crusade, toward which we have striven these many months. The eyes of the world are upon you. The hopes and prayers of liberty-loving people everywhere march with you. In company with our brave Allies and brothers-in-arms on other Fronts, you will bring about the destruction of the German war machine, the elimination of Nazi tyranny over the oppressed peoples of Europe, and security for ourselves in a free world.

Your task will not be an easy one. Your enemy is well trained, well equipped and battle-hardened. He will fight savagely.

But this is the year 1944! Much has happened since the Nazi triumphs of 1940-41. The United Nations have inflicted upon the Germans great defeats, in open battle, man-to-man. Our air offensive has seriously reduced their strength in the air and their capacity to wage war on the ground. Our Home Fronts have given us an overwhelming superiority in weapons and munitions of war, and placed at our disposal great reserves of trained fighting men. The tide has turned! The free men of the world are marching together to Victory!

I have full confidence in your courage, devotion to duty and skill in battle. We will accept nothing less than full Victory!

Good Luck! And let us all beseech the blessing of Almighty God upon this great and noble undertaking.

Dwight D Eisenhower

Eisenhower's message to the troops signed by some of the crew of HMS Mauritius.

Royal Marines Museum, Southsea. 7/19/5

The Bénouville Bridge was later renamed Pegasus Bridge, after the mythical winged horse of the British airborne forces.

0018:
The Merville German battery is attacked by 5 Lancaster bombers of the 7th Squadron, Royal Air Force.

0020:
60 pathfinders of Major Lennox BOYD's 22nd Independent Parachute Company jump over Normandy to mark the three Drop Zones that will be used for the 6th British Airborne Division paratroopers.
Drop Zone "N" to the north-west of Ranville,
Drop Zone "V" west of Varaville,
Drop Zone "K" west of Touffréville.

Once landed, the pathfinders have 30 minutes to scout out and mark their assigned Drop Zone with beacons and radars, especially the "Eureka" transponders. The signals from these beacons are to be received by "Rebecca" receivers aboard planes carrying the paratroopers.

Unfortunately, due to strong winds and German Flak disorienting the crews, the jump does not go exactly as planned and pathfinders are scattered all over the French countryside. The Varaville team make it relatively close to Drop Zone "V" but all their beacons are either broken or lost in the surrounding marshes. None of the Ranville pathfinders land anywhere near Drop Zone " N" but one of the Touffréville team is dropped by mistake over Ranville but thought that they were in the correct place and started transmitting the "K" signal instead of the "N" one which then caused massive disorganisation and chaos during the main jump.

8th Parachute Battalion - Touffreville: Two Recce parties drop on the allocated drop zone. Slight opposition is met at the rendezvous which was quickly overcome and one German killed. One German on a bicycle was taken prisoner.

The first pathfinders of the 101st Airborne (Screaming Eagles) jump over Normandy, led by Captain F. Lillyman, to mark their Division's Drop Zones. The C-47's carrying the Division are scheduled to arrive 45 minutes after the first pathfinders land. The 101st paratroopers are provided with "crickets" a few days before 6 June 1944 to aid recognition and communication. The cricket was a popular toy at the time which consisted of a steel spring blade emitting a click clack when pressed. The response would be a double click clack.

0030:
One hundred RAF Lancaster and Halifax bombers attack the Merville Battery with 4,000 lb bombs in the hope of destroying the position altogether or at the least inflicting considerable damage upon the defences. Some of recce party are caught in this but suffer no casualties.

One of these Lancaster's, E for Easy, has a War Correspondent on board and reports back for The Times *"I am in the co-pilots seat and can get a glimpse of the early stages of the opening of the second front. Most of the way across the channel the sea was obscured beneath cloud but now I can see the wakes of the ships and flashes of gun fire coming from the coast. We are on our way as one of 100 aircraft to "soften up" an enemy heavy gun emplacement. For miles in every direction, north, south east and west the sky is filled with heavily laden Lancaster's all heading for the mouth of the Orne.*

"E for Easy weaves its way gently through the not very frightening flak and took its place in the queue of Lancaster's moving steadily over the target. After the usual direction of 'right, right, steady, steady'

From the bomb-aimer laying prone in the nose of the fuselage, the bomber gave a slight lurch as it was relieved of its burden of 1000 pounders. After what seemed a long interval the bombs exploded among the earlier ones which had already ignited an ammunition dump."

The Café Gondreé at Pegasus Bridge is the first building to be liberated in France. Troops there were offered champagne by the owner.

USS Bayfield - breakfast for Boat Crews and Troops served in the mess (men reminded not to go on deck but to pass through compartments to get to mess.) Breakfast is served for officers in the Wardroom.

0040:
"At about 0040 hours on Tuesday June 6 1944, I thumped onto a corn field in Normandy, an illegal immigrant without a passport but nevertheless welcome, I hoped, at least to the locals. I discarded my parachute harness and fumbled with the kitbag cord from my belt. I realised that my right hand was a bit messy. I crouched down and took stock. Aircraft were still coming in and I got my bearings by noting their flight path. There was no one near me and I reckoned that was probably because I

Above - Horsa Glider at Ranville.
G Lugg Personal Collection
Left: Bill Cheall

"On the morning of D-Day, reveille was about 0330 hrs. Everybody was soon on the ball, wanting to get going. We checked all our kit was to hand, then made sure we had a good breakfast, not knowing when we would eat again that day."
Bill Cheall, Green Howards

had jumped No. 1, and therefore was at the extreme end of the "stick". To the east I could just make out the dark line of a wood, and concluded that I was a good half-mile from the battalion rendezvous. Meanwhile, the Dropping Zone was being raked by small-arms fire, so I decided to get into that wood. I put my Sten gun together and loaded it.

"Once in the wood I heard voices and froze momentarily, only to realise that they were speaking English. In a little clearing, there stood Colonel Pine-Coffin and about a dozen others. The CO said there was no way of knowing if the glider-borne attack on the bridges had been successful and we must get to the rendezvous as quickly as possible. We broke out from the woodland and set off at the double." Taken from Lieutenant Richard Todd's personal account.

0045:
3rd Battalion of the 919th Infantry Regiment, led by Lieutenant Colonel Hoffmann, report the presence of enemy parachutists in the area.

0048:
Mission Albany - The paratroopers of the 101st Airborne Division now start dropping. Their objective is to secure the four causeway exits behind UTAH Beach, destroy a German coastal artillery battery at Saint-Martin-de-Varreville, capture buildings nearby at Mésières, believed to be used as barracks and a command post for the artillery battery, capture the Douve River lock at la Barquette (opposite Carentan), capture two footbridges spanning the Douve at la Porte opposite Brévands, destroy the highway bridges over the Douve at Sainte-Come-du-Mont, and secure the Douve River valley. Mission Albany was to be followed one hour later by the 82nd Airborne Division Drop – Mission Boston.

The drop zones of the 101st are east and south of Sainte-Mère-Église and lettered "A", "C", and "D" from north to south (Drop Zone "B" had been that of the 501st PIR (Parachute Infantry Regiment) before changes to the original landing plan made on May 27).

0050:
Lieutenant-Colonel Terence Otway lands near a German H.Q. and hurries to the rendezvous point in nearby woods. He is slightly late arriving and is greeted by his batman Wilson who offered him a small flask *"Shall we take our Brandy now, sir?"*

Otway manages to gather together only 150 of the 750 parachutists assigned to him and heads towards the Merville battery. The drop is a complete disaster losing most of his men and equipment who had been dropped in the wrong place, some of them managed to regroup later but many were never heard of or seen again, presumed drowned in the marshes deliberately flooded by the Germans. He now had only 6 Bangalore Torpedoes instead of 60 and one Vickers medium machine gun. His orders are to neutralize the guns of the Merville Battery at all costs before the beach landings at Sword which was within range of the battery.

Dropping in with the 9th was Private Emile Corteil, A Company, known as Les, and his Alsatian dog Glen who was used for patrol and guard duties. Glen had his own parachute and was trained to sit and wait when he landed for Les to come and find him with the aid of a little red light that he had on his collar. Apparently Glen had no fear of jumping and trusting his handler totally he would happily jump out of the aircraft with little if any encouragement. However, the night of the 5th June was different, Glen was very agitated in the aircraft and could sense something was wrong and had to be actively encouraged to jump that night. Both Les and Glen are known to have completed their parachute descent. Les was killed later on D-Day, and Glen died at his side. Private Corteil was 19 years old. He and Glen are buried together at Ranville War Cemetery.

Also landing was Private Robert Johns, from Portsmouth. He was shot dead as A Company, 13th Parachute Battalion, defended Le Mesnil crossroads on the 23rd July 1944. He was just 16 years old and had lied about his age to join up aged 14.

Colonel Richard Geoffrey Pine-Coffin drops with the 7th (Light Infantry) Parachute Battalion, their task was to reinforce Major John Howard's 181-strong coup de main force.

8th Parachute Battalion watch the main body arrive and state that aircraft were flying in every direction at different altitudes and all flying well above dropping speed.

12th and 13th Parachute Battalions drop and are also scattered. When they move from their rendezvous each battalion is not more than 60 percent strong, though odd parties join up during the day.

The 12th Parachute Battalion seize the Le Bas de Ranville area and 13th Parachute Battalion the Ranville-Le Mariquet area. The Germans react swiftly against these units and attack Ranville almost at once, but they are repulsed with the loss

"Sie Kommen!"

> *Troops are not permitted to imitate bombs by whistling whilst on deck.*
> Orders to the troops on LST 529

A convoy of Landing Craft Infantry (Large) sails across the English Channel toward the Normandy beaches on "D-Day", 6 June 1944. Each of these landing craft is towing a barrage balloon for protection against low-flying German aircraft. Among the LCI(L)s present are: LCI(L)-56, at far left; LCI(L)-325; and LCI(L)-4.

US National Archives. Photo #: 26-G-2333

of a number of enemy prisoners of war and one German tank destroyed.

0100:
On the east flank, thousands of British paratroopers are now landing in the dark and regroup to accomplish their missions: clear and secure the glider landing zones, destroy the Merville battery, blow the 5 bridges on the Dives River and reinforce Major Howard's party at Bénouville. To the west, 13,000 US paratroopers descend on Normandy but units are scattered, men are drowning in the flooded areas and 70% of the heavy equipment is lost.

Ranville - 7th Parachute Battalion complete their drop but go into action with Companies at half normal strength due to some plane loads being dropped in wrong places and one load not dropping at all. *"Our group, numbering by then some 50, was at the rendezvous. A bugler repeatedly blew our rallying signal, and men came stumbling towards us, shadowy, bulky figures. But still no mortars, no machine guns and no wireless."* Lieutenant Richard Todd's personal account.

Royal Navy hands ordered to man battle stations. Landing craft begin to be lowered into the water; paratroopers cut phone lines and take down telephone poles.

RAF 88 Sqn: Navigator Sqn Ldr George Louden is woken and given the usual big fry up before going for the mornings briefing, his task is to lay smoke at sea level, for which their aircraft had been specially adapted with canisters in the bomb bays and funnels projecting out through the bomb doors, to protect the Royal Navy Ships and also the troops as they forged ashore.

591st Parachute Sqn: Royal Engineers land by parachute and carry out main task of clearing area of poles for a Landing Zone for a glider borne assault commencing at 0330. Lt Thomas receives bullet wounds in his shoulder and two other ranks are injured during the drop.

HMS *Largs* reports that progress is very satisfactory. Heavy swell running and too much wind blowing to be comfortable for small craft, one or two that were being towed have broken adrift and having to make way under their own power.

"A" Company 1st Canadian Parachute Battalion drop, its objective is to protect the left flank of the 9th Parachute Battalion in its approach march and conduct an attack on the Merville battery. Lieut. Clancy, upon reaching the Company rendezvous, finds only two or three men of the Company present. After waiting for further members, unsuccessfully, of the Company to appear, he decides to recce the village of Gonneville sur Mer. Taking two men he proceeds and penetrates the village but can find no sign of the enemy.

Sergeant Ludwig Förster spots the allied fleet from his Widerstandsnest WN 62 (German strong point - see page 24 for location) on the very eastern edge of OMAHA Beach.

These strong points are located all along the Atlantic Wall as a first line of defence against an attack by the Allies. No two strong points were the same, each one designed for the location with whatever equipment was available. They were aimed along the beach to the west and had large concrete walls protruding to the seaward side at the front to protect them from an attack. WN 62 was to prove to be a major cause of concern for the troops landing on OMAHA.

German Navy radar spots a large fleet opposite the Pas-de-Calais.

0104:
224th Parachute Field Ambulance attached to the 3rd Para Brigade drop over a wide area around Varaville.

0105:
225th Field Ambulance H.Q. flight crosses the coast at Cabourg. Some flak is experienced. Pilot fails to see Drop Zone lights so heads to sea and makes a second run-in.

0110:
36 Free French parachutists, within 4 teams, jump over Brittany, in the Duault forest close to Plumelec, alerting German troops of the 84th corps, from the Orne river to Saint-Malo.

0111:
Chief of Operations of 716th Division calls General Marcks at the 84th Corps Headquarters in St Lo informing him that enemy paratroops had landed east of the Orne estuary in the Breville-Ranville area and in his opinion were heading for the Dives bridges and the crossings over the Orne. After much thought General Hayn decides that it could not be groups linking up with the Resistance and that it therefore had to be the invasion. General Marcks decided to "wait and see."

0115:
US 1st Division - 16th Regiment - 2nd Battalion - G Company are alerted aboard the USS Henrico and begin preparations for disembarking into assault

Private Emile Corteil, and Glen

RAMC attending to the wounded. As this photo would have been published at the time, you will notice that the Regimental insignia on the arms of their uniforms has been painted out.

R.A.M.C./PE/1/WALL/4

95

craft. Breakfast was given to all Army personnel consisting of meat sandwiches and coffee. All equipment was then secured.

0120:
Touffréville - 8th Parachute Battalion CO arrives at the rendezvous and situation is that there are about 30 men present and one Royal Engineers Jeep and trailer. Recce Party reports that the Battalion appears to be very widely dispersed and that no container Aircraft have dropped on Drop Zone. The rendezvous signal was a red and green Verey light (a type of flare) put up at frequent intervals which could be seen a considerable distance away.

The green light went on for the 225th Parachute Field Ambulance and the unit dropped on or near their DZ.

The sirens of the Pointe du Hoc battery sound to announce the sighting of allied bombers.

0121:
Pathfinders of the 82nd Airborne Division jump over the Cotentin peninsula to mark out 3 drop zones for the rest of the division (Drop Zones "N", "O" and "T").

0125:
First ships arrive off UTAH Beach following convoy routes opened by minesweepers and marked by beacons.

0130:
"The CO gave the order to move off to the bridges even though we still numbered only 150 men, a quarter of our strength." Lieutenant Richard Todd

Corporal Emile Bouëtard, parachutist of the 4th battalion, Free French airborne, is killed at the Moulin de Plumelec, in Brittany.

General Dollman orders the general alert of the 7th German Army.

0140:
Pine-Coffin's 7th Battalion begins to arrive at the bridges taking up positions in Bénouville and Le Port, west of Caen Canal. With 7th Battalion's arrival, Pine-Coffin succeeded Major Howard's command of the bridges' defence. The 5th Parachute Brigade's position is precarious; 7th Battalion have been scattered and can only muster about 40% of its strength, while the 12th Battalion is in a similar situation at Ranville, east of the Orne. Pine-Coffin's battalion come under sustained attack by the 716th Infantry Division and elements of the 21st Panzer Division but they, with difficulty, hold their positions, awaiting the arrival of Lord Lovat and the 1st Special Service Brigade.

"All seemed quiet as we reached the bridge and trotted over it. I got my first sight of a D-Day casualty: a legless German lay at the roadside, a groaning sound coming weirdly from him. Internal gas, I supposed. Normally, the sight of blood turns my stomach, yet I felt only mild curiosity. We doubled along the causeway towards the canal bridge, a large iron structure that could be opened to allow the passage of sea-going craft. Later it was to be named Pegasus Bridge. Suddenly, all hell erupted on the road ahead. Heavy explosions, flashes and tracer bullets rent the night like a spectacular firework display. "Christ!" I thought. "This is it. Here we go!" We speeded up our jog-trot. Then, as quickly as it started, the tumult died down. An old tank probing the bridge had been hit by a PIAT and this was its ammunition exploding."

"We reached the little café-bar at the west end of the bridge, and the CO directed me to set up Battalion H.Q. 300 yards away below the hamlet of Le Port, whose church could be seen on the crest. Here, in the darkness, the remnants of our H.Q. party began furiously to dig in, my own efforts somewhat hampered by my skinned right hand, though we used explosive charges to blow our fox-holes. So far, so good. Phase one of our task had been accomplished. The bridges had been captured intact and the western bridgehead established. Now we had to hang on until some time later that day." Richard Todd's personal account.

HQRAMC (Headquarters Royal Army Medical Corps) Assistant Director Medical Services and party leave Harwell Aerodrome in Berkshire in Glider No 81.

0145:
8th Parachute Battalion, Sgt. Fesq is sent into Touffréville to get information from the local inhabitants. He reports back that Troarn is held and also Escoville and Sannerville. The prisoner being held is also interrogated and he confirms the statements of the local inhabitants. He also states that the formation in Troarn is a mobile company with half-tracks, strength of about 200 and that all main roads are covered by machine gun fire. During this period elements of the Battalion are arriving slowly at the rendezvous and there is considerable machine gun fire on the Drop Zone. Everybody reports that they have been fired upon on the way to the rendezvous.

> *"I got out in water up to the top of my boots. People were yelling, screaming, dying, running on the beach, equipment was flying everywhere, men were bleeding to death, crawling, lying everywhere, firing coming from all directions. We dropped down behind anything that was the size of a golf ball. Colonel Canham, Lieutenant Cooper, and Sergeant Crawford were screaming at us to get off the beach. I turned to say to Gino Ferrari, 'Let's move up, Gino,' but before I could finish the sentence, something spattered all over the side of my face. He'd been hit in the face. I moved forward and the tide came in so fast it covered him and I could no longer see him."*
>
> A soldier of the 116th Infantry Division

Mired M4 "Sherman" tank on a Normandy beach, 12 June 1944. This tank, which bears the name "Cannon Ball", is fitted with raised air intakes for amphibious use.

USNA 80-G-252802

General Marcks receives new information concerning more enemy parachutists, this time located between the villages of Sainte-Marie-du-Mont and Sainte-Mère-Église. He calmly informed his staff *"sie kommen."*

0150:
In Paris, close to the Bois de Boulogne, the Western Naval Group Chief of Operations, Admiral Hoffman calls an emergency meeting after receiving numerous reports from the various radar stations. At first this is dismissed as interference or weather as there are so many ships coming in and a huge amount of blips on the screen, they could not believe that there could possibly be so many ships. Hoffman, after studying all the evidence sends the following message to Germany: *"Announce to the Führer that the invasion is on."*

0151:
Mission "Boston" a parachute combat assault conducted by the US 82nd Airborne Division commences. The intended objective is to secure an area of roughly 10 square miles located on either side of the Merderet River. They are to capture the town of Sainte Mère Église, a crucial communications crossroad behind UTAH Beach, and to block the approaches into the area from the west and southwest.

In addition they are to seize causeways and bridges over the Merderet at La Fière and Chef-du-Pont, destroy the highway bridge over the Douve River at Pont l'Abbé (now Étienville), and secure the area west of Sainte Mère Église to establish a defensive line between Gourbesville and Renouf. To complete its assignments, the 82nd Airborne Division divided itself into three forces:

- Force A (parachute): the three parachute infantry regiments and support detachments, commanded by Assistant Division Commander Brig Gen. James Gavin.

- Force B (glider): the glider infantry regiment and artillery battalions, and airborne support elements, commanded by Division Commander Major Gen. Matthew B. Ridgway, and

- Force C (sea borne): remaining combat elements, division support troops and attached units including tanks, landing at UTAH Beach, commanded by Assistant Division Commander Brig Gen. George P. Howell.

Gavin was to describe the operation as having two inter-related challenges - it had to be *"planned and staged with one eye on deception and one on the assault"*. The success of the mission lay in balancing these two factors to near perfection.

Some buildings in Sainte Mère Église are on fire, set alight by the pathfinders and previous aerial bombardments, illuminating the sky and the descending men making them easy targets. Some are sucked into the fires and others get tangled onto buildings, trees and utility poles and are shot before they can cut themselves free. The most famous being John Steele of the 505th PIR whose parachute gets caught on the spire of the church, he feigns death and hangs there for two hours watching the scene beneath him. In addition the German garrison were alerted to the airdrops as a detachment as the 101st had dropped earlier arousing their interest.

0155:
The wind in the channel is now blowing 32 kts and the sea is getting very rough.

The first bombers of the 8th US Air Force take off from England to support the ground forces. 1,198 aircraft are bound for the French coastline and 163 for the city of Caen. The mass take-off will continue until 0529 hrs.

0200:
USS Bayfield anchored in the Transport area, condition set to "One Able", all boats lowered. Boat orders issued:
1. Damage Control and Repair 1 and 2 will see that no unauthorised person goes on deck and that complete darkened-ship condition prevails throughout. When troops are ordered on deck - watch opening closely.
2. All Hands will wear impregnated clothing and carry all equipment (Possible gas attack)
3. As soon as boats are lowered, prepare to debark troops and equipment promptly as LCM's and LCVP's come alongside.
4. Prepare to receive causalities.
5. As soon as Boat Teams are debarked, lower starboard and port accommodation ladders.
6. Food will be delivered to the General Quarters Stations.
7. BE PREPARED TO EXECUTE ALL EMERGENCY ORDERS PROMPTLY, CALMLY AND QUIETLY.

Generalfieldmarschall von Rundstedt is informed that parachutists have been observed.

Above; 6th Airborne Cemetery at Ranville 1944.

Capt. G. Lugg personal collection.

Below: Ranville Cemetery 2013

0202:
505th PIR complete its drop. Most of the troops land on or near the drop zone, but a few are widly dispersed over the countryside. Assembly is rapid and the battalions move off towards their objectives.

0208:
3rd Battalion 508th PIR commence their jump.

0210:
Parachute elements of Airborne Division Artillery jump and join up with the 508th PIR upon landing and assist in the attack on La Fiere bridge.

0214:
Parachute elements of the 82nd Airborne, part of Force A, drop near the west bank of the Merderet River and set up a command post.

A German officer of the 716th Infantry Division phones General Marcks in St-Lô and reports:- *On the left of the sector held by the 914th Infantry Regiment, the equivalent of a paratrooper battalion occupies the canal area of Carentan southwest of Brevands. Isolated paratroopers, who have obviously missed their target, are found near Cardonville. In all other sectors, calm prevails.* Marcks issues the signal for invasion "Alarm coast"

0215:
Colonel Hamann, officer in charge of the 709th Infantry-Division phones St-Lô and reports that enemy paratroopers have landed around Ste-Mere-Église. Every German battalion, batteries and regimental headquarters are placed on full alert.

0220:
3rd Battalion, 508th PIR complete their jump and separate into 4 groups. One group is in the vicinity of La Fière, fighting along the railway and attacks La Fière bridge. Two other groups join forces west of the Merderet after taking part in some very heavy fighting. An Officer of this group shot and killed the Commanding General of the German 91st Division. The fourth group fought with the 507th PIR to take the Chef du Pont bridge.

0229:
USS *Bayfield*, flag ship of Rear Admiral Don P. Moon and carrying the Commander of the UTAH Beach assault force (U Force) Major General Joseph L. Collins, drops anchor 11.5 miles off the coast of the Cotentin peninsular. Field order 1 stats "7th Corps assaults UTAH Beach on D Day at H-Hour and captures Cherbourg with minimum delay.

0230:
Heavy combat starts in the locality of Ranville between the troops of the 6th British Airborne and the 716th Infantry and 21st Panzer Divisions.

341 Battery, 86th Field Regiment, Royal Artillery; Reveille on the LSI followed by eggs and bacon at 0300. In the bowels of the ship, lit only by weak orange lights, sleepy soldiers load onto L.C.A.'s.

225th Parachute Field Ambulance; Majority of unit make R.V. in copse. There is some confusion on the D.Z. owing to enemy action. Some opposition is experienced and there is some mortaring in the later stages. Unit proceeded in rear of 12th Para Battalion to LE BAS de RANVILLE.

CO with Capt WILSON and 4 RASC carry out recce of chateau. The inhabitants are woken and are friendly. Three German officers are captured in bed. The unit is brought in as a Main Dressing Station establishment. D.Z. casualties were treated at once

0232:
The first element of the 1st Battalion, 507th PIR commence jumping.

0240:
Generalfieldmarschall von Rundstedt transmits to the 7th German Army that he does not believe that it will be a landing on a huge scale.

0245:
Transmitters "Bag Pipe" and "Chatter" located in England kick into action and scramble the Kriegsmarine (German Navy) and the Luftwaffe (German Air Force) communications.
Off GOLD Beach men begin to climb down from the ships into their landing craft. *"The landing craft was rolling in every possible direction; the sea-sickness pills had failed. Lying still only made one feel worse"* Eric Broadhead Durham Light Infantry

The German 352nd Infantry Division report that 50 to 60 more parachutists have now dropped south of the Carentan Grand Canal.

0246:
352nd Army Postal Service report spotting two aircraft pulling gliders heading southbound.

0250:
Strength of 9th Parachute Battalion now approximately 150 all ranks. Battalion Commences march to Merville Battery. All of Otway's men have a luminous Skull and Crossbones patch stitched

"We were going towards the coast of France, 7 Cruisers and 4 Destroyers, led by Belfast, Diadem, Orion, Emerald, Ajax, Argonaut and Flores. Passed hundreds of craft of all shapes and sizes. There were 4,000 craft of all kinds. Arrived 6 miles off shore between Le Havre and Cherbourg without being seen, stopped engines and waited for daylight. At about 4 o'clock our bombers came over and in 30 seconds Sur Mer was one mass of flames, it was a terrible sight, seemed so unreal. One bomber came down in flames. As dawn broke Belfast opened fire followed by us and the other cruisers followed suit. Our third salvo put a German battery out of commission.

Then the landing craft went in but we were unable to see the shore as it was one cloud of smoke. The Wrestler TDR struck a mine and went up in a cloud of smoke and flames. We have been firing off and on all day and the small craft have been running backwards and forwards all day long, unloading the big transports which are behind us. We have had 2 Red warnings so far but no planes were seen, our fighters have been over all day long.

I had no sleep last night and only a couple of hours today, feeling rather drowsy but don't expect any sleep tonight. Jerry will certainly do something, this has been too quiet to be true.

Signalman John Emrys, HMS Diadem

http://aberth.com/diadem/

Top: Signalman John Emrys Williams

Above: HMS Diadem

Below: John and his HMS Diadem Crew Mates

on their front so that once in the battery they can distinguish themselves from the enemy.

0251:
USS *Ancon*, flagship of the OMAHA assault force, drops anchor 11 miles off the coast undetected. Soldiers are roused for assembly. Sergeants shout the order, *"pick it up and put it on."* Everyone starts loading up. At the last minute, Pvt. Fred Reese has an idea. He grabs a large roll of toilet paper and sticks it under his helmet.

0255:
914th Infantry Regiment: *Between 8 and 10 paratroopers spotted near the IV/352e Artillery Regiment. Near Cardonville, two paratroopers equipped with parachutes and dressed in camouflage uniforms were captured. It seems that near Isigny, 70 more paratroopers landed. Waiting for confirmation.*

0300:
Gliders begin to reinforce paratroops

The Royal Air Force bombs targets at Caen.

"The word came through at 0300, that "They are filling the boats" Our spotting plane came over us as the bombers finished and we blasted three 6" batteries in as many minutes from 11 miles out.

I remember the hundreds of gliders going over towed by Dakotas, Stirlings and Halifaxes. Most aircraft went over the fleet at 3000 plus feet painted with black and white 'invasion' stripes. Bombers and heavies went over at 10,000 feet and lowered wheels over the fleet.

Some fighters strafing disobeyed the order to climb before they left the beaches and zoomed in over the landing ships at zero plus feet. Anything coming at you from the beach was considered by many to be the enemy, resulting in 157 allied fighters shot down in 5 days. Admiral Kirk sent a Signal "All ships to identify before opening fire or he would withdraw low level support". I was on the upper deck when I saw our No 1 4" High Angle Gun open up on a Mustang coming from the shore. It flipped over and crashed. My comments to the I/C. gun got me a bollocking." Royal Marine WCS Hiscock, PO/X112968 - HQ192 Squad aboard HMS Hawkins

American "O" Force (OMAHA) commanded by Rear Admiral Hall, USN, comprising of 3300 vehicles and 34,000 men with a follow up force of almost equal numbers begin to put landing craft into the water some 12 miles off the shore. The sea is rough and almost immediately 10 of the smaller craft founder and 300 men are fighting for their lives in the choppy sea. In the flimsy landing craft men are bailing frantically to stay afloat. Tired and suffering from sea sickness, these are the same men that in a few hours time are expected to storm the beaches with their wits about them.

"U "Force (UTAH troops start loading into the landing craft.

OMAHA: Sergeant Ludwig Förster fires three white rockets from the WN 62 strongpoint located close to Colleville-sur-Mer to ask the ships to identify themselves. The other defence points in the area do the same. Unsurprisingly there is no response from the ships.

Some S-Boote (Schnellboot) of the German Kriegsmarine start patrolling in the English Channel, following the arrival of allied parachutists, but find nothing.

The 352nd Infantry Division report that new groups of paratroopers are spotted south of Brevands and other units are located near Cardonville.

0309:
Ten large craft are reported seven miles north of Port en Bessin. This together with other reports convinced Admiral Krancke that a large scale operation is in progress and the following orders are issued.

- Vessels of West Defence Force to patrol coastal waters
- "Landwirt" submarines[1] to be in immediate readiness
- 8th Destroyer Flotilla (Narviks) to move from Royan to Brest
- 5th Torpedo Boat Flotilla from le Harve to reconnoitre in Port en Bessin-Grandcamp area. This was later changed to the Orne estuary.
- 5th and 9th Motor Torpedo Boat Flotillas from Cherbourg to patrol off Cape Barfleur and west of Cape de la Hague respectively. [2]

0310:
Report sent from Pointe du Hoc to the H.Q. of the 352nd Division of the German Infantry: *"Landing of enemy parachutists on both sides of the Vire river".*

---
[1] A group of 36 submarines based on the west coast of France earmarked for use against the invasion
[2] The flotillas left Cherbourg at 0445 but bad weather compelled them to return at first light.

American soldiers with full equipment leap into the surf from a landing craft and wade toward Utah Beach, Les Dunes de Madaleine.

USNA

General Marcks orders in reserves headed up by S.S. Standartenführer Kurt Meyer, Commander of the 25th S. S. Panzergrenadier Regiment, to move in to the OMAHA and UTAH junction to deal with the paratroopers, stating that the 352nd Infantry Division must maintain open communications with the 709th Infantry Division through Carentan and for this purpose, the start of the movement must be reported.

0312:
1st Battalion, 507th PIR land east of the Merderet River and are fairly dispersed.

0313:
The 84th German Army Corps H.Q. S.S. are informed that all sectors are quiet except south of Brévands where the equivalent of a battalion has dropped and near Cardonville where isolated units have been identified.

0315:
Glider No 81 with HQRAMC on board lands after an uneventful crossing until fired on by flak ships which registered two hits on glider. No causalities.

Reveille for the Queens Own Rifles of Canada onboard the S.S. Monoway, a Red Ensign ship from New Zealand. The Channel is rough; the spirits of the men boisterously high. An excellent breakfast was served...few managed to hold it down.

Order sent to S.S.-Standartenführer Kurt Meyer, *"The entire Detachment of Meyer's reserves must be placed in order of battle and move to the bridge west of Neuilly Forest to Montmartin sector Deville. The approach march to be organized in small groups and multiple columns. A report must be sent as soon as the unit sets off. "*[1]

0322:
Reports from the 352nd Artillery Regiment states that they are the target of bombing.

0325:
Ranville - 7th Parachute Battalion occupy objective and hold it against various counter-attacks "A" and "B" Companies being heavily engaged.
Causalities - killed 3 Officers, Capt Parry (Padre), Lt Bowyer and Lt Hill, plus 16 Other Ranks.
Wounded - 4 Officers, Major Taylor, Capt Webber, Lt Hunter & Lt Temple & 38 other ranks.
Missing - 170 Other Ranks did not rendezvous after drop.

---

[1] S.S.-Standartenführer Kurt Meyer, nicknamed "Panzermeyer" was not a tank officer, he was given the name in reference to his aggressive and fearless attacks.

914th Infantry Regiment: Instruction on the arrival of Meyer's reserves. *"Acknowledgments must be made in the area of depression South of Carentan, where enemy forces were parachuted."*

0330:
Major-General Gale, Commander British 6th Airborne Division, and his HQ unit arrive in one of the Gliders. He has his jeep on board but this was stuck in the wreck of the glider that has landed heavily. Supply HQ in the UK was said to have received an urgent request for a horse!

Touffréville - 8th Parachute Battalion reports situation as follows:-
Battalion Strength 11 officers and about 130 Other Ranks, 1 Officer and 2 Other Ranks (OR) are wounded and 6 ORs had Drop Zone injuries and are not in a condition to fight. The Commanding Officer is wounded in the hand.

Naval Force "S" arrives and takes up positions off the Normandy Coast.

Reveille for Bill Cheall and those onboard the *Empire Lance* Everybody was soon on the ball, wanting to get going. They checked all their kit was to hand, then make sure they had a good breakfast, not knowing when they would eat again that day. *" Our gear consisted of our 303 Lee Enfield rifle or, in my case, a two-inch mortar and six bombs. We all carried two filled Bren gun magazines in case there was a hold up in the supply chain, three hand grenades, a bandoleer of fifty rounds of 303 ammunition, an entrenching tool, a filled water bottle, a gas cape and groundsheet, gas mask, a full small pack and our webbing equipment, plus bayonet and steel helmet. Section leaders carried a Sten gun. We never travelled far without our small pack on our back; it contained a change of clothes and personal things. If anybody had spare capacity, more ammunition was carried because nobody was certain how things would go once we had landed and we were moving into uncharted waters against a formidable enemy."*

OMAHA - The sea is now very rough. Waves are three to four feet high, some even reaching over six feet. Wally Bieder was one of the first men down the side and into the landing craft. He held the bottom of the rope ladder for the other solders as the craft bobbed up and down and smacked against the side of the ship. Lt. Spalding took his place at the front of the craft, behind the ramp. Next to him is Sgt. Fred Bisco.

When all the men are aboard, the equipment is lowered from the ship. Pvt. Vinny DiGaetano saw the flamethrower coming down. He grabs the

The Smiling Assassin.

S.S.Standartenführer Kurt Meyer (Panzermeyer)

Whilst leading the first battle group to make contact with the Canadians he ordered that no prisoners be taken. He was later tried and found guilty for the shooting of 41 Canadians over the 6th and 7th June 1944

Bundesarchiv, Bild 101III-Ludwig-006-19 / Ludwig / CC BY-SA

weapon and straps it to his back. Fully loaded, the craft circled until finally the order came: "All boats away!"

The 91st Infantry-Division H.Q. near Picauville reports being under attack.

0335:
Gliders containing the reinforcements of the 6th British Airborne Division land in the area of Ranville.

The 716th Infantry-Division reports enemy paratroopers near Amfreville, Breville, Gonneville and Herouvillette.

Report sent to the headquarters of the 352nd Infantry Division in Germany: "*Very heavy bombings on Le Guay, Pointe du Hoc and Grandcamp*".

0344:
Report of the Naval Command in Normandy: "*A reinforced battalion of paratroopers spotted SW Brevands, here only a small detachment landed. The bombings are ongoing*".

0345:
Royal Artillery L.C.A.'s lowered into the sea which tossed the 25' craft around like corks. It was a 7 mile journey that would take some three hours.

Off OMAHA beach "G" Company was called by the boat teams to their respective debarkation stations and begin loading into the LCVPs'. A very heavy sea is running, which creates considerable difficulty in loading the personnel from the "USS Henrico" into the assault craft. Loading is affected by means of loading all heavy equipment and ten men into the assault craft before lowering away the boats. The remainder of the boat team personnel is then loaded over the side of the "USS Henrico" by scramble nets. This is extremely difficult, due to the weight of the equipment carried by each man in his assault jacket and the slippery footing created by the wooden rungs of the scramble nets.

0353:
Reports to the Chief of Staff of the Army Corps: *Meyer's reserves should start 04.15 H., a battalion to Carentan and two battalions to the area Montmartin-en-Graignes.*

0354:
Mission "Chicago": 52 CG-4 (WACO) gliders towed by C-47s from the 434th Troop Carrier Group land on Landing Zone "E" north of Hiesville. They bring 158 men, 16x 57mm antitank guns of the 81st AA battalion, 1 baby bulldozer, 1 advanced surgical unit, 1 radio jeep and 1 trailer carrying an SCR 299 for long-distance communications with England. All this material is for the 101st Airborne.

0355:
The German 914th Regiment of Grenadiers report two paratroopers are trapped near Cardonville while about 70 paratroopers have jumped near Isigny.

0400:
British warships put to surface action stations

HMS *Largs* waits for a signal to come from the midget submarine pointing the way to the beach (SWORD) this will be done by the submarine firing Verey lights in the direction they are to land.

225th Field Ambulance is now established in the chateau and is starting to receive casualities from various units.

MERVILLE BATTERY: The 9th Para Battalion, under Lt. Col. Terence Otway arrive at the Merville Battery. Initially composed of 700 men, after a dreadful drop only 150 are able to regroup with a single heavy machine gun instead of 5. Regardless, they continue their attack, they have trained hard, "to the limit of their abilities".

Otway had built a mock-up of the battery on a forty-five-acre site below the Iron Age fort of Walbury Hill, four miles south-west of Newbury in England and had the surrounding woods and fields bulldozed and made to replicate the battery exactly. He and his men trained for several months before D-Day, going over and over the same thing time and time again until it was second nature. Otway, needing to be 100% sure he could trust his men and even set "honey traps". He need not have worried, the women reported back that not a single man revealed any element of the plan. They were trained to take on anything and showed exceptional courage to continue with the very limited resources they had. Failure did not cross Otway's mind for one moment.

The northern end of the Battery is protected by an anti-tank ditch, 14 feet wide and 300 feet long, with the remaining circumference protected by two rings of barbed wire, the inner ring being 8 feet tall, and in between these lay a 50-75 foot deep minefield. Otway's party have also lost the tape that would mark the way through the minefield. After clearing a path through his ever resourceful men then slid out on their backsides dragging their heels into the ground and leaving a path marked out through the minefield.

*D Day for me began at approx 0500hrs. I was awakened by the raucous blare of the ships ever present tannoy system, "Hear this, hear this, wakey, wakey rise and shine, lash up and stow". In other words, wash up, dress up and get rid of your hammock! The last item provided in lieu of a bed. Once I got used to it I must say it was pretty comfortable. However, this call brought reality to the fact that the TIME had come. I couldn't believe it. It's all a game, I thought. We shall see…

Royal Marine John B Wetjen.

Q Troop, 47 Commando

* Lay at Ease, held at Royal Marines Museum, ACQ280/06 11/13/393

L.C.T. beached at La Breche, ramp pierced by shell.

Capt. G Lugg personal collection

The garrison, of gunners and sentries, amounted to one hundred and sixty men, and they are supported by numerous machine-gun emplacements and 20 mm anti-aircraft guns.

Otway gives the order to "get in" and a torrent of fire rained into the battery. Grenades are thrown in, Sten gun fire, explosions, screams, smoke, dust, shouting. Some Germans come out to surrender, others continue the fight.

"Booby traps and mines were going off all over the place, fierce hand-to-hand fighting was going on inside the battery, and I had to keep dodging a machine gun in the tower which was shooting at me." Lt Col. Otway.

Major Alan Parry of Otway's 9th Battalion Pathfinders, who had been shot earlier, dragging his wounded leg, started to neutralise the guns by placing explosives in the breech. After the explosion, he went to verify the extent of the damage. Suddenly a shell whistled in and exploded close to casemate n°1. Major Parry felt a pain in his hand so sharp it felt sure it had been blown off but upon checking was somewhat relieved to see that his hand was still attached to his arm but badly gashed. They are being subjected to counter-battery fire from another German Battery, ordered by Battery Commander Lieutenant Raimund Steiner in the Forward Observation Bunker on the beach at Franceville who has been contacted via the armoured underground telephone cables.

After looking over casemate No 1, Major Parry, in great pain from both his leg and arm injuries, summoned all his strength to look at the other three. More counter-battery fire comes in, the noise was deafening. He then supervises the safe withdrawal of the Battalion, only handing over command, when unable walk.

Otway went from casemate to casemate to ascertain the state of the guns. He wants reports of the numbers of dead, wounded and fit men.

Dawn was breaking and Otway knew that if the cruiser HMS *Arethusa* receives no signal from the 9th Battalion of a successful neutralisation of the Merville guns, her Captain would assume the attack has failed and would fire upon the battery. Unfortunately, the Naval gunfire observation party, who would establish radio contact with *Arethusa* and direct the firing, has not turned up at the rendezvous point and to make matters worse, the 9th Battalion no longer has a radio…

3rd Battalion, 505th PIR arrive at St Mere Église, the town is securely held and out posted within the hour.

After assembling the 2nd Battalion, 505th PIR start to move out to take Meuville au Plain, but orders are received from the regiment to stand by.

The Royal Winnipeg Rifles. (The Little Black Devils) are at sea, its cloudy and cool with strong NW winds and a heavy sea. Tea and a cold snack is served as breakfast to all in the Battalion however, few are able to keep their meals down due to the rough sea. Patiently, each man waiting for his serial section to be called to board his respective landing craft. As each group is called the tension mounts.

Report from the Operations Centre of the Luftwaffe in Caen: *In the area on the right, the 716th Infantry Division, we can see a pack of four-engine large aircraft towing gliders approaching, heading southwest to Houlgate, Cabourg. Parachute jumps near Morsalines, St Cosmas and St Mere-Eglise on our left, the 709th Infantry Division. Three prisoners are captured, carrying maps of the mouth of the Vire.*

Marshal von Rundstedt asks the Supreme Command in Berlin for authorisation to send two divisions towards the coast.

Violent air raids on the WN strongpoints 44, 47 and 48.

Hitler went to bed giving orders not to be woken up before 0900 hrs

0405:
80th Airborne Anti aircraft Battalion lands.

0407:
Mission "Detroit": 52 gliders land on Landing Zone "O" north west of Ste-Mere-Église. They bring "A" and "B" batteries, 80th AA Battalion and headquarters for 82nd Airborne, artillery and signals. 3rd Battalion, 505th PIR under Lt.Col. Edward C. Krause captures the town.

0408:
General Don Forrester Pratt, second in command of the 101st Airborne Division, becomes the highest ranking Allied Officer to be killed in Normandy on D Day. The glider he was a passenger in, along with his aide 1st Lieutenant Lee John May, is piloted by Lieutenant Colonel Mike Murphy. It is flown successfully on to its designated landing zone, two miles west of Sainte-Marie-du-

This morning the Commander gave us the daftest talk I have ever heard on the loudspeaker. He complained about us wearing overalls and overcoats during the day and gave an order that all men must be in the rig of the day and look as smart as possible as an example to the soldiers who pass by us in the landing craft. Fancy worrying about dress when there are hundreds of young fellows losing their lives only a few miles from us. What is this an invasion or a beauty competition?

Signalman John Emrys Williams, on-board HMS Diadem

Maj. Gen. RFL Keller of the 3rd Canadian Division accompanied by members of his staff, arriving at Bernières-sur-Mer, 6th June 1944.

Canadian Archive.

Mont, but when Murphy applied the brakes, wet conditions beneath cause the glider to skid without slowing, over running the landing zone and crashing into 40-foot-tall (12 m) trees. Murphy broke both legs. Pratt, sitting in the Jeep, died from a broken neck. The Jeep was not chained, but was tied down with nylon rope and did not break loose or flex thus causing whiplash when it suddenly came to a violent stop. Lt. May was riding on the jump seat behind the Jeep and survived the crash having been thrown forward.

0415:
82nd Airborne Division H.Q. Initial glider serial landed and is scattered and does not reach the Command Post until late afternoon. The Chief of Staff is injured in a glider crash and was later evacuated.

0413:
The 352nd ID H.Q. orders the departure of the 915th Regiment of Grenadiers spearheaded by S.S.-Standartenführer Meyer towards Montmartin-Deville, through the bridge to the west of Neuilly, moving in columns and small groups.

0420:
224th Parachute Field Ambulance now come under the protection of 1 Canadian Parachute Bn. at the Canadian R.V.

915th Infantry Regiment: *"S.S.-Standartenführer Meyer with the 915th IR and the Reconnaissance Battalion (plus an artillery battery of the 352nd Regiment) - have started their march. Arrival in the area in three or four hours.*

Gunfire is heard in the sector held by the 726th Grenadier Regiment."

0425:
352nd ID HQ order the 914th Regiment to attack the paratroopers south of Carentan.

0430:
All Fighter Direction Tenders are now in position.

Royal Artillery's night came to an end on the L.C.T., blankets stowed away, hasty breakfast for those able to eat it, ammunition prepared and guns checked.

R.A.M.C.. Medical, 224th Field Ambulance Div H.Q. is now up and running.

CO 225th Field Ambulance visits No 3 Section at the Church in Ranville. There is some sniping going on and one of the Section had been wounded by enemy Light Machine Gun. Capt Tibbs has organised his Section to clear the DZ of causalities.

The lowering over side of the manned assault craft commences from the 'Empire Battleaxe' and from the 'Glenearn' in accordance with the pre-arranged timetable. The assault Companies of the 2nd Battalion East Yorks. go first and as they pass the remainder of the Battalion, they were given a hearty cheer.

OMAHA : 1st Division - 16th Regiment - Cannon Company - The six howitzer sections loaded on Dukws aboard LST 376 are driven into the sea approximately twelve miles out from the beach. As the Dukws are driven down the ramps of the LSTs, they are filled with water because of the steep angle of the unloading ramp. Every effort was made to bail out the Dukws as they were driven toward the rendezvous area.

Others Dukws of the Company take the stalled ones into tow and continued on. Later, the heavy load of towing two loaded Dukws causes the towing vehicles to also stall. The two ropes are then cast off and furious efforts made to start the motors again. Success is achieved with two of the Dukws and these continue on. The stalled vehicles sink under the heavy seas. Most of the men from the Dukws are rescued by Navy small boats. Of the four remaining, one sinks en route whist going to help the men in the water from the sunken vessels. Most of these men are also picked up by Navy small boats. One sinking DUKW reached a Rhino Ferry and is unloaded. The two remaining Dukws reach the Rendezvous area and proceed toward the beach. Twenty four men are missing.

914th IR - *Report on the beginning and progress of the attack by two companies of the 914th Infantry Regiment against paratroopers southwest of Brevands. We have no details yet. At Canal de Carentan the enemy tries to force a passage from The Mill to the south.*

0434:
First P-47s take off.

UTAH - Corporal Harvey S. Olson, Private Tommy Killeran, Sergeant John W. Zanders and Corporal Melvin F. Kenzie of the 4th Cavalry swim ashore on the Iles St. Marcouf and become the first men to invade Europe by sea. Armed only with knifes they wade ashore from two man canoes to mark the beach for the incoming landing crafts. After the landing, the men do not find a single German soldier or battery but get trapped in the minefields covering the beaches. When they had verified that

> *"It is very difficult to describe the attitudes, reactions or feelings of what went through the minds of the crewmen. Some thought of their wives and sweethearts, and others were in dread of drowning.*
>
> *Looking into the faces and eyes of my mates, I could see that some were scared shitless, others fiercely proud just to be part of it, anticipation and nervous excitement showed everywhere."*
>
> Mne. Norman G. Marshall.
>
> ACQ 44/00 RM Museum.

Canadian Infantrymen aboard a landing craft heading for JUNO Beach. The fear and apprehension on their faces is plain to see.

National Archives of Canada

the islands were unoccupied, 132 men from the 4th and 24th Cavalry Squadrons, under Lt. Col. Edward C. Dunn land on the (mined) beaches of the Saint-Marcouf islands.

About 4 miles off the coast from UTAH Beach. Three weeks before D-Day, SHAEF believed the Germans might have built heavy batteries on them and did not want to take any chances as they could have greatly impeded the main landings had they been defended.

Whilst the first men were killed or wounded by the German S-mines, Colonel Dunn was able to send the "mission accomplished" message. At the end of the day there would be 19 killed or wounded in the process of taking the two islands from the mines the Germans had left behind.

Being the first man ashore Corporal Harvey S. Olson was later awarded the Silver Star medal for his actions. His citation reads as follows:-

"Sgt. Harvey S. Olson, Troop A, 4th Cavalry Reconnaissance Squadron, Mechanized. On June 6, 1944, Sgt. Olson with one companion, displaying the highest courage in the face of unknown dangers, became one of the first American soldiers of the ground forces to land on French soil. He volunteered for the mission of the landing on D Day on the Iles St Marcouf, a strategically placed island commanding the beach where the assault was to be made. Sgt. Olson and his companion paddled through heavy surf and mined waters in a small two-man rubber boat to within 100 yards of the island.

Sgt. Olson then destroyed his craft by slashing it open, and swam the remaining distance armed only with a knife. Once on the island, which was heavily covered with anti-tank and anti-personnel mines, Sgt. Olson and his companion signalled the assault forces and marked the beach with lights. The skill and courage with which he carried out his hazardous assignment, made possible the successful landing on schedule of his detachment; denying the use of the island to the enemy. This was a vital factor in the opening phase of fortress Europe".

Field Marshall von Runstead orders the 12 S.S. Panzer Division and Panzer-Lehr to move immediately to Calvados.

0435:
16th Infantry Regiment report: *"We have captured an American Lieutenant near the WN Le Guay. He says that fake parachutists that exploded on contact with the ground, were dropped with the real paratroopers."*

Gruppenkommando West orders reconnaissance patrols in the Baie de Seine with the 5th Torpedo Boats, the 15th Patrol Boats, the 38th Minesweepers and, on each side of the Cotentin Peninsula, the 5th and 9th Speed Boats Flotillas.

Commander Heinrich HOFFMANN, commanding the 5th Torpedo Boats Flottilla, leaves Le Havre with three boats: T28, Jaguar and Möwe.

Air raids on Le Guay, Pointe du Hoc, Grandcamp and Maisy.

0436:
RAF 88 Sqn are airborne from RAF Hartford Bridge heading to Selsey Bill where they descend to "wave height" and then head for the beaches. "L" for Louden with Sqn Ldr George Louden on board is to contact the battleship Ramilles and inform them that they are ready to lay smoke. However they do not get the response they were expecting and instead Ramilles gave them everything she had got by way of tracer gunfire, despite the aircraft being painted up like a "humbug" (black and white stripes painted overnight on the wings and fuselage of the aircraft for identification purposes.) Fortunately, they escaped unscathed, they found out later that 75% losses were expected from the smoke laying operation.

0445:
Lieutenant G. Honour's HMS X-23 midget submarine surfaces a mile off the Normandy coast. 20 miles away it's sister ship, Lieutenant K.R. Hudspeth's HMS X-20 does the same. Those two ships mark the limits of the Anglo-Canadian sector. Their task is to raise a mast equipped with strobe lights and to set-up optical and radio-electrical guiding devices. They will then lead the way for the fleet. Since they got under way from Portsmouth on 2nd June, the crews had spent 74 hours at sea.

HMS Belfast reports fires & flack on starboard beam.

LCT's carrying the DD tanks arrive at their transport area for UTAH beach some 45 minutes after they should have left it due to the weather.

0445:
OMAHA - landing craft proceed in line toward the beach. All the craft are heavily loaded, and the very rough sea causes the personnel and equipment to become thoroughly drenched and all boats ship

> We have captured an American Lieutenant near the WN Le Guay. He says that fake parachutists that exploded on contact with the ground, were dropped with the real paratroopers.
>
> 916th Infantry Regiment report.

Nazi propaganda photo which was originally described as follows:
Glider - shattered on the ground.
Many gliders used in the Anglo-American invasion were shot down by our flak and crashed.
This glider went down between German troops and ran against a rear wall. Some of those onboard were dead, the rest could be overpowered and taken prisoner by our troops immediately.

Bundesarchiv, Bild 146-2004-0176 / CC-BY-SA

more water than could be pumped out, causing them to be constantly in danger of foundering.

0453:
The 352nd Infantry Division signals to the 84th Army Corps that it is no longer able to locate the warships.

War Correspondent in E for Easy: *"This is definitely the invasion, I noted the time, it is precisely 4.53am. Above the cloud a full moon made the sky so light that one could read the identification letters on the nearest aircraft. Not a German fighter to be seen."*

0455:
224th Parachute Field Ambulance party move off down the main Varaville - Herouvillette road. Capt. T.G. Gray, RAMC, joins this group soon after the march commenced. An enemy machine gun post is located on the main road west of Petitville and so the whole party moves off the main road into the school. A small Brigade H.Q. party under Capt. Woodgate joins the main group here.

0500:

"At 0500 hrs, the ship heaved to. The message came across for everybody to be on deck at their attack platoon positions. We were now standing waiting for further orders, almost weighed down with equipment, ready for the fray. Suddenly, 'Come on lads, let's go!' from our officer brought me back very quickly to why I was there; it was time. We had dropped anchor seven miles from the coast and could see a red glow in the distance. The Air Force had begun to play their part, as had others we did not then know about, and the endless roar of bombers and fighters passing overhead was deafening, interspersed with the roar of the guns from the battleships; we had great difficulty hearing commands.

Then I found myself with my leg over the side, trying to get a footing onto the scrambling net. I had fastened the mortars and bombs onto my equipment and my Number Two on the mortar was alongside me. The practice we had done for this day was nothing like the real thing and endeavouring to get a foot onto the landing craft was beset with danger. The sea was very rough and there was a three-foot rise and fall of the craft against the side of the ship. It was a hair-raising experience but, luckily, nobody suffered any injuries. Somehow, we made it and pulled away from Empire Lance and then waited until all assault craft were in line abreast. There were fourteen assault craft to land on GOLD beach, with thirty men in each.

I was on the port side, fifth from the front of our boat. How could I forget? The first thing we all did was to get out our sick bags from on top of the grenades, in the right pouch of our equipment. As soon as we were all settled on the bench seat, the order came, 'Craft away'. We were only seven miles from our objective. This, then, was what we had trained for. The whole operation was fantastic; the sea seemed to be covered with ships of every description. The run in was to take two hours and our H-hour was 0725 hrs, with the Americans on our right and because of the differences in the tide they had started their invasion at 0630 hrs. God help us, lads! " Bill Cheall - Green Howards

Glider elements of 82nd Airborne Division Artillery land and move directly to the Division Command Post

0501:
Several bombers towing gliders over Houlgate and Cabourg are reported, in addition to the air drops at Morsalines, St. Côme and St. Mere–Eglise. Three paratroopers with maps of the Vire river are captured.

0502:
352nd Artillery Regiment: *"Off Port-en-Bessin; a large naval unit and four smaller units are sighted and off Grandcamp light naval units are also spotted".*

0503:
352nd Anti-Tank Battalion: *"Isolated personnel transport gliders are observed at an altitude of 2000 meters in a westerly direction."*

0506:
726th Grenadiers: *"The WN's, at Arromanches Saint-Honorine and Colleville are under continual air attack as well as the bombing of the highest calibre. Parachutists are observed, probably the crew of a downed aircraft."*

0507:
716th Infantry Division reports more and more gliders landing in the Orne sector.

A War Correspondent on board a British Destroyer starts to report the day. *"Events have started to move rapidly since 0400 this morning, I shall keep a report of everything in my diary. We are presently lying eight miles from the lowering position for the invasion craft."*

0510:
Naval artillery guns commence firing against German coastal positions first by *Orion* cruiser off GOLD Beach, then by the cruisers *Ajax, Argonaut,*

View from the Command Post at Pointe du Hoc showing the cliffs the Rangers needed to scale.

Lieutenant Commander Knapper and Chief Yeoman Cook, of USS Texas (BB-35), examine a damaged German pillbox at Pointe du Hoc on D-Day, 6 June 1944.

Emerald plus the Dutch warship *Flora* and 13 destroyers.

18 Marauder bombers of the Royal Air Force attack the German battery of the Canisy Mount. Allied aircraft streak low across the eastern flank and lay a most effective smoke screen to shield the force from the heavy batteries at Le Havre.

The Free French warships *Montcalm* and *Georges-Leygues* bombard the German battery of Longues-sur-Mer, after it started firing upon US *Arkansas*.

914th Infantry Regiment: *"The II/914e Infantry Regiment captured three Americans they are carrying maps and aerial photos of the Cotentin Peninsula, especially in the sector of the mouth of the Vire. Prisoners can not be transferred at this time because the enemy blocks the route."*

0515:

A *Very light was fired from the Merville Battery by the 9th Battalion to signal their success. An aircraft circling over the battery spots this and relayed the message to the Navy. They had achieved their objective. All they have to do now is to clear the area and progress to their next objective.

In addition a very battered Carrier pigeon was used but did not get back to the UK until the 7th June. The poor pigeon, later named the Duke of Normandy, was encased in a large cardboard cylinder, with a hole for his head to poke out, on the 1st June. Here he was incarcerated until the morning of the 6th June. The poor thing had been parachuted down tied to a radio operator under his smock, endured some dreadful battle noises, and then with a message tied to its leg thrown into the air amidst more gunfire from all angles. Despite all this and the awful weather in the channel this little bird made it back and for its efforts was awarded the Dickin medal, being the animal equivalent of a Victoria Cross. It took him 26 hours and 50 minutes to return to his loft with the message.

Sadly, after capturing the battery, and losing a further 75 men in the process, it was discovered that the guns were First World War vintage and did not have the range to seriously trouble the landings, although they could just about reach SWORD Beach.

Otway found a barn and set to removing the injured men, both British and German, one of the German survivors was a Doctor who did what he could until supplies ran out. He set off alone back to the battery to where he knew there were extra medical supplies and was killed on the way by a German shell.

For his actions at the Merville Battery and in general throughout D-Day and beyond, Lieutenant-Colonel Otway was awarded the Distinguished Service Order. His citation reads:

For conspicuous bravery and outstanding leadership. This officer led 150 men of his battalion on the successful attack of the Sallenelles battery. He personally directed the attack and organised the successful cleaning up of the enemy strong points under heavy enemy mortar and machine gun fire. He led the attack on and successfully held Le Plein until relieved by another formation. On arrival in the Le Mesnil area he succeeded in beating off two major enemy attacks of several hours duration by his magnificent leadership of his numerically very weak and tired battalion. His utter disregard of personal danger has been an inspiration for all his men.

Otway was sent to a hospital in Cardiff to recover, however he was deemed to be unfit for active service. He was given duties at the War Office.

All LCA's for The Canadian Winnipeg Rifles are now manned and lowered into the choppy sea. Still 10 miles from shore only the hardiest rifleman is able to keep his stomach in check and not reach for his vomit bag.

709th Infantry Division: *"There is no enemy in the town of Carentan at present, but significant forces are parachuting north of Carentan. Sainte-Mère-l'Église is completely occupied by paratroopers."*

0516:

Assistant Director Medical Services (ADMS) visits Main Dressing Station 225 Para Field Ambulance where reception and treatment of causalities is well under way and proceeding to plan.

St. Mère-Église was the first French town to be liberated by the American soldiers of the 3rd Battalion of the 505th Parachutist Infantry Regiment led by Lt. Colonel Edward C. Krause. The stars and stripes are hoisted at the town hall. They hold the town until reinforcements arrive on the afternoon of the 7th June.

Henry Langrehr is also involved in the capture of St Mere Église, he was depicted in The Longest Day parachuting into a greenhouse. He had to wait 63 years before being presented, with 5 others, the Legion of Honour from Nicolas Sarkozy.

---

* A pyrotechnic signal in a system of signalling using white or coloured balls of fire projected from a special pistol

Army glider pilots, among the first to land in Normandy and disrupt enemy communications, are on their way back to England. They are shown in a LCVP, which is taking them to larger craft off the Normandy coastline.
USNA

Fallschirmjaeger with MG42 machine gun
Bundesarchiv, Bild 101I-587-2253-15 / Schneiders, Toni / CC BY-SA

"(American) paratroopers began jumping out by the hundreds. I saw one paratrooper land in the road but a German killed him before he could get untangled from his parachute. Another paratrooper was also killed near me. I will never forget the sight." Raymond Paris, resident of St. Mère-Eglise.

0520:
352nd Artillery Regiment reports to the HQ of the 352nd ID : *"Forward observers of the 2nd and 4th Artillery Groups report noises, probably from Naval Units moving in the direction of the estuary of the Vire river. Moreover, near Le Guay-Pointe du Hoc, 29 ships are observed including 4 large warships (destroyers or cruisers), at a distance from 6 to 10 km. 3 or 4 aircraft have crashed at Formigny, 1 (Polish) pilot is captured. The number of landing craft in front of Port-en-Bessin is now in excess of 50."*

War Correspondent: *Its Dawn and innumerable assault ships appear smudgily."*

0522:
The three torpedo boats of Commander Heinrich Hoffman cross the artificial fog protecting the allied ships and emerge in front of the invasion fleet. Hoffman decides to attack immediately.

Report received from the Naval Command of Normandy: *"We opened fire on targets at sea. An enemy ship is sinking."*

The German flotilla fire a salvo of 18 torpedoes. One torpedo could just be seen approaching H.M.S. *Largs*. The Divisional Commander's ship was saved by putting her engines to full astern, and the torpedo passed a few feet ahead. A second torpedo hits the destroyer *Svenner* of the Royal Norwegian Navy sailing about two hundred yards astern of the *Largs* and she starts to go down immediately. The Germans turn tail and disappeared into the fog.

0525:
HMS *Arethusa* receives a frantic message from their liaison officer stationed on the task force bombardment control ship HMS *Largs*; he reports that a reconnaissance aircraft had spotted yellow smoke coming from the Merville battery. The message has arrived with five minutes to spare before HMS *Arethusa* commences firing.

0527:
War Correspondent: *"The night bombings have ceased and the great Naval bombardment begins."*

HMS *Belfast* opens fire again with full broadside to port.

0530:
The soldiers of the first assault wave of the S Force (SWORD Beach) leave their transport ships and load into the assault craft that will take them to the beaches.

For the first time that day an allied fighter attacks ground targets close to Falaise.

HMS *Largs* off SWORD beach receive the signal from the midget submarine. Assault craft are ready to move in. Battleships, Monitors, Cruisers, Destroyers etc are all pounding away at the beaches. Rocket ships are also moving up.

Naval bombardment of Pointe du Hoc begins with the 14" guns of USS Texas, each shell costing in the region of $10,000.

0531:
The ships of Eastern Naval Task force, acting on orders from Rear-Admiral Phillip Vian, open fire on the British and Canadian beaches of GOLD, JUNO and SWORD.

0532:
LSI's anchor off JUNO Beach.

0533:
War Correspondent: *"We are beginning to move in slowly."*

OMAHA - 916th Infantry Regiment: *"In the Bay of Colleville-Vierville, landing craft are approaching the beach. Many larger ships are observed heading west. It seems that the enemy protects himself behind a smokescreen."*

0535:
German shore batteries open fire; Allied naval forces, now massed along entire Normandy coast, begin bombardment.

In the Eastern Task Force area, Forces "G" and "J" arrive at the lowering positions without any trouble. The *Bulolo* (Naval Commander Force "G") and leading LSI's anchor up.
The Sherman DD Tanks of the 741st Tank Battalion begin to leave their LCT's.

Report of the Chief of Staff : *"Transmission of the report sent by the 916th I.R. in addition, five large ships are now seen off Saint-Laurent-sur-Mer three of them approaching accompanied by a large*

Right: Lt. Col T. Otway statue at the Merville Batterie

Top: : The Duke of Normandy pigeon

Below: Merville Batterie June 2012

number of landing craft ashore. So far, twelve prisoners are captured."

0536:
UTAH - Ships commence firing after receiving the first rounds from the German coastal artillery, and methodically crush the coastal defences. The USS *Nevada* fires its 380mm cannon continually at the Azeville battery, destroying one of the the casements. They bomb their targets with extreme precision with the guidance of the Navy forward observers who had parachuted in with the airborne troops during the night. In less than an hour they complete their task just before the Rangers are due to assault Pointe du Hoc which would have been fired upon had they not succeeded.

War Correspondent: *"Cruisers open fire I can now recognise the Belfast and the Mauritius."*

0537:
Norwegian Destroyer *Svenner*, after being torpedoed by one of the E Boots from La Harve, broke in two and sunk in less that five minutes. 32 Norwegian and one British crew were killed, 185 (15 wounded) were rescued from the crew of 219. A further torpedo narrowly misses HMS *Largs* by a yard.

0540:
HMS *Arethusa* (positioned off SWORD Beach) starts firing upon hotels on the sea front. The Germans used them for spotting for the artillery.

0545:
Naval Artillery bombard the Houlgate, Mount Canisy and Villerville batteries.

0546:
War Correspondent: *There are at least a thousand ships in our sector alone. Naval bombardment intensifies. Big battleships join in. I can see the Warspite of Salerno fame belching fire. Orion, Mauritius and another cruiser, the Black Prince are belting away."*

0548:
USS *Hobson* off UTAH commences indirect area fire on allocated targets. Due to light haze and flat landscape no direct targets were discernible.

0550:
Warships open fire on the UTAH Beach Batteries. USS *Satterlee* fires upon Pointe du Hoc and the *Texas* opens fire on the beach defences in the Dog sector, with the *Arkansas* attacking the D3 exit. In addition the *Georges Leygues* (Free French) and the *Tanant Side* aim at E1 on Easy sector, sadly most of the firing fell a mile too far inland killing a field of Cows.

276 B-26 Marauders of the 9th Air Force drop 4,404 250lbs bombs on seven targets from les Dunes-de-Varreville to Beauguillot. USS *Hobson* reports seeing one aircraft catch fire and blow up although no AA fire was observed.

Report to the Chief of Staff of the Army Corps : *"The Division Commander suggests to halt the movement of S.S.-Standartenführer Meyer in view of the deteriorating situation. The General commanding the corps agreed to the request and ordered the detachment to stop its movement."*

War Correspondent: *"I see the first flash from a German gun battery. So far not one enemy plane has arrived. It appears have taken the enemy by surprise."*

0552:
352nd Artillery Regiment: *"Between WN 60 and WN 80 landing craft are approaching the beaches near Colleville. Our artillery can not reach these targets. Region Maisy held under fire from large-calibre naval batteries. The same goes for the region Marcouf. The enemy ships are too far away and can not be reached by our artillery."*

0555:
480 B-24 Liberator bombers carrying 1,285 tons of ordnance are due to obliterate the strongpoints on the coast between Port-en-Bessin and the Pointe de la Percée but because of the low ceiling and visibility, the mission is a complete failure with the bombs dropping too far inland. The OMAHA beach's WNs are intact and 117 B-24s return to England with full bays. The troops coming ashore believe that the German strongpoints have been dealt with, sadly this was not the case.

UTAH – PC1261, the primary control craft for the landing force on Red Beach, UTAH is sunk by an explosion. It is not known if it was a chance hit by a shell or a mine. Due to the failure of the back up control craft, Red Beach was now without a guide. Shortly after an LCT heading for Green Beach was destroyed in a similar manner. As the shell fire was not heavy the LCT's managed to get 2000 yards nearer the beach than had originally planned and launched the DD's at 3000 yards.

OMAHA - The Allied Naval barrage and bombing raids on the German defences are ineffective.

(LB(K)) Landing Barge Kitchen, a converted Thames Barge

Below, extract from Section IV, Depot Ships, Standing Orders. Landing Barges, Kitchen

7/19/5 RM Museum Southsea

4. L.B.(K) will provide hot dinner, hot tea, hot supper and cold breakfast. Dinner will be ready at 1200, supper at 1700. The issue of meals should be completed as soon as possible after these times. It is realised that there must necessarily be some stragglers but S.C.F.B., Squadron Commanders and Flotilla Officers are requested to ensure that no vessels draw meals later than 1330 and 1830 respectively, unless this is absolutely unavoidable.

With dinner will be issued tea and the days allowance of bread, butter, jam (or syrup or paste) and marmalade. With supper will be issued cold breakfast. This there will be only two issues of food per day. To fit in with this routine, S.C.F.B. must arrange for running craft to take over their duties after breakfast and before dinner daily. If it is found possible to issue hot breakfast this will be done, but it must be realised that L.B.(K). have limited facilities, limited staff and large numbers to cater for. To avoid the difficulty of very small issues, jam, syrup and paste and marmalade may be drawn on a weekly basis. Craft with primus stoves may also draw an extra allowance of tea, sugar, milk and biscuits on a weekly basis. Hot tea will be available throughout the day for craft with primus stoves, and when night work is heavy, special arrangements will be made to provide hot tea at night also.

916th Infantry Regiment: *"Off Vierville forty four landing ships (small and medium) are observed which open fire on the coast."*

War Correspondent: *"A thin line of stout tank landing craft heads towards the shore. Minesweepers are returning. They have got plenty of guts these fellows."*

0556:
914th Infantry Regiment: *"Located ten to fifteen miles north of WN 88, three large naval vessels are observed. They bombard the area Maisy".*

0558:
Sun Rise. It is grey, cold and rainy. The wind is Force 3 to 4 and stirs up 2 metre waves on the sea.

The *Hilary* (Naval Commander Force "J", H.Q.) anchors up off JUNO beach..

0600:
The wind has dropped slightly but the sea is still producing waves of three to six feet in height. For many, the sea sick pills are in effective.

Rocket launcher barges approach the beaches, spraying them with salvoes of rockets: 20,000 in the British sector (GOLD, JUNO and SWORD Beaches) and 18,000 in the American sector (UTAH and OMAHA Beaches). Allied landing craft approach the beach. LCT's launch the DD tanks.

H.M.S. *Largs* in company with LSI's *Princess Astrid* and *Maid of Orleans* reach their lowering positions preparing for touch-down at 0725 hrs

War Correspondent: *"The enemy coast is clearly visible. Enemy batteries are firing spasmodically. Big fires are burning ashore."*

2nd Battalion, 505th PIR move into position North of St Mere Église and assist the 3rd Battalion in holding the town.

The Queens Own Rifles of Canada silently board their LCA's manned by the Royal Marines, they are seven miles off the French Coast.

0602:
The 352nd Infantry Division reports that a group of ships together with four smaller convoys start moving, and small ships gather in front of Grandcamp.

0603:
Order passed by the Divisional H.Q. 352nd Reconnaissance Battalion (which is connected to the telephone network): *"Stop the battalion! Expect additional orders from the Commander of the 915th Infantry Regiment. The Reconnaissance Battalion is currently positioned in the woods near Cerisy."*

0604:
916th Infantry Regiment sight 140 ships in the Bay of Vierville. Coastal defences are subjected to heavy bombardment.

0605:
OMAHA - LCH 168 report aircraft passing overhead towards the shore, wind 280 and Force 5, no firing from the shore. Too rough to land DD's.

OMAHA - Heavy day bombers of the 9th Air Force bomb enemy strongpoints in the vicinity of Colleville-sur-Mer

UTAH: Bomber attacks on the beach commence.

0606:
The 726th Regiment of Grenadiers informs its headquarters that the crew of a shot bomber was located north of Sully.

0615:
"D", "E" and "F" Companies of the 2nd Ranger Battalion head towards Pointe du Hoc, their mission is to climb the 100' cliffs and disable the six 155 mm guns that could cause havoc on UTAH and OMAHA beaches with their 25 km range and was considered as the German defensive position most dangerous to their plans and had to be neutralised at all costs. The Germans considered Pointe du Hoc as un-reachable from the sea and the area was so heavily mined that it could not be reached from an overland attack. They had not taken the Elite American Rangers into consideration who did not see the 100' cliffs as unassailable.

The Rangers have been at sea in their landing craft for over three hours. The bad weather, equipment failure and unpredictable tides have caused misdirection and they are heading too far to the east. A kilometre out they notice they are heading towards Pointe du Percée and have to make a hard turn to the west and at speed and parallel to the beach through flanking fire, head towards their disembarkation point at the foot of the cliffs at Pointe du Hoc. The delay means they are running late, it has been 30 minutes since the Naval bombardment lifted and the Germans have come out of their bunkers and are taking up their position and manning their guns.

Queen Beach looking towards Lion Sur Mer.

Capt. G. Lugg personal collection.

"I had about five hundred yards to go to reach the head of the beach. My slanting course was also taking me four hundred yards to the left, to the end of the seawall. As I flew along, I felt no fear. I must have been using up all my nervous juices as fast as they were being secreted.

Within a few yards, I was surprised to meet two screaming, naked men making for the water at high speed. They were hairless, burned bright blue, and wore only smoking boots. I assume they were a tank crew. We passed on opposite courses with never a second glance. I then picked my way through a zone where many bodies lay. These were evidently machine gun victims, in numbers approaching an entire Company."

Brian Moss. 233 Field Company, Royal Engineers

USS *Texas* starts firing upon the exit at the Western side of OMAHA beach.

JUNO - Landing craft start heading towards the beach.

726th Grenadier Regiment: *"WN 60 is currently the target of a violent bombardment. In the area of WN 37, twenty small landing craft are approaching the beach."*

0620:
Four Allied aircraft are destroyed near Formigny, a Polish pilot is held prisoner.

Longues-sur-Mer falls after coastal shelling from HMS *Ajax*. It took 114 six inch shells to do the job.

UTAH - USS *Nevada* starts shelling the sea wall over the heads of the troops approaching the beach in the landing craft.

0620:
OMAHA: 916th Grenadier Regiment: *"In the Bay of Vierville, landing craft are clearly visable."*

0623:
OMAHA - 726th Grenadier Regiment: *"Landing Craft arriving at WN 59, 61 and 62 and in front of Asnelles. The enemy has positioned smokescreens at sea to protect its vessels and other on the beach. Until now, our losses are very small."*

UTAH - Aircraft start laying a smoke screen to the northwest of St. Marcouf screening fire support area and transport area from batteries on Cotentin Peninsular.

0625:
USS *Fitch* reports seeing USS *Corry* hit.

Squad 14 of the Special Engineer Task Force have arrived on Easy Red, the beach is completely deserted due to their early arrival. Their LCM was then hit by a shell and all on board are either killed or wounded, they were the first Americans to die on OMAHA beach.

The 726th Regiment report sighting 30 ships moving at slow speed 10 kilometres off the coast of Port-en-Bessin.

0626:
OMAHA: Report received from the 352nd Artillery Regiment: *"The coast areas WN 59 and 60 are under intense fire from enemy artillery. Major naval formations are observed. Due to heavy bombing, several artillery positions are buried, three of them have been identified and are operational again. For now, the artillery regiment maintains good connections with the observation posts."*

0627:
The Naval bombardments off the coast at OMAHA lifts and shifts inland.

0629:
USS *Corry* is reported as still being under fire

0630:
8th Parachute Battalion : PIAT (Projector, Infantry, Anti Tank) detachment reports six half-track vehicles moving on the road from Troarn - Le Mesnil and approaching their position. They open fire and score hits on all six vehicles causing their crews to dismount and take up a position on the far side of the road. A fire fight then ensues and after a spirited action the enemy withdraw with their casualties leaving 3 dead who were identified as 21st Panzer Division and six half-tracks, four of which were inadequately destroyed as they were recovered by the enemy that night.

War Correspondent: *"The whole invasion fleet is now awaiting just seven miles off Courseulles."*

H-Hour for UTAH and OMAHA

OMAHA - LCT 535 lands the first tanks. The 1st and the 29th American Divisions land over a 6.5 kilometre stretch of beach. The 1st to the East (Easy and Fox) and the 29th to the West (Dog). Out of 29 amphibian (DD) tanks on which the Americans had placed great faith, that put to sea, 27 sink due to the unexpected swell and because they are landed too far out. Conditions could not have been less favourable for this novel weapon, but even so the general consensus of Naval opinion was that ordinary water proofed tanks landed on the beach in the normal matter would have served the purpose equally well.

The smoke, swell and wind cause the landing craft to drift to the east, forcing the infantry to come ashore opposite places they did not recognise. Some sectors had no landings at all.

A mile off shore, the LCVP's pass several men tossed about in the rough sea, supported in life belts and in small rubber rafts. It was first believed these men, increasing in number in the water, were shot-down airmen, but before long they were recognized as DD tank men. Their tanks had been sunk or swamped.

> "Ships large and small were spread around us, the tiny dots of L.C.A.'s scattered like confetti on white-crested rollers all steering towards the Normandy coast. LST's, frigates, corvettes, destroyers, cruisers, battleships and minesweepers plus many more which I could not identify. One if particular, peculiar looking, ugly, a menacing framework of steel at a 60 to 70 degree angle, seemingly stationary until bursting into a wall of flame as a volley of missiles hurtled towards the coast. I had seen my first rocket ship in action. "How do you like it Jerry? Up yours!"
>
> Mne. John B Wetjen, 47 Commando.
>
> RM Museum Southsea ACQ 280/06

Scene on Omaha Beach during the afternoon of 6 June 1944

USNA 80-G-45714

1st Division, 16th Infantry Regiment - First wave lands and meets fierce resistance on the beaches which is under heavy machine gun and rifle fire. No advance made inland as the whole area is covered by pill boxes and mine fields just inland from beaches.

Official reports state Force "O" Left flank launched 6000 yards off shore, all but two or three founder. Right flank; lands on beach but quickly put out of action by enemy fire.

The German blockhouses resist bombardment and the landing troops are subject to constant heavy fire. The survivors shelter behind rock levies or other obstacles on the beach. Troops continue to stream onto the beach despite enemy fire, and are blocked on the beach or massacred as they leave their landing craft. They suffer heavy casualties.

The sea is beginning to turn red. Even among some of the lightly wounded who jumped into shallow water the hits prove fatal. Knocked down by a bullet in the arm or weakened by fear and shock, weighed down by sodden heavy back packs they they are unable to get up and are drowned by the tide. Other wounded men drag themselves ashore and, on finding the sands, lie quiet from total exhaustion, only to be overtaken by the tide and eventually drown in the water. A few manage to move swiftly through the swarm of fire to the beach but find that they cannot hold there. They have no alternative but to return to the water to use it for body cover. With their faces turned upward, so they can breathe and feigning death they slowly creep toward the land at the same rate as the tide. That is how many of the survivors make it.

Lt. John Spalding, E Company, the 16th Regiment, jumps into waist-deep water. His heart is racing as he steps forward with legs that move as slowly as in a nightmare. An artillery shell explodes somewhere close and a spout of water shot up by Spalding's side. The sweat on his skin turned ice-cold and he offered a silent prayer, *"I can do this, please God, I can lead these men."* Two hundred yards ahead was Omaha beach. Behind him, the last soldiers jump from the landing craft and spread out. It had been drilled into their heads. *If you get hit, don't take a buddy with you.* Each man struggles alone and fights to control his fear. Pvt. Reese drops his rifle as he fought to the surface. He gasped for air and was blinded by wet toilet paper. It streamed out from under his helmet where he had put it earlier. Somehow, he doesn't lose his glasses as he pulls lumps of sodden tissue off his face. *

---
* Courtesy of USNA

UTAH - All bombardment stops. The strong currents have scattered the 4th American Division during the first wave of assault. By mistake, they have deviated 1800 meters to the south, this actually works in their favour as German defences here are less concentrated. Brigadier General Theodore Roosevelt, Jr. decides to land the following convoys in the same place.

1st Battalion, 505th PIR set off for the bridge over the Merderet river.

Three companies of the US Rangers head for a small strip of land beneath the cliffs at Pointe du Hoc. If they signal that they have successfully scaled the cliffs a further two companies will follow them as reinforcements. The contingency in the event they did not get the signal was to land on OMAHA beach slightly to the East and fight their way across land to Pointe du Hoc.

B Company, 1st Battalion Canadian Parachute Regiment, after being guided to their target by a French woman, successfully blow the Robehomme bridge over the Dives River.

JUNO - 8th Canadian Infantry Brigade sights Bernières and St Aubin whilst heading for the beach. The landmarks which have been carefully memorised from air photos are clearly recognisable - the jetty at the harbour of Courseulles - the flat expanse of marsh land to the East - then the church steeple amid a profusion of trees, which marks Bernières and on down the coast to the cluster of buildings surrounding the next church which marks St Aubin sur Mer. As the coast draws nearer the wind increases and a heavy sea makes it necessary to consider whether or not the DD Tanks are to be launched or whether the troops should go in without their immediate assistance.

General Alfred Jodl angered by Runstead's orders to move the 12 S.S. Panzer Division and Panzer-Lehr to Calvados, cancels it and decides to wait for Hitler to wake up.

General Feuchtinger, Chief of 21st Panzer German Division, after waiting for official orders that did not arrive, took it upon himself to order to attack the 6th British Airborne Division beyond the Orne river.

WN 62 overlooking OMAHA Beach commences firing upon the landing troops. WN 62 The best armoured of the 15 strong points on the 6km long bay of Omaha beach sectors Dog, Easy and Fox, was permanently manned by 28 men from 3rd Company of the Grenadier Regiment 726/716th Infantry Division. Soldiers of this Division were

V-MAIL

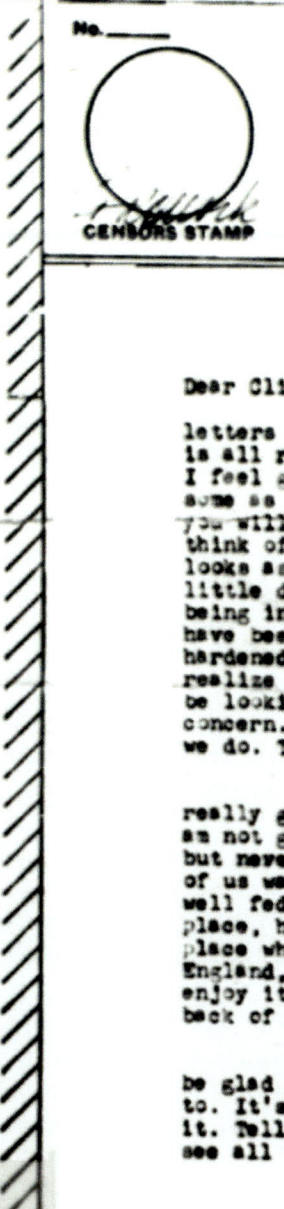

Mr. Clinton N. Searl
Box #213
Boothwyn, Penna.

24 May 1944
England

Dear Clint:

I haven't written to you for a few days, your letters haven't been coming in either. I hope everything is all right back there. Things are about the same here, I feel great. This waiting is getting to be a bit tiresome as you can understand. Makes you wonder at times if you will ever come out of it on top. It's funny, we always think of the other guy getting all the Hell; now that it looks as though we will get a little, the picture has a little different color. You know, if I ever thought about being in a position like this, a few years ago, I would have been scared as Hell. The way that a person can be hardened to face such a dubious future is remarkable. I realize that maybe in days, weeks, or even months, I may be looking death in the face, yet, it is of hardly any concern. No matter how hard we try not to change, I guess we do. This mess certainly has played Hell with things.

When this thing gets started, Clint, it is really going to be a big show. I'm glad in a way, that I am not going to miss it. That may sound sort of crazy, but nevertheless, true. I think the real reason for all of us wanting this to get started, is that we are pretty well fed up with this place. England may be a beautiful place, historic and serene, but to us it is just another place where an army day dawns. I always wanted to come to England, but being here this way is hardly the way to enjoy it. Things take a different perspective from the back of a GI truck.

Well Clint, that's about all for now. I will be glad when I can write you the kind of letter I want to. It's Hell when so much is going on and I have to skip it. Tell Mary and Clinty that I send regards, and hope to see all of you before 1945. I wonder!

Your Brother,
– Bob

Sgt. Robert H. Searl
56th Signal Battalion.
V Corps

V-Mail letter written by Bob Searl to his brother in USA on May 24, 1944, one day after leaving base Camp in Taunton, England and arriving at one of the many marshalling area camps on the coast of England preparing to board the Initial Assault landing ships. The Camp was near Truro, with complete isolation and temporary housing in tents, with no cameras, outside contact and complete strict security. "*Somehow we all knew that this was the real thing, no more rumours or guessing. Our time had come to do what we had been trained so long ago to do. With many anxious, but with silent apprehension, the unit was moved out in the early morning hours of June 1, 1944 to the seaside port of Falmouth, England and loaded on LST #54 on June 5, 1944 and headed for the Normandy coast of France. The craft subsequently returned to the port due to bad weather and sailed the following day, arriving at Omaha Beach - Easy Red Area at 11:00 am on June 6, 1944.*" "Due to stiff resistance by hostile coastal artillery forces, the Battalion was prevented from landing on schedule and remained offshore, disembarking on the beach the morning of June 8, 1944.

Bob Searl's personal collection

distributed in the strong points WN59 to WN64, the command post was situated in WN63 which was situated over a km further inland. One bunker is armed with a 75 mm gun, the second was empty. Two 50 mm anti-tank guns, two 50 mm mortars and a double barrelled anti-aircraft gun completed the heavy armaments. There is also 4 machine guns which fire upon the landing US troops.

0631:
UTAH – Landing craft fire a heavy rocket barrage on the beach area. However, the barrage is 500 yards short, at least 30% of the rockets fall in the water.

0633:
USS *Hobson* reports that *Corry* appears to be hit amidships and stops heading seaward. At the same time her artificial smoke generator starts working. With the off shore breeze, the smoke screen effectively hid the *Corry's* actions and condition from *Hobson* for several minutes.

0635:
As the great armada of ships approach the French coast on the dull mist of the dawn, many flashes can be seen on the coastline as allied bombers and fighter-bombers fly in to engage enemy coastal batteries and target that may hinder the landing.

*OMAHA - "G" Company boats reach the line of departure 2000 yards from the beach and deploy with all boats abreast and head toward the beach at the best possible speed. Intense enemy fire is seen falling on the beach and as the Company comes to within 1000 yards of the beach this fire begins to land in and around the craft, increasing in intensity as they move closer. Great difficulty is experienced by the coxswains of the assault craft in maintaining the boats formation, and one of the craft capsizes about 200 yards from the beach, necessitating the boat team to swim ashore without a great deal of their assault weapons. The remainder of the boats, however, succeed in almost reaching the shore before lowering their ramps, and most of the Company was able to walk ashore.

Approximately 200 yards inland from the waterline a small shingle mound about ten feet in height gives the Company some shelter from the intense machine gun and small arms fire that rake the beach. A large amount of Troops are already ashore but are unable to advance onto the steep, high bluff overlooking the beach, due to enemy fire.

* Landing craft were loaded in a certain way with Officers/NCO's at the front with the intention of leading their men forward, however, as the ramps went down they were the first to be shot and many units found themselves leaderless.

Most of the units are disorganised due to losses of Officers and NCO's on the beach.

The 84th German Army Corps reports that 12 enemy soldiers are captured while three warships are getting closer to the coastline, surrounded by many landing craft.

0636:
OMAHA - landing of the second assault wave of the 116th Regiment of the 29th Infantry Division.

UTAH – USS *Hobson* switches fire to the battery believing to be firing at *Corry* which ceases firing shortly after.

OMAHA - 726th Grenadier Regiment: *"The first landing craft approach the beaches opposite WN 65 and 69. Some of them are carrying tanks."*

0640:
Eisenhower awakes after a short nap. He receives an optimistic call from Admiral Ramsey who informs him that so far it is all going well.

UTAH: With the ship sinking, USS *Corry's* Commander now orders abandon ship.

OMAHA - "F" Company 1st Section land in the vicinity of Colleville sur Mer. Smoke laid down by the Navy and Artillery has already lifted, which is working in the Germans favour. Enemy machine guns, rifles and mortars fire at the assault teams as they run out of the LCVP's. The sea is chest high as the men wade across 30 yards of water and cross the beach of approximately 150 yards under constant fire. The cost in casualties is 6 officers and about 50% of the Company.

The 2nd, 4th and 5th Sections land approximately 400 yards too far to the left of their planned position. These three sections play a major part in silencing beach defences. Staff Sergeant Strojny picks up a rocket launcher from a wounded soldier and fires it unassisted at the pillboxes and open emplacements. A has a direct hit into the embrasure of one of the pillboxes causes them a lot of trouble and sees it go up in flames. Staff Sergeant Piyo, mortar squad leader, 4th Section, knocks out several emplacements and after using all his ammunition, together with a few other NCO's, leads an assault on further enemy positions. As a result approximately 15 Germans are captured and taken prisoner.

The 2nd Section land at their allocated position on the beach and display courage and initiative. When the section leader is killed the assistant section

The Fire and Control Post for the German Gun Battery at Riva Bella, protected by the strongpoint built at the Casino.

Rufty Hill

"One of our sergeants, in D Company, was called Rufty Hill and as he jumped off the ramp into the sea he landed in a shell hole. At the same time a wave made the assault craft surge forward and he was forced beneath the boat. Rufty was drowned and probably crushed beneath the boat. I knew that chap and knew he would have given a very good account of himself had he lived to go into the assault. He was 'one of the lads'. It was awful to think that Rufty had survived Dunkirk and from Alamein to Enfidaville then through Sicily, only to be killed in such a tragic way."

Bill Cheall, Green Howards

leader takes over ordering the wire man to blow the barbed wire, which he does after crawling 30 yards exposed to small arms and mortar fire. Shortly after the section Sergeant is also wounded and the next senior NCO assumed command and leads the section to higher ground overlooking the beach. This section then attached itself to "G" Company and moves inland destroying enemy snipers and isolated machine gun nests between the beach and Colleville sur Mer.

Company Headquarters and the 3rd Section land directly in front of the strongpoint assigned to Company "F". However, they have lost all of their special equipment. Therefore, only small arms fire can be used against the enemy emplacements, with little effect. No support is received from the tanks as none have landed at that sector of the beach.

0642:
American Admiral Kirk, chief of the Western Naval formation, announces that *"all is held in accordance with the plan"*

0645:
914th Infantry Regiment: "T*he attack by II/914e Infantry Regiment against the paratroopers southwest of Brevands is progressing slowly due to the heavy ground. Grandcamp is under fire from naval artillery."*

OMAHA - Company "C" of the 2nd Rangers land after losing about a third of their strength when an LCA sunk. Some of the men drowned but others were lucky enough to be picked up by the US Coastguard and evacuated.

0647:
USS *Fitch* fires 4 salvos at the battery seen to be firing at *Corry* but it is out of range.

0650:
UTAH Beach: 32 DD tanks of the 70th Armoured Battalion reach the shore, twenty minutes later than scheduled having made up some time after setting off late due to the weather.

The B-25 bombers of 8th and 342nd Squadrons of the Royal Air Force drop a smoke screen which protects the allied armada.

War Correspondent: *"The destroyers - now close to the shore are bombarding any target they can see. A string of tank landing craft pass us. Soldiers sitting on the turrets of their tanks give the thumbs up sign. Weather is worsening, big clouds are coming up, Spitfires roar overhead."*

0652:
OMAHA - The 352nd Artillery Regiment reports: *"Between 60 and 80 landing craft are approaching in front of Colleville-sur-Mer. The Regiment cannot counter the entire enemy units. Maisy and Saint-Marcouf are under fire from the Naval artillery. According to statements from the prisoners, an airborne division was dropped in the area of Carentan, and aims to capture the city."*

0655:
JUNO - 13th Field Artillery Regiment fires upon a fortified position on the west of the cliff at Juno. Among the men of the Regiment is 24 year old Lieutenant James Doohan. (Scotty in Star Trek.) Shooting two snipers, Doohan leads his men to higher ground through a field of anti-tank mines.

0656:
UTAH – *Hobson* reports the landing beach is covered with thick black smoke and dust extending out over the water. Although the pre-arranged black smoke rocket has not been observed (it would probably not have been seen anyway) it was assumed that the first troops have landed so they switch their fire to their next target.

OMAHA - The 914th Regiment reports that now there are three warships bombarding the Maisy sector.

0657:
914th Infantry Regiment: "T*wenty landing craft approaching the coast in front of WN 92."*

0658:
The bombing over GOLD Beach and the west of JUNO Beach begins. 385 B-17s of the 1st Bombardment Division strikes the coastal batteries and strong points between Longues-sur-Mer and Courseulles-sur-Mer. At the same time, 322 B-17s of the 3rd Bombardment Division operate in the east of JUNO sector and over SWORD Beach, striking the batteries and defences between Bernières and Ouistreham.

The Royal Navy and the landing craft carrying the self-propelled guns of the 3rd Canadian Division open fire on the the enemy's shore defences. Everything from cruisers to landing craft carrying rockets fire salvo after salvo into the enemy targets. This support fire in Courseulles' sector begins to fall short or long of the Germans positions.

0700:
The Supreme Commander, General Dwight D. Eisenhower receives an emergency transmission

Royal Marine WCS Hiscock.

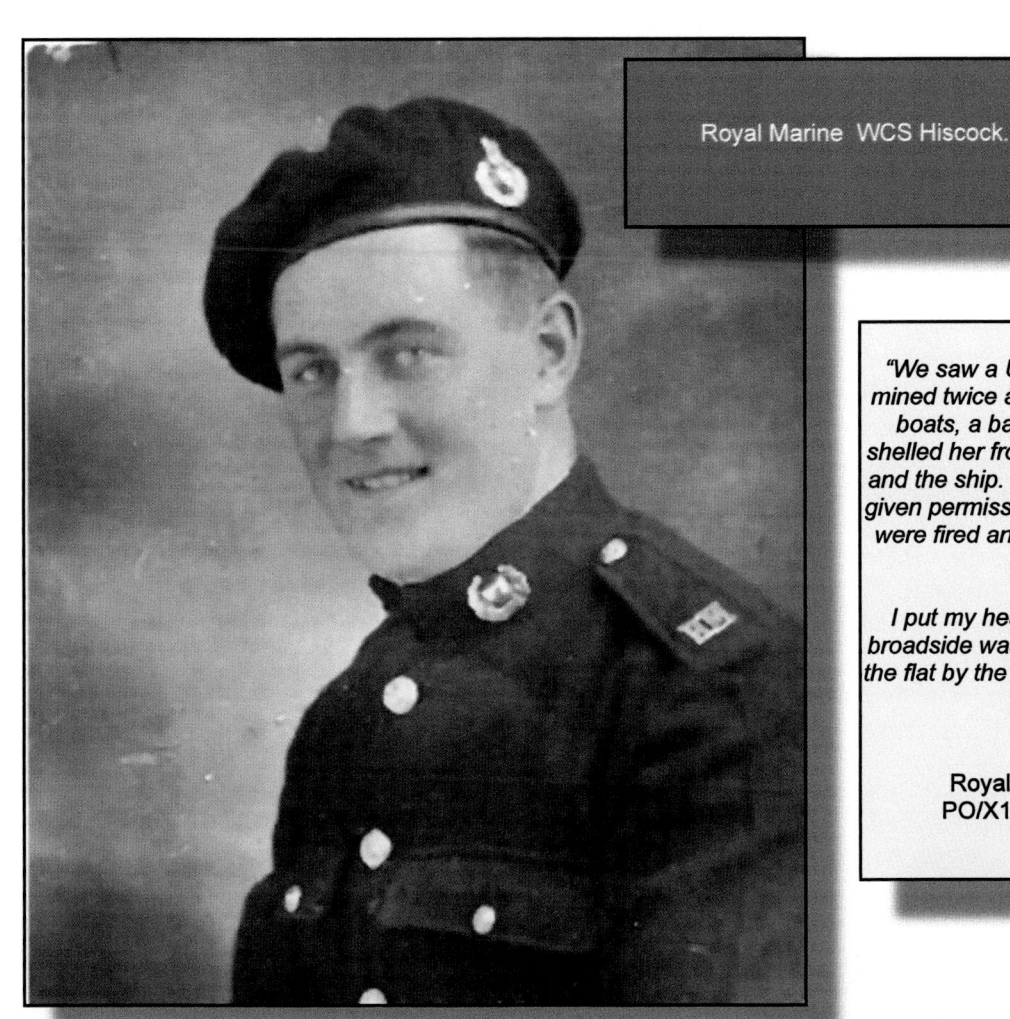

"We saw a US Destroyer, USS Glennon mined twice and while her crew took to the boats, a battery of 88mm mobile guns shelled her from the shore, hitting the boats and the ship. It was a while before we were given permission to open fire but two salvos were fired and the first hit the mobiles and destroyed them.

I put my head out of the hatch just as a broadside was fired and was thrown across the flat by the blast. I was given two aspirins for concussion."

Royal Marine WCS Hiscock
PO/X112968 - HQ192 Squad

Mine damaged USS Glennon off Normandy Coast

from Sir Trafford Leigh Mallory, the Air Marshal. The message is brief: *"Parachuting has gone well."*

SWORD: HMS *Arethusa* reports German cruisers astern attacking the landing ships, fortunately there are no direct hits. *Arethusa* turns her 4" guns upon the enemy destroyers whilst maintaining her shore bombardments with the 6" guns.

War Correspondent: *"The first wave of Fortresses come in. One pattern of bombs flattens out the beach section opposite our destroyer."*

The CO of 225th Field Ambulance proceeds to the Orne Bridges to visit the Regimental Aid Post (RAP) of the Coup-de-Main party who have landed in gliders alongside both bridges. Capt. Jacob RAMC has established the RAP in ditch and bank. He has some dead + 15 casualties. The position is being heavily sniped. Arrangements are made to evacuate these casualties to Main Dressing Station.

The second assault wave at OMAHA Beach begins. The situation is chaotic as troops are pinned down and take cover behind mined beach defences. Engineers are unable to clear obstacles.

UTAH – *Hobson* reports the smoke screen on the *Corry* is thinning and observes that she is definitely in trouble with her back broken between the stacks, she is awash amidships and is still under fire.

OMAHA - "G" Company reorganise the assault teams and the 60 mm mortars and light machine guns are placed in firing positions. A huge effort is being made by a few Officers and NCO's to build up a volume of fire on the enemy to enable movement forward. A few of the elements of the 1st wave have succeeded in advancing approximately 100 yards in front of this position, but are pinned down and seem unable to move in any direction because of the terrific fire descending on them.

The Rangers, Company "A", now make their way up the cliffs from OMAHA with a rope that was secured after one of them scaled the cliffs using his bayonet and a knife, come under fire from WN73, a fortified house about 200 yards to their east. 20 men from the 116th Company "B" come to assist and the house is soon taken.

JUNO – 8th Canadian Infantry Brigade decide not to launch the DD tanks as the visibility was lessening. Troops start loading into their landing craft.

The tide is beginning to change and beach obstacles are becoming submerged.

0704: OMAHA - 916th Regiment report that the fortifications on the beach are under a continuous barrage of the Naval artillery and that Near WN 68 at East Vierville an enemy force of about fifty men are landing.

JUNO - 8th Canadian Infantry Brigade receive a signal stating that the Armoured Vehicle Royal Engineer's (AVRE's) are late. H hour for J2 [second assault group of Force J] was set back an additional 10 minutes. To give the leading Infantry the support at the correct time, orders are issued to delay fire from the Self Propelled artillery to conserve ammunition for the assault. The armada slowly approaches the shore

0706: OMAHA - 726th Regiment: *"The enemy near the WN 60, North East of Colleville, landed forty men and a tank. WN 60 exchanges fire with the troops."*

0708: 2nd Ranger Battalion, Companies "D", "E" and "F" land at Pointe du Hoc, LCA 888 is the first craft to land containing Lt. Col. Rudder and members of Easy Company. Large craters along the 30 meter stretch of beach from the Naval bombardment make landing more difficult than it should be but also provide shelter.

Rudder and 225 Rangers start to attack the eastern face of the cliff at Pointe du Hoc, their mission is to take out the German battery situated at its summit that was a threat to troops landing on the nearby beaches. A tirade of machine gun fire and grenades are launched at the Rangers. USS *Satterlee* and HMS *Talybont* warships swing in dangerously close to the shore and launch salvos at the top of the cliffs at the Germans defending the battery, providing supporting fire for the Rangers. Further down the beach near Point du Percée, C Company comes under heavy fire and takes 35 casualties just attempting to get ashore.

The 5th Ranger Battalion, reinforcements for Pointe du Hoc, having not received the signal from 2nd Rangers by the appointed time, revert to their contingency of landing at OMAHA beach leaving the men at Pointe du Hoc with no immediate reinforcements.

914th IR with four companies, continue its attack against the paratroopers. Faced with a tough opponent they report that they are gaining ground, albeit slowly.

Sgt Bob Searl

Chas Townsend [NJ] & Steve Mason [NJ]
56th Signal Battalion. V Corps

Bob Searl, Victor O, Communications point, Normandy.
All the above are from Bob Searl's personal collection

0710:
A,B,C,D Companies and Battalion HQ Green Howard's make their hazardous dash for the mainland in a sea that did not favour a landing so important, whilst allied cruisers and destroyers heavily engage enemy shore batteries.

OMAHA - Sergeant Turner G. Shepperd in one of the two DD Sherman tanks that haven't sunk, manages to come ashore on the beach near strong point WN 61. The Sergeant located in the turret gives the order to fire: a direct hit, and the 88 mm of WN 61 is taken out of commission.

OMAHA - "G" Company are ordered forward and managed to pass through a narrow gap between the mine fields, the shingle mound and the cliff overlooking the beach. The section of "E" Company, 16th Infantry, under command of 2nd Lieutenant Spalding and remnants of two sections from "E" Company, 116th Infantry, are pinned down at the base of the cliff. They are told by the Company Commander that their organisations are supposed to be 500 yards to the right of this position, and to move inland, and to the right if possible. They then begin to move forward and slightly to the right. As "G" Company sections reach this point they are directed to seize the high ground to the immediate front and to deploy from right to left as they clear the crest of the hill and move forward as quickly as possible; and to maintain contact with the two sections of "E" Company, 116th Infantry, on the right.

Two machine gun nests are destroyed and one prisoner is taken by 5th section, "G" Company, and they secure the immediate crest of the bluff, thus enabling the remainder of the Company to reach this high ground and deploy in their movement forward. The Company move out from this position in the following order from right to left: Sections 5, 3, 4, 1 and 2, with the light machine gun section attached to the 2nd section. Movement forward is accomplished under artillery fire and a number of snipers firing machine guns. One enemy machine gun is destroyed on the left flank of the Company, and a light machine gun section and three enemy soldiers are killed. This engagement takes place about 200 yards from the deployment position. Two more enemy are destroyed by the 1st Section as they progress inland.

OMAHA: The 121st Engineer Combat Battalion, less Company "A", with the 112th Engineer Combat Battalion attached, land as part of the 116th Infantry Combat Team, which is part of the First Infantry Division Landing Team. The first units of this Battalion to land are two platoons of Company "B" with Lieutenant Colonel Ploger, the Battalion Commander, and a small staff, from two LCM's. (Landing Craft Mechanised) These platoons are closely followed by an LCM containing one platoon of "B" Company and one platoon of "C" Company landing ten minutes later.

0715:
GOLD: landing craft provided with 127 mm rocket launchers open fire on the coastal defences.

JUNO – Duplex Drive Sherman tank "Bold"of the Canadian First Hussars Regiment is launched into the water some 4.5km from the beach to lead 8 Sqn's first wave attack on the heavily fortified German positions at Courselles-sur-Mer. Onboard was B Sqn Ldr Major Duncan and his crew. The run into the beach is described by Sgt Leo Gariepy. *"At about 2.7 km from shore I looked about and saw Major Duncan bout 30 yards to my starboard and the rest of the DD's behind us. We had been showered by small arms fire but suddenly I saw two pillars to the right near Major Duncan's tank, the first shell fire we had received on the way in, I looked ahead again and when I turned around the Majors tank had disappeared."* When the Bold started to sink, the men were trapped inside and could not get out until they hit the bottom and the tank flooded, one man died but the others were picked up in the water by either landing craft or rescue boats. The Bold was later raised from the sea bed and is now a memorial in Courselles-sur-Mer.

OMAHA: The 726th Regiment report that WN 60 is severely bombed and that 20 landing craft are approaching.

0720:
Supreme Allied H.Q. states:- *"The Royal Navy, with the aid of strong Air Forces began landing allied armies on the North coast of France this morning".*

SWORD: The flails of the 22nd Dragoons (79th Armoured Division) are the first ashore, accompanied by teams of sappers.

SWORD - The 1st South Lancashire's land on Queen White Beach and, despite losing the Commanding Officer and well over one hundred other casualties, they make good progress through German beach defences and press inland to capture Hermanville.

War Correspondent: *"It is by now light. I can see the spire of the Bernières Belfry. Buildings are crumpled. "*

OMAHA Beach: The 916th Regiment report that amphibious tanks are identified in the Vierville Bay.

When a soldier is going into action, it is not a time to think of the past, or the future. The present is the thing that is uppermost in his thoughts; what is happening now; today is all that matters and God willing there would be another time for his tomorrow. The probability of death does not come into the equation. Get on with the job.

Bill Cheall - Green Howards

Members of a chemical unit get ready to fire high explosive mortar shells at a German pillbox which forms part of the coast defense of a beach in France. At extreme right is the M-29 "weasel." USNA

OMAHA - 1st Division - 16th Regiment - Headquarters Company: The ramp on the LCM is dropped too far from the shore leaving the troops a considerable distance to cross under heavy fire to reach cover on the beach itself. In addition there is a sand bar some 25 yards wide which has to be crossed to reach the beach proper.

As the ramp drops, Lieutenant Hill is first off into the water, waist high, followed by men from his I&R Platoon. The communication group follow, carrying all its equipment, followed by Company Headquarters group, field artillery, and other attached men. There is very heavy fire. Officers and NCO's are trying to disperse the men, and get all the equipment off the boat. Approximately 35 officers and men are killed or wounded from the time the ramp went down until the beach was reached. When the men eventually reach the beach there is total confusion as it is totally over crowded and there is no open exit. One pill box is still firing. There are dead and wounded all over, on the beach and in the water. Equipment and men are floating and lying around all over the place. Examples of bravery, courage, heroism and initiative during this period are too numerous to mention.

OMAHA: Lt. Spalding leads his men on the first advance over the bluffs left of Draw E-1. He and his men are the first to attack German defences from the rear. For his actions on D-Day, he was later awarded the Distinguished Cross.

0721:
British troops land on SWORD Beach. Commandos led by Brigadier The Lord Lovat head towards Pegasus Bridge.

7th Armoured Division (Desert Rats) come ashore, above the din of the bombardments can be heard "Roll out the Barrel" on the tannoy of a rocket barge!

"H-Hour was 0723 but we arrived 2 minutes early and received some spasmodic friendly fire. After hitting the beach we commenced to discharge our petard tanks. Our landing point was nearly opposite a pillbox which we thought contained an 88 mm anti-tank gun. Our suspicions were confirmed when the first tank off L.C.T. 896 had its turret destroyed when it reached the beach. The tank was totally disabled." Sub Lieutenant Victor Bellars*

The 50th (Northumbrian) Infantry Division under Major General D. H. A. Graham lands on a 5-kilometre length of GOLD beach. The German artillery and machine guns slow down the offensive. Graham's mission: establish a foothold in the cliffs at Arromanches and quickly take Bayeux. Liaise with the 3rd Canadian Infantry Division to the East and the American Troops to the West on OMAHA Beach.

GOLD: The first units of 231st and 69th Brigades touch down on King and Jig beach. DD tanks and beach clearance groups, delayed by bad weather, land directly on to the beach.

As part of the beach clearance Group, Trooper Jim Smith (C Sqn, Westminster Dragoons) lands on GOLD Beach just east of La Riviere. The two Churchill tanks in front of him edge their way off the landing craft onto the beach, but are immediately hit by shells and explode instantly killing the crews. Jim was not scheduled to land on D-Day but volunteered when the tank's gunner fell ill. Upon landing he looked east along the beach and in the distance spotted a German defence bunker (WN33) firing shells over his head towards the other troops and tanks landing further along the beach.

Jim was driving an American Sherman tank known as one of Hobart's Funnies as it had a 10-foot boom on the front with chains spinning around to sweep the mines out of the sand and clear a path for the following troops. His gun was facing out towards the sea to keep the way clear for the fast turning chains.

The Germans - having not seen a contraption like this before - were more concerned with the tanks landing further down the beach. This gave Jim the chance to stop the chains and turn his gun towards the bunker. He fired two high explosive shells at it, but they appeared to ricochet off. He then loaded an armour piercing shell and fired as he saw the barrel of an 88 mm gun turn towards him. Having aimed at the barrel of the gun while it was being reloaded, the shell deflected off the gun barrel, entered the emplacement between the gun and the mantle concrete and spun around inside killing all the crew. Jim then progresses into the town and was soon asked to assist in taking out a German sniper hiding in the belfry of a small church picking off the British troops as they entered the town. Jim spots him through his sights and takes out the side of the belfry with one shot.

USS *Hobson* reports that *Corry* is now sinking, *Hobson* changed position and continued firing. USS *Fitch* came to stand by *Corry* as it was considered that *Hobson's* mission of covering the landing beach flank was vital. Most of the batteries have stopped firing all bar one that starts firing upon *Fitch* as she approached the stricken ship.

---
* www.combineddrops.com

"We were fed very well. The cooks made gallons of bacon and pea soup. We had hot steamed tinned meat pudding and sandwiches etc. Bread was made fresh on board by the bakers."

Royal Marine WCS Hiscock
PO/X112968 - HQ192 Squad. Onboard HMS Hawkins

Army troops on board a L.C.T., ready to ride across the English Channel to France. Some of these men wear 101st Airborne Division insignia.
Source: US Naval Historical Center Photo #: 80-G-59422

Corry sunk and settled on the bottom with the bow and stern remaining well clear of the water and sadly with 24 of her crew entombed aboard her. For her actions on the date of her loss, USS Corry received her fourth and final Battle Star for World War Two service

Three German destroyers leave Le Harve, chased by Scylla

OMAHA - 726th Grenadier Regiment: *"Landing of enemy forces on the beaches opposite WN 60, 61, and 62, and further west. The enemy, the size of a company, remains on the beach, which is under the fire of our artillery. The antitank gun 8.8-cm WN 61 was knocked out by a direct hit."*

GOLD - *"At WN 37 on the right boundary of the division, landing craft approach the coast, the landing of such units is imminent. WN 37 was the target of heavy bombing and artillery rockets."*

0725:
JUNO - Landing Craft Guns (LCG's) open fire on the beach defences. The orders are to fire until 0807. Bernières sur Mer and St Aubin receive a terrific pounding though the main effect seems to be more inland and not on the immediate beach defences.

OMAHA - 726th Grenadier Regiment: *"An enemy attack on WN 60 and 62. Near WN 61 four additional barges docked, a barge was burned by an antitank 5-cm. The enemy has entered WN No. 62, while No. 61 is under assault from the beach and back position. Telephone connections to Port-en-Bessin are cut".*

726th Grenadier Regiment are asked by H.Q.: *"When and by what unit will there be a counter attack between WN 61 and 62 to push the enemy into the sea?"*

War Correspondent *"I am looking through my glasses and I can see the first wave of assault troops touching down on the waters edge and fan up on the beach. Men leap out of craft and move forward. Tanks follow them."*

0726:
SWORD - La Brèche. A flotilla of ten landing craft carrying assault engineers and their armoured vehicles, under command of a Lieutenant of the Royal Naval Volunteer Reserve, touch down one minute late. All craft succeed in unloading with the exception of one which only manages to unload one flail; as a second was about to move down the ramp it was hit by a mortar shell which exploded the Bangalore torpedoes being carried. The explosion killed Lieut-Colonel Cocks, the Royal Engineers' Commander, and two other ranks; seven other ranks are wounded; three vehicles are disabled on board which prevent further unloading. None of the other craft are seriously damaged though two were hit by shells and mortar fire.

0727:
USS *Fitch* under fire whilst attempting to pick up survivors from *Corry*.

OMAHA - "H" Company reaches the beach, they are originally scheduled to hit the shore at Easy Red at 0710 hours, but had to contact the Navy control boat and lost some time in doing that. After finding the exact direction from the control boat the company starts towards shore at full throttle.

They are immediately hit by machine gun fire and heavy casualties ensued. They too have landed too far left of where they were supposed to be. The tanks are on the beach to the right of where they landed, but are not giving too much support. There are obstacles on the beach and around these are anti-personnel mines and Teller mines[1] on top of them. The tide was rising at this time and many of the wounded, who probably could have been saved, are drowned. Quite a bit of equipment is lost. All off the radios are either lost or destroyed.

The situation on the beach is critical. One of "H" Company's machine guns set up to the left and starts firing at the pillbox and open emplacements that are on the left flank. Enemy mortar fire is dropping on the beach, but is fairly ineffective. There is machine gun fire coming from the extreme left. This sector is supposed to be taken up by the 3rd Battalion. Every time a move was made this gun would open up and keeps the company pinned down. There is also a lot of mines going off.

0730:
SWORD: The British 3rd Infantry Division under the command of General T.G. Rennie lands on time. The Naval and aerial bombing on German defences is effective, but heavy fighting slows down the soldiers' progress. Rennie's mission was to take the right bank of the Orne River, liaison with the 6th British Airborne and the Canadian 3rd

---

[1] Teller mines were attached to the top of poles. Each 20-pound mine carried about 11 pounds of explosives, triggered to explode when a pressure of about 330 pounds was put on the detonator in the centre of the mine. The blast could destroy a jeep, or blow the tracks off a tank.

Wilf Shaw and his radio.

"At one stage of the fighting in Normandy a shell came over. I was down in the trench but, of course, the 18 set had to be above me. I lay in the bottom of the trench, flatter than a pancake, sweating, cursing and praying. This shell came over and exploded, hellish close, the 18 set went for a Burton. I gathered it all up, 3 or 4 holes in it, "Can't possibly be working" I thought. I pressed the pressel switch, " Dog 7 ! report my signals" - pregnant pause - back came the reply, "Dog 7, hear you strength 5, over". I just couldn't believe it! *"

Wilf Shaw, 6th Green Howards

* Reproduced with the kind permission of his family.

Infantry Division, take Caen as rapidly as possible and the Carpiquet aerodrome by nightfall.

Royal Marine Commandos land after the Norwegian destroyer "Sevland" went in close to the shore and blasted away at the sea front machine gun posts. As the ship is heading back into the bay she hits a mine and sinks. Most of the crew are saved. With the ship going in and shelling the gun posts it saved many of the RM Commando lives.

"There was so much happening now and so swiftly. Every second was vital; let's get out of this coffin! We were getting so near now and felt so helpless, just waiting for our fate one way or another and at that time we were keeping our heads down. Enemy shells were now landing on the shoreline and machine gun bullets were raking the sand. Then, at the top of his voice, the helmsman shouted: 'Hundred to go, seventy-five to go, all ready, fifty to go!' He was now fighting hard to control the craft, avoiding mined obstacles showing above the water, as well as the ones just beneath the surface. One boat had already met disaster on the approach. 'Twenty five yards', and suddenly, 'Ramp going down – now!' And the craft stopped almost dead in three feet of water and our own platoon commander shouted, 'Come on, lads,' and we got cracking. That was no place to be messing about. Get the hell out of it. Jumping off the ramp we went into waist-deep water, struggling to keep our feet. We waded through the water looking for mined obstacles, holding rifles above our heads. I was trying to keep a very cumbersome two-inch mortar and bombs dry as well as making certain I didn't drop it." Bill Cheall - Green Howards

UTAH - The men of the 3rd Battalion 502 PIR (101st Airborne) under Lt Colonel Robert COLE occupy Exit 3 of the Beach near Audouville-la-Hubert.

OMAHA: 1st Division - 16th Infantry Regiment Forward CP lands. Beach still under small arms and heavy machine gun fire. No advance can be made inland. Casualties are extremely heavy. Slight artillery fire on beach. Heavy machine gun fire covering all exits and the entire beach. The second wave of troops is coming in fast but as the first wave can not get off the beach there is nowhere for them to go which adds to the confusion and over-crowding.

OMAHA - Surviving Rangers of C Company reach the top of the beach, east of the D-1 exit (Vierville-sur-Mer) and assault the fortified house on the cliff top. They have lost 35 men. From the top, Cpt Goranson spots a section of Coy "B" 116th and sends a man to guide them to the ropes they had used. Their first objective was to secure the fortified house and the bunkers at Pointe de la Percée.

UTAH - The parachutists of the 3rd battalion of 502nd PIR (101st Airborne Division) control the #3 causeway west of beach, near Audouville-la-Hubert.

USS *Hobson* and USS *Fitch* lower boats to recover survivors of *Corry*. *Hobson* then returned to position and continues firing.

OMAHA - An advance element of 121st Engineer Combat Battalion Headquarters lands under heavy mortar, artillery, and machine gun fire on Dog Green and part of Dog White beach. A direct artillery hit on the bow of the LCI(L) is made just as unloading begins.. It is estimated that 50% of this initial force are casualties, and 75% of the equipment was lost.

General Cota of the 116th Command Group lands at Dog White along with Colonel Canham. They found most of the 29ers huddled behind the seawall unable to move. Knowing that the position was vulnerable to German artillery, they split up to gather the men and find a way off the beach.

JUNO - As the flotilla moves in towards the shore, men put on their equipment and camouflaged their faces and hands. At first it appears that the landing will be unopposed and most craft dismount the 2" mortars which are prepared to cover the landings with smoke. Then machine guns open up from the Strongpoint at St Aubin, which is almost opposite the Easternmost landing craft and perhaps 2000 yds from the Westernmost, and the craft are subjected to mortar and shell fire; the 'Z' Transport craft received a direct hit amidships. The Oerlikons reply and the craft put down smoke on the beach, with 2 inch mortars.

Rommel's Chief-of-Staff calls to announce the arrival of paratroopers in Normandy. He ends the call with the remark that he will call back when there is more news.

Report received from the 352nd Artillery Regiment: *"For the moment, communication is cut with the observation post near Colleville. The landing craft that landed between WN 61 and 62 are destroyed by concentrated fire. Between ten and fifteen small landing craft are approaching the mouth of the Vire".*

0731:
The two LCIs (Landing Craft, Infantry) transporting the French troops of No. 4 Commando land

I don't think it is possible to find adequate words to describe everything that happened on that beach, it was impossible to notice everything and the multitude on noises were unintelligible.
I followed a line of dripping men carrying rucksacks and wearing green berets like myself (we had enough to carry without wearing tun hats) until we came to a gap in the wire where the mines had been cleared. Brigadier the Lord Lovat was standing there sorting us out. He was as cool as the proverbial cucumber, and except for his wet clothes, might have been standing in Piccadilly Circus.

"D" Tales by J.K.Emmerson. Staff reporter with the Commandos, RM Museum Southsea.7/19/5

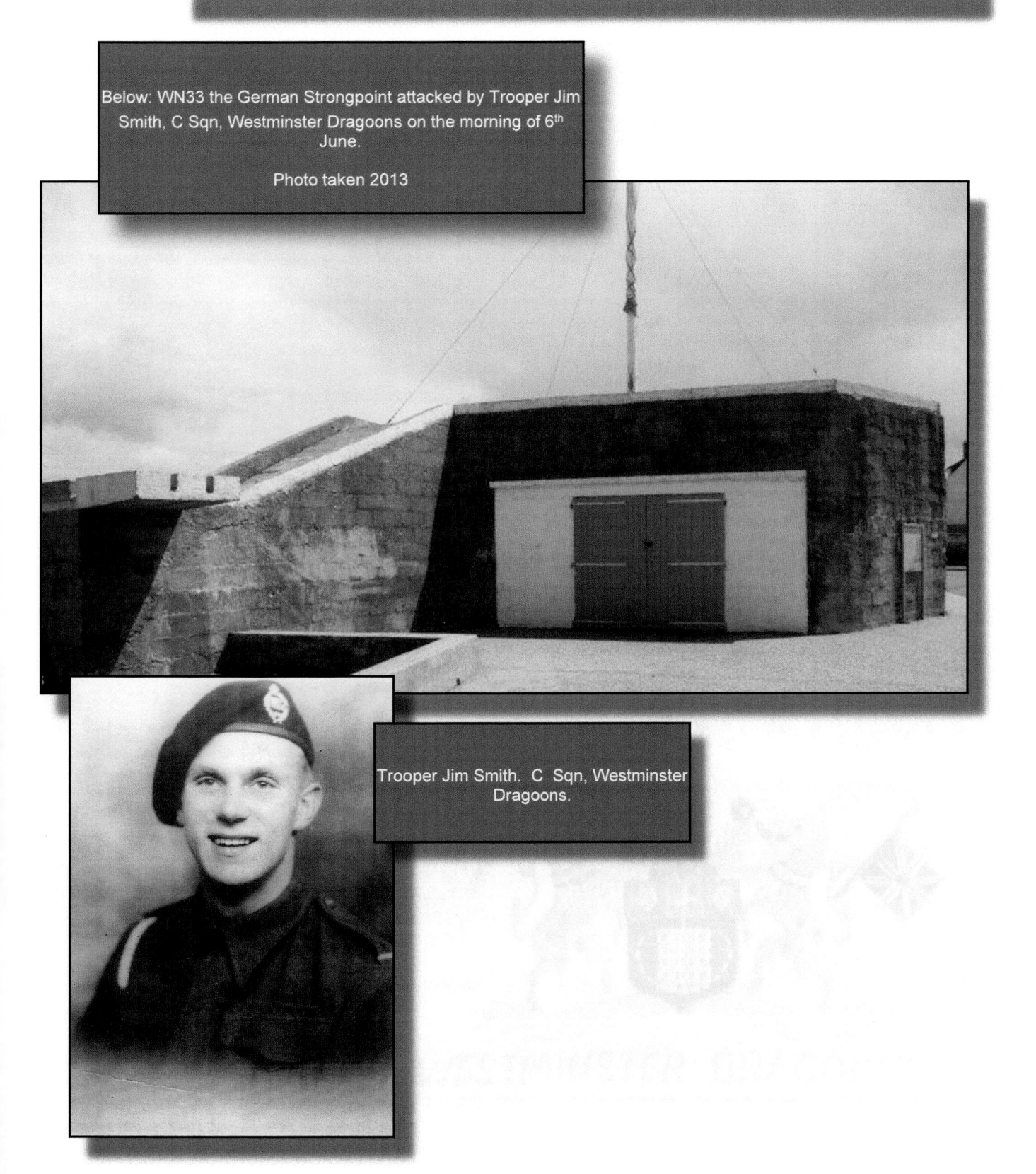

Below: WN33 the German Strongpoint attacked by Trooper Jim Smith, C Sqn, Westminster Dragoons on the morning of 6th June.

Photo taken 2013

Trooper Jim Smith. C Sqn, Westminster Dragoons.

0733:
OLD - King sector, the 6th Battalion Green Howards with CSM Stan Hollis land as part of the first wave. They have as part of their training been told to look out for a German Pill box on the beach right in front of where they were to land. Hollis later recalled *"As we were coming in I lifted a stripped Lewis gun off the floor of the landing craft and pelted a pillbox with a full pan of ammunition."* It turned out that the "pillbox" was nothing more than a small shed used for the tram that ran along the beachfront.

Also landing on Gold beach was Private William Buckland, REME. Sadly he was shot and injured as soon as he stepped on the beach. He lay behind a wall in pain for many hours until a doctor came and treated him before evacuating him straight back to the UK. He later refused his medal as he felt that he had not done anything. Forty years later he was taken to Haslar Hospital in Gosport as since the war he had suffered from pieces of shrapnel floating around his body and this was one of his many visits. Incredibly, the doctor that came to treat him was the same one that tended to his wounds on Gold beach. William was the only man the Doctor had met that he had treated in Normandy. They stayed in touch until William died in 2003.

0735:
British UDT (Underwater Demolition Team) and Royal Engineers land at GOLD Beach, followed by Infantry from the 50th Division

"We were landing at low tide on Gold Beach. To my right, I was surprised to see a marine taking cover behind the stern of an LCA.. He was hanging oddly over the stern, so that only the upper part of his body was clear of the water. Many months later, I read of a marine, Cpl. George Tandy, (coxswain of L.C.A. 786) who had been decorated with the DSM (Distinguished Service Medal) for having steered his craft all the way into the beach with his feet. The steering gear of his LCA had apparently been damaged as the craft was released from the ship. He was dubbed the "human rudder". And I had thought he was taking cover!" Brian Moss, Sergeant, 233 Field Company, Royal Engineers, attached to the 5 East Yorks
War Correspondent: *We are now moving out on patrol and the fight goes on."*

UTAH – USS Barnett[1] reports first boats returning from the beach: commences hoisting boats and receiving casualties.

H Hour for JUNO.

"As my closest pal Bill (William Cuthebertson Calbert and his crew left the barge in their carrier heading for the beach at Berny-sur-Mer they fouled a sea mine and became a blinding ball of flames and twisted steel sizzling in the sea, it was a hard thing for me to watch from the shore. Only then did I realise what was taking place around me, the terrible waste and destruction of war and loss of human life. Anything and everything became expendable". Robert J G Comber, Rifleman, Queens Own Rifles of Canada. "

To the Chief of Staff : *"Near Arromanches on the right sector of the division limit, landing craft are approaching the coast, their landing is imminent. Nearby WN 60-62, NE Colleville, an enemy from 100 to 200 men penetrate our lines. In the Bay of Vierville, no enemy unit is present, but a large number of landing craft are approaching quickly. We ask that a battalion of S.S.-Standartenführer Meyer reserves (I/915) is assigned to an attack against the sector to WN 60-62."*

0736:
GOLD - On the Jig sector, the assault companies of the 1st Hampshire land without the supporting tanks which have been delayed.

0737:
GOLD: A and D Companies Green Howard's assault the beach on King Green sector. A Company attack the fortified strong point at Hable de Heurlot and D Company press on to Mount Fleury.

OMAHA - German report sent by the 726th Regiment *"The first landing crafts have landed in front of the WN 65 and WN 69 with amphibious tanks".*

UTAH – Having determined which gun battery was firing upon them whilst trying to pick up survivors, USS *Fitch* starts rapid fire upon it. From then until 0845 they continued manoeuvring among survivors whilst maintaining fire upon the battery.

0739:
Juno - 19th Field Artillery Regiment commence firing upon the fortified position at Saint-Aubin. For 30 minutes they fire above the heads of the infantry and over the LCA's that are on the shore. Taking

---
[1] Troop ship that carried injured and KIA back to England.

"I sped along, dodging and ducking, the grenades swinging madly in my pockets. There was no sign of 2 Platoon at all. I wondered if they were sheltering behind the beach obstacles somewhere. Steel helmet bouncing on my nose, I covered the last few yards and collapsed on the sand next to figures in khaki under the sea wall. Panting like a dog, I was shocked to see only half a dozen men there: just the Yorkie CSM and a handful of his men. Where had our invasion gone? Where was 2 Platoon? Where was our officer?"

Brian Moss 233 Field Company, Royal Engineers

Meal time by 56th Signal Battalion Forces at Communications Test Point located in the Cerisey Forest, a few miles from the Beaches of Normandy and near St. Lo. The station was located adjacent to a damaged concrete bunker as a result of a direct hit by Allied Artillery. It was used only a few days before by the German Forces. The shaved head of Stan Szczepanik of Elizabeth, New Jersey is clearly visable.

Bob Searl personal collection

Scrap at La Deliverande.

Capt. G Lugg Personal Collection

advantage of the surprise, the first assault troops silence the 75mm and 88 mm guns and ensure access to the beaches.

0740:
OMAHA - LCI number 91 is hit by a mine and by the German artillery, killing 73 soldiers.

USS Satterlee and HMS Talybont continue firing at Pointe du Hoc, the soft side of the cliffs start to collapse causing a large mound that reach a third of the way up the side of the cliff helping the Rangers ascent. Ropes and grappling hoots are used and fired with rockets to the top of the cliff, however in some cases these had become too waterlogged to use and they revert to ladders they have carried ashore. Rangers reaching the top throw ropes down for others to use. Within thirty minutes of landing and under heaving attack they reach the top of the cliffs.

5th Ranger Battalion (Pointe du Hoc reinforcements) lands on OMAHA beach Dog White sector virtually unscathed.

"C" Company of the 2nd Ranger Battalion successfully scales the rock face at Pointe du Purcee and become the first troops on the high ground above OMAHA beach.

After landing and finding the assault waves still on the beach Captain Pence (16th Regiment - 1st Battalion - "A" Company) orders the Company to pass through the assault waves and beach obstacles and seize the first high ground. In moving his Company off the beach, Captain Pence is wounded and the Company carries on under Lieutenant Dillon, all the time being under heavy enemy concentrations of artillery, mortar, machine gun and sniper fire. While moving through a mined anti-tank ditch and then through a mine field, Lieutenant McElyea and Lieutenant Webne are wounded together with approximately 45 EM (Enlisted Men) from mines and small arms fire. The company pushes on to the high ground and toward a sector of the 2nd Battalion's objective.

OMAHA: Two officers and thirty-four enlisted men, an advance traffic section of the 29th Infantry Division Military Police Platoon, attached to the 116th Regimental Combat Team, debark from LCI 94 and go ashore but due to poor visibility debark approximately two miles east of their intended landing position. The advance traffic section mission on landing was to control the traffic on the beach, beach exits, and the roads leading to the vehicle transit areas in the zone of the 29th Infantry Division.

On landing, the assaulting troops are met by continuous heavy artillery, mortar, and small arms fire, and the military police fight with the infantry in their advance from the beach to their objectives until following morning.

0745:
GOLD - Troops make slow progress against raking fire, but three beach exits are cleared within the hour.

"On the beach, lads were falling all over the place. Resting with his back against the tank was our company commander, Captain Linn, who had been wounded. He was waving his arm for us to get off the beach. Tragically, while he was in that position, he was hit again and killed. Captain Chambers, now took over and he, too, was wounded but was able to carry on his duties. He was shouting and waving his arms: 'Get off the beach – off the beach, off the bloody beach. Get forward lads and give the buggers hell!' Bill Cheall - Green Howards

POINTE DU HOC: The Rangers establish a provisional H.Q. in a crater in front of the anti-aircraft bunker (37 mm gun), West of the German battery.

OMAHA: The German soldiers of the strongpoint WN 70 announce the breakthrough of six American tanks including 3 in front of WN 66.

Task force "C", made up of "A" and "B" companies of the 2nd Battalion of Rangers, are about to land in the extremity of Dog Green and Dog White sectors. All the 5th Rangers battalion moves towards Dog Green.

St Martin de Varreville in American Hands

914th IR report *"fifteen landing craft near Le Grand Vey."*

0749:
JUNO - Rocket ships manoeuvre into position and fire their salvoes, but owing to poor visibility and smoke the effect is not clear. A few moments later, word is received that the assault companies are ready for the dash to the shore and Royal Marines Forward Observation Battery orders fire on strongpoint at Bernières. Lack of opposition from beach is encouraging and assault companies are ordered in.

Despite the air support which failed to materialise and the erratic Royal Navy bombardment, the rockets falling short and the DDs and AVREs' being late, "C" Company of the 1st Canadian Scottish

Reconnaissance photo of the hut. The road leads up to Mont Fleury Battery

The Hollis Hut

King sector, Gold Beach. In 2006 The Green Howard's purchased this small hut and it now stands as a memorial to Stan Hollis who went on to gain the only VC awarded on D Day.

land at the junction of "Mike and Love." They quickly head towards the beach defences and the Chateau Vaux.

"D" Company (Maj. L. Fulton) with a pioneer section land to the left of "Mike Green." "B" Company (Capt. P. Gower) with No. 15 platoon and 2 sections of the 6 Field Company RCE land at "Mike Red" — all within seven minutes of one another.

"As the doors were lowered, these companies advanced through a hail of bullets. Spandaus and Nazi rifle spat furiously at the invaders. During the run-in some assault crafts were swamped on the reefs in front of Courseulles. Thoroughly submerged and weighed down by extra ammunition, Capt. Gower virtually walked under the water until he reached the beach. Many others were in the same situation.

Rushing the enemy, B Company encountered heavy enemy fire. Cpl. J. Klos, badly shot in the stomach and legs while leaving the assault boat, made his way forward to an enemy machine-gun nest. He managed to kill two Nazis before he was mortally felled. His hands still gripped about the throat of his victim produced a chilling sight!

Rfn. Kimmel, a signaller, showed outstanding courage in disposing of a beach pillbox with the rifle and bayonet.

Over 15 machine guns and five concrete emplacements were encountered by the Battalion on the Courseulles beach. Some of the enemy positions were quickly taken, while others had to be fought over in hand-to-hand struggle. Working their way down the trenches, sections of Little Black Devils ferreted out Nazi defenders." 1st Canadian Scottish War Diary entry.

"The German machine gunners in the dunes were stupefied to see a tank emerge from the sea, some ran away or just stared, mouths wide open." Sgt Leo Gariepy

0750:
GOLD: 1st Hampshires and 1st Dorsets are pinned down on Jig beach and take heavy causalities from the L e Hamel strong point WN38.

The County Regiments, Suffolk, East Yorks and South Lancs land on SWORD Red Queen beach and meet intense opposition from the strongpoint and are pinned down by concentrated machine gun and mortar fire at the waters edge, some being in 2 ft of water.

JUNO - Nos. 4 and 10 (Free French) Commando land. Heavy fighting on SWORD.

The Commander 726th Grenadier Regiment : *"Meyers Battalion is moving towards Colleville in support of WN 60-62. He will attempt to push the enemy back. His arrival will be in about an hour and a half."*

0755:
352nd Artillery Regiment signal that *"The situation in WN No. 60 is uncertain."*

0756:
JUNO: 3rd Canadian Division, 7th and 8th Brigades land. General R.F.L. Keller's Division lands in two waves. They are running slightly behind schedule due to the natural offshore reefs. They were due to land at 0745 hours, so that the landing craft could clear the reef on the rising tide. This delay presents the invading Canadians with a difficult situation as the beach obstacles are already partially submerged, and the engineers are unable to clear paths to the beach. The landing craft are therefore forced to feel their way in, and the mines took a heavy toll. Roughly 30 percent of the landing craft at JUNO are destroyed or damaged.

As the troops waded ashore, there was little fire at first—mainly because the German gun positions did not aim out to sea but were set to enfilade the coastline. As the Canadian soldiers work their way through the obstacles and come into the enfilading killing zones, the first wave took dreadful casualties. Company "B" of the Royal Winnipeg Rifles is cut down to one officer and 25 men as it moves to reach the seawall. In the assault teams, the chance of becoming a casualty in that first hour was almost 1 in 2. By mid-morning, hard fighting had brought the town of Bernières into Canadian hands, and later Saint-Aubin is occupied. Progress inland past the towns is good, and, as some armoured units arrive in later waves, they briefly interdicted the Caen-Bayeux road.

No sooner had the troops cleared the area round a shop in Bernières than the proprietor popped up from the cellar and, with bullets still flying, started to sell wine!

0757:
GOLD - Report received from the 726th Grenadier Regiment: *"On our right, in the area of the 716th Infantry Division, thirty tanks have already landed. between WN 35 and 36."*

OMAHA beach was about three miles long with cliffs at each end. The US Rangers scaled them and got a foot hold quite quickly. The central beach was swept with a crossfire from Spandau machine guns and 88mm guns. Horrendous!

RM WCS Hiscock
onboard HMS Hawkins

US Army Rangers resting in the vicinity of Pointe du Hoc, which they assaulted in support of "Omaha" Beach landings on "D-Day", 6 June 1944. Note Ranger in right centre, apparently using his middle finger to push cartridges into a M-1 carbine magazine. The carbine and a backpack frame are nearby

US Navy Photo #: 80-G-45715

0758:

JUNO - The 1st Hussars Tanks land ahead of the Regina Rifle Infantry and, firing at close range, take on the German guns.

Peering out his periscope, a soldier of the 1st Hussars sees another tank… *"waddle right up to this fort thing. The tank fired twenty-eight rounds before it was holed. We came alongside him. The fire was very heavy. Guns were popping off everywhere and machine gun bullets pelted our hull. We broke through the wire into the dunes and among the fortified houses. We wheeled around and spotted an anti-tank gun behind the casement. The Jerry's were manning it, but we crashed through a brick wall and surprised them."* Two direct hits passed through a gun shield and the German gun blew up.

0800:

At GOLD, JUNO and SWORD, the British and Canadians clear the beaches and begin their progress inland.

*"*I went on watch at 8 o'clock, things were very quiet until about 9 then hundreds of our planes and gliders came over in clouds. They cast off the gliders and dropped their parachutists. What a sight it was, hundreds of different coloured parachutes came down in one mass. 4 or 5 of our planes were shot down in flames. I shall never forget the sight. The town was in flames"* Signalman John Emrys Williams on-board HMS Diadem.

SWORD - The midget submarine X23, commanded by Lieutenant Honour, approaches and ties up alongside HMS LARGS after laying submerged just off the beach-head for more than 48 hours.

The first of Lord Lovat's Commandos land on Queen Beach.

Eisenhower sends a message to General Marshall on the situation in Normandy as at 0800.

UTAH - The offensive begins. Patrols advance behind the dunes to join forces with paratroopers from both American Divisions.

Brigadier Theodore Roosevelt orders in follow-up troops. He is later awarded the Congressional Medal of Honour.

USS *Fitch* reduces firing to the rate of 2 salvos a minute and then to one a minute and then to one every two minutes.

---
* Reproduced with kind permission of his family.

OMAHA - Troops are slowed up by German artillery as the rising tide forces reinforcement's to advance under fire. Destroyers and rocket launcher barges approach the beach in an attempt to destroy the German blockhouses. Losses are enormous. The assault up the cliffs begins, assisted by tanks and destroyers firing from close inshore.

American soldiers arrive at the top of the dune in front of the WN 60 strongpoint.

29th Cavalry Reconnaissance Troops Mecs. attached to the 116th Infantry Combat Team land It was divided into seven (7) groups and operate a Commanding General's Radio Voice Net reporting the advances, locations, and resistances met by the assault companies.

US 1st Division - 16th Regiment - 1st Battalion - Headquarters Company - the forward C.P. group of the 1st Battalion 16th Infantry land on the left side of Easy Red – OMAHA Beach. The machine gun and rifle fire is terrific and men are being hit from the front and flanks as they leave the LCVP's. Men who are carrying the heavier loads of equipment such as wire and radios are hit more often as being weighed down they could not move as fast as the rest, they are sitting ducks. Upon reaching the beach it was found that there are many men from the first assault unit still laying there. Some are going back into the water to get wounded men, ammunition and equipment. There are not sufficient exits cleared through the wire entanglements and mine fields to remove the men quickly and as as result the beach was filling with nowhere for the men to go. They had to make their own exits by blowing wire and going through mine fields.

"E" Company, the 16th Regiment; According to the plan, nearly 400 men should have landed side by side as a fighting force. Instead most of E and F Company are scattered for 800 yards in a murderous crossfire on the wrong section of Omaha. Scores of soldiers become casualties before they even leave the water.

Just north of Utah Beach, one of the two 210 mm Skoda K52 guns (from Czechoslovakian origin) of the Azeville battery is destroyed by allied ships.

0804:
The 716th IR HQ receives information that The Orne bridge near Bénouville is now in enemy hands.

0805: SWORD - 246 Field Company clears the first exit off Queen White Beach

"Glancing along the beach, I could see no one else on their feet, only the dead and the dying. There were a few figures scuttling about in the distance, but that was all. The CSM threw what I realised was his last grenade over the wall, so I pulled out a couple more from my pockets and handed them to him.

"Good lad," gasped the CSM, "let's give them some more of these buggers!" and he sent them over the wall. I hurled my other two grenades to join them. I also gave the housetops a squirt from my Sten gun, not because I saw any particular target there, but because it seemed the right thing to do."

Brian Moss 233 Field Company, Royal Engineers

Bursting in flame when machine gun fire exploded a hand grenade, this Coast Guard-manned LCVP, packed with troops, was piloted safely to the Normandy beach on D-Day by a 23 year old Texan Coast Guardsmen. He unloaded his cargo of invaders and, assisted by his engine man and bowman, put out the fire and made the run back to his Coast Guard-manned assault transport in a hail of German machine gun and mortar fire. USNA

OMAHA - 1st Division - 16th Infantry Regiment Rear Command Post lands and establishes on the beach which is still under heavy fire. Infiltration starts through the right flank of area at a small break through. The mine field is cleared out and all troops on the beach commence moving off to flank.

JUNO - Sixteen shells every minute hit the Mike Green beach sector. AVRE (Armoured Vehicle Royal Engineers) Group J2 land. However, the Senior Officer of the DD's in J1 group revises his decision and launches them 1000 yards from the beach. Some confusion ensued and they touch down between 0759 and 0810. The AVRE which has gone astray in the night, arrives six minutes after the infantry some 30 minutes late on their deferred time.

The Regina Rifles land under heavy fire on NAN GREEN beach at Courseulles sur Mer. Landing time had been set so that the low tide would expose obstacles on the beach which now left some 400 yards for them to cross before they reached the sea wall. On the Battalion's right, are the Royal Winnipeg Rifles with a company of the Canadian Scottish Regiment coming in on MIKE RED beach. The remainder of the Canadian Scottish, the reserve battalion for 7th Brigade, wait to come ashore at MIKE RED, later in the morning. On the Battalion's left, to the east, are the Queen's Own Rifles of 8th Brigade landing at Bernières, on NAN WHITE beach. To the flanks, the Sherman tanks of the 6th Canadian Armoured Regiment (1st Hussars) give support, with B Squadron assaulting along side of the Reginas.

916th Grenadier Regiment *"A rather weak enemy infiltrated Pointe du Hoc. The 1st platoon of the 726th Infantry Regiment is engaged for an immediate counter-attack"*.

0806:
OMAHA: 726th Regiment reports that WN 60 is under fire and that 40 soldiers with an amphibious tanks have landed in front of this strongpoint.

0809:
OMAHA: All the amphibious tanks intended to land on Fox Green sink between their starting point and the beach.

JUNO - The two assault companies ("A" and "B") The Regina Rifle Regiment touch down at 8:09 and 8:15 respectively. "A" Company, which is directly opposite the strongpoint, immediately meets heavy resistance. The strongpoint gives it a hard struggle, and the help of the tanks of "B" Squadron of the 6th Armoured Regiment proves invaluable. This is supported by the later examination of the German positions by the Special Observer Party which reported, with respect to the 75-mm. position at the east end of the strongpoint, *"The gun had fired many rounds (estimated 200 empties) and was put out of action by a direct hit which penetrated the gun shield making a hole 3" x 6". ... It is probable that the gun was put out by a direct shot from a DD tank."*

0810:
JUNO - The two assault companies of the North Shore (New Brunswick) Regiment sprint across a 100-yard open beach in the face of fire from Saint-Aubin. "A" Company suffers the heaviest casualties, incurring many fatalities from beach mines.

Nan White sector. The Queen's Own Rifles. Rifleman Doug Hester and Rifleman Doug Reed are singing "For Me and My Gal" as they approach the shore. The ramp goes down, suddenly Doug Reed is dead. Three other men are also killed in the first few seconds. One was Fred Harris, the son of a Toronto doctor, who had turned down every opportunity to be somewhere else on D-Day. Hester jumps from the craft into the freezing water. A burst of gunfire went through Corporal John Gibson's back pack. Corporal Gibson turns to Hester, grinned, and said, "That was close, Dougie." Then another burst of gunfire killed him.

0812:
JUNO - As it became evident that the assault Companies are achieving some success, the reserve Companies are now ordered in. Stiff resistance is now being encountered along the narrow coastal strip and progress is slow. As they run across the beach under under heavy enemy machine-gun fire, the men are quick to forget their sea sickness. However, the bad weather still had an impact on the operations: landing the tanks is causing a problem and the LCTs have to move in closer with the risk of hitting a submerged mine.

As they set foot on the beach, men of "B" Company of the Queen's Own Rifles have to run 200 metres against a hail of fire from a German Strongpoint that was not silenced earlier. They are struggling due to the Sherman DD's not arriving as planned. Almost one half of the company is lost in the initial dash across the beach. A supporting flak ship is wirelessed for support. The flak ship came in so close that it almost runs aground and began firing at point-blank range. Finally, Lt. W.G. Herbert, Cpl. R. J. Tessier and Rfn. W. Chicoski

~~TOP SECRET~~   ~~TOP SECRET~~   **EYES ONLY**

SHAEF
STAFF MESSAGE CONTROL
INCOMING MESSAGE

SHAEF CP   SHAEF 83/06

Filed 060800B June   TOR 060930B June

<u>URGENT</u>

FROM   : SHAEF COMMAND POST, PERSONAL FROM GENERAL EISENHOWER

TO   : AGWAR-TO GENERAL MARSHALL FOR HIS EYES ONLY; SHAEF FOR INFORMATION

REF NO : 90016, 6 June 1944

       Local time is now 8 in the morning.

       I have as yet no information concerning the actual landings nor of our progress through beach obstacles. Communique will not be issued until we have word that leading ground troops are actually ashore.

       All preliminary reports are satisfactory. Airborne formations apparently landed in good order with losses out of approximately 1250 airplanes participating about 30. Preliminary bombings by air went off as scheduled. Navy reports sweeping some mines, but so far as is known channels are clear and operation proceeding as planned. In early morning hours reaction from shore batteries was sufficiently light that some of the naval spotting planes have returned awaiting call.

       The weather yesterday which was original date selected was impossible all along the target coast. Today conditions are vastly improved both by sea and air and we have the prospect of at least reasonably favorable weather for the next several days.

       Yesterday, I visited British troops about to embark and last night saw a great portion of a United States airborne division just prior to its takeoff. The enthusiasm, toughness and obvious fitness of every single man were high and the light of battle was in their eyes.

       I will keep you informed.

<u>DISTRIBUTION</u>:

1. SUPREME COMMANDER ✔
2. CHIEF OF STAFF
3. SGS
4. Gen. Strong (G-2)
5. Gen. Bull (G-3)

DECLASSIFIED
DOD DIR. 5200.10, June 29, 1960
NE by *WGL* date 6-29-67

~~TOP SECRET~~

COPY NO 1
SUPREME COMMANDER

SHAEF Incoming Message from General Eisenhower to General Marshall concerning the first reports of the Normandy landing, June 6, 1944
[DDE's Pre-Presidential Papers, Box 133, Cables Official (GCM/DDE February 19 - October 18, 1944) (4)]

do a good job in silencing the strongpoint with grenades and Sten guns.

0815:
GOLD: 2nd Devons, Notts Yeomanry and 7th Green Howard's arrive on Jig and Mike and proceed inland.

The Rangers at Pointe du Hoc quickly take the gun emplacements, only to find that the guns have been moved inland, they fan out and isolate the main bunker and destroy its antennae.

OMAHA: 1st Division - 16th Regiment - HQ Company's boat is about 50 yards from the shore when the ramp is lowered. The boats have been under some artillery and machine gun fire on the way in, but as the ramp is lowered there is no immediate fire . The men went off in an orderly fashion , into waist deep water . All equipment is taken off. As the last few men are leaving the LCM it is brought under fire, but fortunately no one is hit. There is no sand-bar to cross as the Advance Group experienced, and the distance to the beach is much shorter due to the fact the tide has risen considerably.

The rear CP group gets to the beach to find the same confusion and chaos which existed when the Advance Group hit. The group moved to the left in an effort to join up with the Advance Group. Contact is made, but it is difficult to marshal the men together into any organized group, as they are too spread out. The primary task at this point is to take what cover is possible, save what equipment could be saved, rescue what men from the water that could be rescued, and last but not least, to try to get off the beach.

Midst all the confusion, one beach exit is opened, and the men start to move off the beach up onto the hillside, where there is more cover. Most of the Headquarters and Headquarters Company men join up at this point. The hillside is crowded with troops, but everyone has a hole, and there are several opportunities to use it.

JUNO - empty L.C.A.'s returning, Wind drops to Force 3.

JUNO - LCT 1008 orders to prepare to beach on Nan White. All securing chains on the tanks are removed. The flotilla sails parallel to the beach then turns 90 degrees and with full power (8 knots) makes for the beach . 2nd Lieutenant Stan Mincher's job is to check that the anchor was ready so that they could pull themselves off later and to oversee the proper operation of the door and the landing of the army. The door goes down 100 yards from the beach dropping the last foot or so when they feel the shudder as they skate up the beach. Stan jumps ashore with dry shoes. However, the tide was coming in fast and by the time he leaves there is three foot of water by the doors. The tanks go off well but have difficulty leaving the beach as the 10 foot sea wall is breached in very few places. The beach is under fire and there are LCA's littering the area plus lorries and tanks broken down and blocking the beach exit. The Army's waterproofed bull dozers help move some of them. A sailor from the RN beach party tells them to cut their barrage balloon adrift as the enemy are ranging on it. As soon as the troops are ashore, many of them are so scared they just drop their bicycles and run, the engine goes astern, the winch pulls on the kedge anchor and back they go. The 2 ton doors have to be winched by hand and it takes four men five minutes to do it. The whole operation has taken 15 minutes.

0819:
POINTE DU HOC -   916th Grenadiers report to the 352nd H.Q: *"Close to Pointe du Hoc, the enemy climbed the cliff (with ladders and ropes launched by projectiles)"*.

0820:
SWORD - N°4 Commando first wave of LCA's arrive. Mortar bombs were falling in and around the landing craft and as the Commando land there are 40 casualties, including the Commanding Officer, Lt.Col. R.W.P. Dawson, who is wounded in the leg. Rapidly forming up under concentrated fire, No.4 Commando fight their way from the beach to the forming up area, putting out of action several of the enemy strong positions and enabling Units of 8 Brigade to pass through.

GOLD - Follow-up battalions and No. 47 Royal Marine Commando land.

OMAHA - 16th RCT H.Q. lands. Col. Taylor starts encouraging the troops to get off the beach.

OMAHA - The 726th Grenadiers report that the 88 mm gun of the WN 61 is inoperable and that landing crafts prepare to land in front of the WN 37 and 37a strongpoint the latter of which is being bombarded by the Naval artillery.

914th I.R. Report: *"The II/914e Infantry Regiment struggle against the paratroopers in Brevands is continuing."*

0822:
Radio Report of the 914th I.R." *Fifteen landing craft are now entering at the mouth of the Vire."*

> *As adjutant I was 'OC Troops' in the boat carry Commando H.Q. and spent the night with he troops in a cramped little mess deck. It was hot and smelly – almost everybody was sick, and although I wasn't I felt so bad I wish I could be. Sitting with my back jammed up against a bulk head thinking what a rotten way to take troops to war.*
>
> Major D.J. Flunder, MC. VRD, 48 (RM) Cdo
>
> RM Museum Southsea 7/19/5

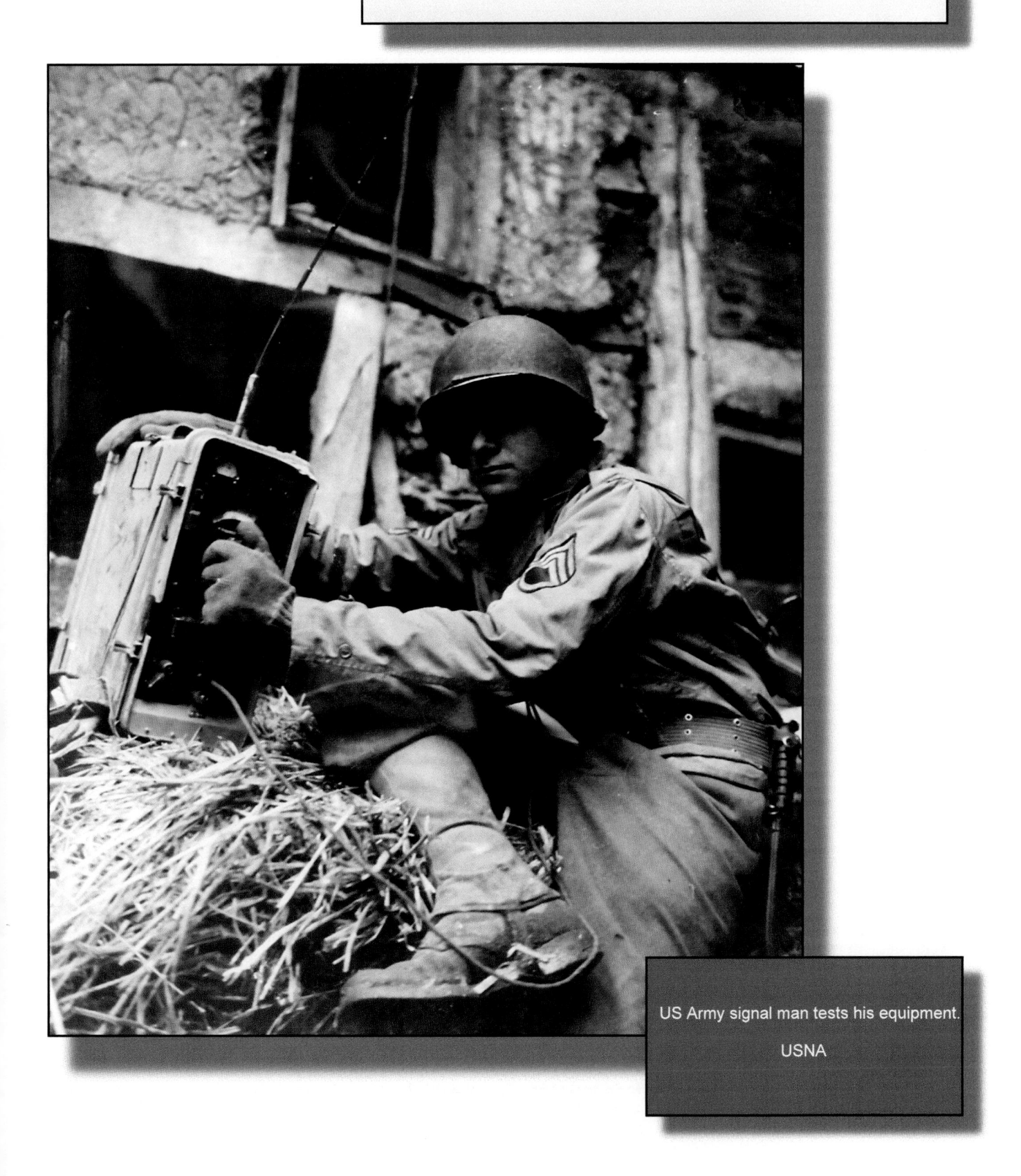

US Army signal man tests his equipment.

USNA

0823:
JUNO - Advanced beach signal station "Mike" Green established.

0824:
OMAHA - Troops are now under fire from the Maisy Gun battery.

0825:
SWORD - Royal Marines 41 Commando approach the coastline and Troop Commanders are able to identify their beach from the briefings. It is in a bit of a mess, littered with dead and wounded and burnt out tanks and with Flails flailing through wire and mines, Bulldozers clearing gaps etc. The beach is quite obviously still under fire as mortar bombs and shells were crashing down in abundance.

352nd Artillery Regiment Report: *"Tanks have now landed opposite WN 35, a number were burned or immobilized by our antitank artillery guns"*

0830:
SWORD - Shells start falling around the landing craft with several reaching the ships and damaging ramps etc. on some craft but fortunately not causing any causalities.

JUNO - The Canadian 7th Brigade's reserve battalion, the 1st Battalion of The Canadian Scottish Regiment, commanded by Lt.-Col. F. N. Cabeldu, finds opposition still alive as its three companies approach "Mike" Beach. The leading companies come under mortar fire on the beach, and one of them is held up there for some time while waiting for an exit to be cleared of mines.

Le Régiment de la Chaudière, begin to land at Bernières, its craft having had a difficult time with the beach obstacles. Captain Otway-Ruthven described "A" Company's experience: *"The LCAs. of the 529th Flotilla (H.M.C.S. Prince David) struck a very bad patch of obstacles and mortar fire on Nan White and all foundered before touching down. The troops, however, discarded their equipment and swam for the shore. They still had their knives and were quite willing to fight with this weapon."* This was not completely true; Canadian Naval records show that one of Prince David's five assault craft did make it to the beach undamaged.

Rangers and 116th Infantry reach top of the cliffs at Les Moulins.

OMAHA - The Beach Master orders a temporary interruption of the landing due to the lack of space on the overcrowded beach, the troops are pinned down and unable to move forward thus prohibiting any further landings. This causes a few Germans to believe that the invasion is failing. The 915 Grenadier Regiment defends an attack on WN 60.

OMAHA - General Cota eventually establishes his headquarters on the beach

OMAHA - Eighty six men and four officers of 1st Medical Battalion, A Company aboard LCI 85, head in to the shore with no enemy opposition. As the boat slides in over the pilings that stuck up there they could see soldiers lined up all along the rocky beach ahead of them. Suddenly they come to a stop and at that instant could hear gunfire and then reports of shell fire. The men in charge at the front of the boat were then determining whether it was too deep to let down the ramps and at this time the first cries of the wounded from up front could be heard. The skipper of the craft, Mr. Henley, then decides that a landing couldn't be affected and so he backed the craft off the pilings and pulled out about a hundred yards for another try. At this time the report of fire is heard and smoke can be seen pouring out from one of the doorways. As the craft went underway again for another try at the beach Captain Rolston was seen standing in the doorway leading from the then smoking number three hold directing the men out of sure death down below to a position along the port side of the boat. This he did while they were still under enemy fire. About fifteen minutes have elapsed between the time they backed off the beach and headed in for another try at the shore. It was also evident at this time that they had suffered a hit below the water line due to a list to the starboard side of the ship.

The second attempt in at the beach was more successful in getting the ship in close enough to disembark. One of the boat crew jumps in with a life line and manages to get to shore via this line but the enemy is still firing, injuring and killing others who are crowded forward and trying to get off the ship.

Fire now broke out in the two forward holds and the craft began to have a more pronounced list to the starboard. The craft was then backed away from the shore quickly, the skipper had evidently decided that no more landings could be made in view of the seriously damaged ship. All during this shelling the Medical personnel are giving what aid they can to the injured aboard the ship.
USS *McCook* sails very close to the shore and attacks the German strong points with its 5" guns. The intensity and danger of the naval bombardment steadily increases throughout the morning.

A casualty of the heavy fire against the D-Day invasion fleet, a Coast Guard L.C.I., loaded with troops, lists heavily to port before sinking in the English Channel. She had time, however, to pull alongside a Coast Guard assault transport and evacuate her troops and wounded before capsizing and going down. The infantry landing craft was fatally hit on a run to the French beach, this picture shown soldiers up on the high rail as the L.C.I .limped to the transport. USNA

1st Battalion, 505th PIR now hold the eastern end of the bridge over the Merderet River against heavy enemy fire from the western approaches.

Colonel Josef "Pips" Priller, one of the Luftwaffe's top aces and his wing man Sergeant Heinz Wodarczyk carry out a single strafing pass over the beaches in their Focke Wulf 190's sending both Allied and German troops scattering. At times they are only about 50' above the ground and have to weave around the barrage balloons. Ships along the coast turned their guns towards them but the German Ace and his side kick disappear unscathed back to their airfield at Lille. It was exceptional flying especially considering they were both nursing hangovers after downing several bottles of excellent cognac at Luftwaffe High Command the night before and not getting to bed until the early hours. Interestingly after the war Priller went on to run a Brewery.

Report of the 352nd Artillery Regiment: *"WN 35 and 36 are overwhelmed. The enemy infantry accompanied by thirty five tanks deploy to Meuvaines. The division on our right sent the Ost Battalion 642nd to occupy the ridge east of Meuvaines. WN 37 continues fighting. WN 40 destroyed three or four vehicles near them, two or three landing craft burning."*

JUNO - "C" Company, Queens Own Rifle land. Half of the LCA's have struck mines but, by a miracle, few of the men are wounded and all swam or wade ashore. B Squadron, Fort Garry Horse, have also landed. An exit is breached in the sea-wall and very soon the armour joins the forward companies of the Queens Own. "C" and "D" companies immediately press forward along the brigade Centre Line: Bernières-sur-Mer, Beny-sur-Mer, Basly, Colomby sur-Thaon, Anguerny Heights. Great stress is placed on the capture of the last mentioned which is of great tactical importance to the division.

0831:
JUNO - Advanced beach signal station "Mike" Red and "Nan" Green established.

916th Infantry Regiment are preparing for an attack on Meuvaines.

0835:
No. 48 Royal Marine Commando land at St Aubin, and heads east. Little beach clearance takes place due to high tides and rough seas and the Landing Craft wooden hulls are damaged. The beaches are congested and under continuous fire. Heavy casualties are suffered by the Commando from machine gun and mortar fire, as the assaulting infantry pass straight through the beach without pausing to mop up, and some of the defences sited to give cross-fire are now beginning to come to life again. Though the Infantry has got across the beaches quickly, there is some delay before exits were established.

OMAHA - The Americans take their first four prisoners, from the 8th company of the 916th Regiment.

The 352nd Infantry Division report that between 100 and 200 soldiers have entered the defence perimeter and that a battalion must strengthen the German positions at Colleville.

The General commanding the division Gen Kraiss reports: *"Situation on the right wing near Meuvaines and Asnelles is difficult; Meuvaines fell to the enemy. At Asnelles our anti-aircraft guns destroyed six tanks. General Kraiss proposes to launch an attack with Meyer's detachment to reinforce the bulk of the 352nd Anti-Tank Battalion, and to push back the enemy infantry and tanks to the coast and sea. Elements of the 352nd Anti-Tank Battalion must be put in order of battle. General Marcks authorizes the proposed plan."*

The wind picks up to Force 4 again.

0840:
SWORD - 2 Troop, No 6 Commando lands on Queen Red and march to the positions at Le Plein taking en route one German battery 16 prisoners and killing 24. Casualties Capt Pyman MC killed, Major Coade wounded, 4 OR's killed and 28 wounded.

352nd Artillery Regiment: *"Connections with the observation posts should be restored as soon as possible and in any case before the high tide because it is likely that the second wave of enemy forces will land at that time. A detachment of the Third Artillery battery connection must be ready immediately with a view to support the attack by Meyer."*

0843:
On Nan Red Beach the obstacles have not been cleared and were well below the water when the Commando landed. Two craft containing "Y" and "Z" Troops, strike the obstacles and as a result are unable to beach. HQ craft also strike an obstacle but are fairly close inshore. The majority of the landing ramps fail, this was either because the end nearest the shore floated or because the movement of the craft on the obstacles shook them off the craft. "A", "B", "X" and HQ Troops have to

Motorised patrols of the Fallschirmjaeger

Bundesarchiv, Bild 101I-585-2182-30A / Zimmermann / CC-BY-SA wade ashore in about 3 feet of water, but "Y" and "Z" Troops can only get ashore by swimming.

Many Officers and men attempt to swim ashore from these craft and a high proportion of these were lost through drowning owing to a strong tide. Some do manage to get ashore. On reaching the beach, troops make for the cover of the earth cliff and sea wall. Here they find a confused situation.

The cliff and sea wall give some protection from small arms fire, but any movement away from them is under machine gun fire. The whole area meanwhile is subjected to heavy mortar and shellfire. Under the sea wall is a jumble of men from other units including many wounded and dead; the beach is congested with tanks, self propelled guns and other vehicles, some out of action, others attempting to move from the beach in the very confused space between the waters edge and the sea wall.

LCT's are arriving all the time and attempting to land their loads, adding to the general confusion. The beach exit to the right of the isolated houses is free from aimed small arms fire except for occasional shots and that a gap is now been clear through the mines. As this is the quickest way to the assembly area, orders are immediately passed for troops to move up to the assembly area by this route. "B" Troop leads followed by "A", HQ. And "X", but in the conditions prevailing, it is largely a question of telling individual men the way to move.

The Assembly area is much quieter and Troop rendezvous is quickly established and Commando HQ. set up. The Commanding Officer returns to the beach to contact "Y" and "Z" Troops. A considerable number of men of mixed Troops are found still under the cliff and these are moved off to the right. He locates "Y" Troop attempting to get ashore from an LCT to which they have transferred from their LCI. Lieut Fouche is already ashore and has orders to pass men along to the right as they come ashore, but he is hit almost immediately by mortar fragments and seriously wounded; his Orderly is killed. However, the landing of "Y" Troop is very slow and few men manage to get ashore before the LCT shoved off, taking with her about 50 men of the Commando back to England despite their energetic protests.

"Z" Troop is more fortunate and about 40 men eventually collect in the assembly area. It is found on calling for reports that "A", "B "and "X" Troops each have about 50-55 men available.

The CO now issues a warning order for the advance and makes his way to the pre-arranged RV.

0845:
SWORD - 41 Commando touch down about 200 yards out to sea on Red Beach, 300 yards away from where they should land on White. Whilst still coming in, Lieut. Colonel Gray foresaw this and does his best to get the craft to slew right on to the proper beach which is in fact drawing less fire than Red. Unfortunately, his efforts were unsuccessful and they come ashore in the wrong place.

"P" Troop commanded by Captain B.J.B Sloley with an Advance HQ move swiftly across to White Beach and within about 5 minutes were off the beach virtually intact. Within 5 minutes a section of "A" Troop with Captain C.N.P. Powell, DSO, Troop Commander have followed. Lieut.Colonel Gray then decides to move this body to a more suitable spot for assembly

The second half of the 86th Field Regiment, Royal Artillery are now due to land but it is getting difficult to find a clear spot on the beach. The strong wind and tide have made the first boats ground almost sideways on to the coast instead of head on and far too much of the beach was covered by ships sides. Also boats which should have pulled away after unloading have been damaged or stuck and the beach was fast becoming jammed. One of the LCT's which has already beached, first vehicle off the ramp has got stuck in the water and as a result none of the other vehicles behind it can get off.

No. 3 Troop, 6 Commando land from its LCI on SWORD beach without casualties. After getting clear of the beach as quickly as possible, amidst a certain amount of confusion, the troop takes up its position as leading troop of the Commando, and consequently of the whole No.1 Special Service Brigade. It is noticed that no troops in 8 Infantry Brigade have penetrated further than the first lateral as they consider that the area before them was under fire. The troop, however, proceed to the Commando forming-up area in the woods, reaching it without casualties and undue incidents. As they run inland shells from the Allied ships are falling beyond and on to various enemy batteries; a six-barrelled mortar is also seen firing fairly close. The ground up to this time has been very marshy and many deep ditches have to be crossed which are filled with water - the rucksacks they all carry are now sodden and weigh far more than they should hindering their progress.

OMAHA - 916th Grenadiers report that the WN 70 strongpoint has fallen into the hands of the enemy.

" The number of targets knocked out was kept on the gun shield and number of rounds chalked up on the barrel of the gun. A CPO was a dab hand at cartoons and on No1 gun there was a picture of Olive Oyl and Popeye, No3 gun had 'Rommel's Runners verses the Hawkins' and No4 gun had an outsized Mrs Mop (of ITMA fame) with a gun rammed up Hitler's arse with the words "I can do you now, Sir!" No3 & No4 guns were Royal Marine guns."

Royal Marine WCS Hiscock
PO/X112968 - HQ192 Squad. Onboard HMS Hawkins

The beachhead is secure, but the price was high. A Coast Guard Combat Photographer came upon this monument to a dead American soldier somewhere on the shell-blasted shore of Normandy.

USNA 26-G-2441

3 tanks have gone through the defences of the WN 66 strongpoint and the upper bunker of the WN 62 is destroyed.

OMAHA - G Company of the 16th RCT (Regimental Combat Team) reach the summit dominating Easy Red sector.

0846:
OMAHA - Report received from the 352nd Artillery Regiment: *"North of St. Lawrence, WN 65, 66, 67, and 70 are probably captured by the enemy. Opposite WN 68, powerful enemy formations are landing from larger vessels with about 150 men.*

Telephone connections to the 916th Infantry Regiment are all suspended for the moment."

0849:
OMAHA - The 1st Battalion of the 116th Infantry Regiment reports that it is stopped by the firing of heavy machine guns and asks for the support of the Naval artillery.

0850:
224th Filed Ambulance Main Dressing Station party move into a farm under the protection of "B" Company 1st Canadian Parachute Battalion. Major YOUNG sees the farmer (M. Barberot) and is immediately given accommodation for the wounded.

JUNO, Advanced beach signal station "Nan" White established.

8th Canadian Infantry Brigade "C" Company reserve battalion lands. Beaches are not cleared as quickly as they should be but casualties are comparatively light considering the congestion. The reserve battalion finally clears off the beach and makes its way forward to the assembly area in the vicinity of the church. Brigadier KG Blackader lands and proceeds to the HQ of Queens Own Rifles of Canada.

0854:
USS *Hobson* is relieved by USS Butler as planned. *Hobson* then goes to assume the sunken *Corrys* fire support mission.

0855:
8th Canadian Infantry Brigade "D" Company come in late, several of its craft are blown up on mined obstacles concealed by the rising tide. Only 49 survivors reach the beach

UTAH – USS *Fitch* ceases firing and completes picking up the rest of the men in the water that have escaped the sinking *Corry*. They then proceed out of the Fire Support Channel and up the boat lane en-route to the USS *Barnett* as directed to deliver survivors.

OMAHA - 352nd Artillery Regiment are having trouble maintaining radio contact with WN 60.

0857:
OMAHA - 30 tanks land between WN 35 and 36 strongpoints.

0900:
The second 210 mm gun of the Azeville battery is destroyed by the Allied ships.

8th Parachute Battalion Patrol arrive back from Troarn. Patrol Commander states that he was moved to Troarn Station and was fired on from the high ground to the south of the Station. The patrol could not move on and lay up, they observe half-track vehicles moving north on Troarn - Le Mesnil road and Troarn - Banneville road. CO decides that most of the mobile Company have probably left Troarn and that as soon as R.E. party are finished with Bures bridges, Troarn bridge could be dealt with.

HMS *Largs* moves inshore to take up the main function as Operational Headquarters for SWORD beach.

"Yank report of very large force of Fortresses bombing about 2 miles inland, along whole 40 miles of beaches. Our fighter cover terrific. Understand very heavy casualties suffered by paratroopers. American casualties on beaches very severe, officer reports troops experiencing trouble with land mines and machine gun nests.

Came off watch. Had corned beef sandwich for breakfast – now at action stations ready to pass ammunition to Oerlikon guns." LAC Leslie Armitage, on board Fighter Direction Tender (FDT) 216 off OMAHA.

Fighter Direction Tenders were, in effect, floating command and control centres which bristled with antenna and aerials for radar, communications and intelligence gathering purposes. They were the eyes and ears for the assault. There were 3 Fighter Direction Tenders designated FDT 13, 216 & 217 at Normandy.

POINTE DU HOC -The Rangers counter an attack led by the first company of the 916th Infantry Regiment.

View of Omaha Beach from WN 62, the German strong point that gave the US Infantry so much trouble.

August 2013

OMAHA - "L" Company - Lieutenant Cutler calls to battalion and tells them that the enemy have been subdued in the strong point.

OMAHA - The first element of the Advance Group of the 29th Signal Company land on Easy Green while the beach is under constant artillery and small arms fire. First communications are established at Brigadier General Cota's initial CP located in defilade on the beach some twenty-five yards from the water line.

UTAH - C T8 (Combat Team) begins to move off the beach by Exit 2.

Many survivors from USS Corry are sighted in a badly damaged whaleboat, clinging to the cork nets, and floating in water supported by rubber life belts. USS PT199 goes to rescue them from the water. They reported "It was a very difficult task as many were suffering from shock, wounds and exposure." They lower a scramble net, for those that could not get up, three men from PT199 jump into the water with ropes that they tied around the men to bring them in. Three very badly wounded men were left in the whaleboat with the Doctor from Corry. A tow is rigged to take them to receive hospitalisation. Of the total taken aboard, 15 needed artificial respiration and only one died.

Below is a moving account by the Corrys Commander G.D. Hoffman, U.S.N. written a few months after the event.

"After passing through the transport area we headed on in towards the beach, acting as lead off vessel for the following craft. By this time the first light of morning had come. Looking behind us one could see several hundred landing craft obediently following in our wake. Looking ahead, the grey misty beach could be seen; all seemed oddly enough, quite peaceful and not at all hostile. Suddenly there was a large splash out on the starboard beam that didn't seem so dangerous as it was more of a rude awakening. The battle was on. We had the mission of proceeding further on in towards the beach, holding fire until a certain time, and taking up our fire support station out of the boat lane, in which we were at this time leading the boats down. Now there were more splashes and they were much closer. Each time we would try to locate the batteries in preparation for opening fire. The destroyer next to us let go with a salvo and so did we immediately thereafter. The shooting had started a bit ahead of schedule and the two destroyers had started it but it was not long before the heavier vessels further out to sea on the other side of the shoal water, also let go, right over our heads.

From now on it was counter battery fire. We had by this time arrived at our fire support station and it was ten minutes past due for our pre-arranged fire at the beach defences, which were about to menace the assault craft. Fortunately, the batteries, opposing us, were silenced and we were able to anchor at short stay and commence firing at beach targets located on our charts. All was going well for a while; we were pouring it into the beach areas, taking them in sequence and had caught up with our schedule. Suddenly a salvo of shells fell close aboard on our port beam. We got going in a hurry and commenced a rapid continuous fire. The shells were going out so fast that the tracers seemed almost like those of machine gun fire. We were endeavouring to shake them off with violent manoeuvres, consisting of hard right and left rudder and alternate flank speed and stopping and backing. The next thing to occur was a tremendous explosion shaking the whole ship, knocking men down wherever they stood. All hands were dazed by the shock and the ship had received a fatal blasting. All power was lost, the compartments were flooding, the gun turrets were deluged by tons of water and had ceased firing.

The boats were ordered into the water for purposes of towing the ship clear and signals were hoisted asking for help in the form of a tow. It quickly became apparent that the ship was done for and no degree of towing would suffice. The smoke screen generator had just been hit and the ship was enveloped in its own smoke screen, thus hiding our plight from the remainder of the assault forces. Abandon ship was ordered the wounded placed in the boats and the crew was ordered into the rafts and floater nets. Finally, when all hands were in the water, I came down off the bridge and stepped into the water on the main deck and swam off using an empty powder tank as a float.

The next two hours were the worse, for the Germans kept up their shelling causing further deaths of our men in the very cold water. The ship had sunk in shallow water and the stacks, masts and the now upright bow were yet sticking out. Apparently, the Germans didn't recognize our predicament. After a trying two hour period, assistance came in the form of destroyers coming in at high speed, dropping their boats and firing at the shore batteries. It was a happy experience getting picked up and witnessing the destroyers bombarding the beach while rescuing us. A memorable sight it was, empty shell cases dropping out of the rear of the turrets on the ship we were being carried aboard.

Our story was at an end, the rest were carrying on the tremendous task. The mist had cleared, the

Personnel of D Company, Regina Rifles, occupying forward position, Normandy.

Photographer: Donald I. Grant (*National Archives of Canada PA 129402 sun had come out, the troops were going in on the ferries and the beach had assumed its original passive appearance.*

The sight cheered us as we were leaving the area, for we knew that, at least in our sector, shore battery opposition had been checked and the Army was landing by the thousands."

JUNO beach under mortar fire. Men bunched inside dunes with DD and AVRE but nothing is moving. The bombardment having failed to kill a single German or silence one weapon, means that "C" Company Canadian Winnipeg Rifles have to storm their positions "cold" and do so without hesitation.

"Bloody fighting raged all along the beaches. On the right, the Winnipegs had to battle their way past five major concrete casements and 15 machine gun positions set in the dunes commanding a long sweep of beach. From dune to dune, along the German trench systems, and through the tunnels, these Manitoba troops fought every yard of the way. They broke into the casements, ferretted out the gun crews with machine guns, grenades, bayonets and knives. The Canadians ran into cross-fire. They were shelled and mortared even in the German positions, but they kept slugging away at the enemy. After a struggle that was . . . bitter and savage ... the Winnipeg's broke through into the open country behind the beach." Regimental Diary

JUNO - Bray-sur-Mer. Maj. Fulton's, Winnipeg Rifles, company have quickly poured through the minefield at La Vallette and head straight for Graye-sur-Mer. They make good progress and some sections even approach Banville. While "D" Company is making this sprint, "A" and "C" Companies have landed, along with half of the Battalion Headquarters. The Beaches are still under fire when they land. For nearly two hours the Battalion Headquarters No. 22 wireless set was the target of much of this fire. It was a rough welcome for Headquarters.

"A" Company move inland towards St. Croix-sur-Mer where it comes under fire by a battery of eight machine guns. "C" Company makes its way towards Banville, where it is met by several pockets of enemy resistance which have been bypassed. They quickly overcome these obstacles and push southwards to Banville where they are confronted by three enemy machine guns which are situated on the high ground near the village. Hard fighting develops but "C" and "D" Companies manage to take the village. The first phase of the operation has been completed.

Bernières had been cleared, so "A" Company Queens Own follow in support of "C" and "D". The few remaining in "B" Company re-organize and are held back in Bernières until the afternoon. In the original plan "B" Company were to remain to form a firm base. Now there is no choice.

The brigade reserve, The Régiment de la Chaudière, have now landed; so too have The 14th Field Regiment RCA with its SP (self-propelled) guns. Their initial progress is held up by an enemy 88 mm on high ground overlooking the town. So deadly was the fire that four Priests (105mm artillery pieces mounted upon Sherman tank chassis) are knocked out. Then a detachment of The Queens Own Rifles of Canada, riding on a tank, outflanks the position and put the quietus on the crew.

Regina Rifles battalion headquarters group come ashore and the HQ is established. The Commanding Officer of the 13th Field Regiment co-locates his Regimental HQ with the Regina's battalion HQ, and from there he is able to direct the fire of the 95mm guns of the tanks of "B" Squadron. His own field guns are to come ashore later.

Troops landing on "Nan Green" Beach, on the left, are having rather rather less difficulty that the other sectors; the Crabs deal with the mines, an anti-tank ditch is filled with fascines dropped by the AVRE's, armoured bulldozers improve the lanes, and both planned exits (leading into the East Courseulles strongpoint) are now operational.

Widerstandsnest WN60 located near Cabourg overlooks the Fox Red sector of OMAHA and is situated some 60 meters above giving a good view of the beach and defending the F1 exit. About forty German soldiers man the position. The main armament is a 75mm gun. There is also a small Fire Control Post which gives an exceptional view of the eastern sector of the beach. At the south eastern corner was a Tobruk on which was installed a Renault tank turret from a R35 tank captured by the Germans in 1940. The four mortars installed on the site are a real threat. This position proved to be not as impregnable as the Germans had hoped. Slightly beneath was a shelf where the Americans troops sheltered, and finally took the position by climbing the cliffs to the east and taking the position from the rear. It was well fortified, it is the first strong point to fall to the Americans.

---
* Ross Munro, frontline reporter of The Canadian Press, in his despatch of that day, June 6, 1944:

Canadian tankers taking a break whilst sat on their Sherman tank

Canadian Archives.

At the headquarters of the 3/16th RCT, the capture of WN60 comes as a surprise as they felt they were impenetrable.

0905:
45 Royal Marine Commando lands at La Breche west of the River Orne as part of the 1st Special Service Brigade. They are to push inland and contact the 6th Airborne Division who were holding the bridges across the Caen Canal and the River Orne.

Each man carries the following rations on landing:
One emergency ration,
Two x 24hr landing rations,
20 cigarettes,
One Tommy Cooker with 6 refills,
Water sterilising Outfit,
one tin of preserved meat and a full bottle of water, with strict orders that rations are not to be consumed before landing and the Emergency Ration was not to be consumed unless permission was given by an officer.

Two days reserve rations are loaded in unit transport but are not to be used unless the normal supply system failed. Orders are that rations must not be removed from causalities before or during evacuation. Rum can be issued with the authority of the Brigade Commander. Local resources must be used as much as possible with the exception of water which will have been tested my a medical officer first.

LCI Nos 289 and 290 are hit near the beach - both start to sink with some causalities to 6 Troop. Further casualties occur on the beach which is under constant shell fire. Nevertheless, Commandos form up under CO (The Lord Lovat) and move to first check point.

The Canadian soldiers who landed on the Red Mike beach sector report that the situation is excellent

OMAHA - 726th Grenadier Regiment: *"WN 62 is presently not in action and only has a single gun intact. Enemy forces make a push between WN 61 and 62 to 63. More troops are landing from about fifty boats opposite WN 62.*

Calm has returned to WN 52, but. WN 37 is calling for reinforcements. Infantry and enemy tanks are heading towards Meuvaines."

0910:
OMAHA - The Rangers landing on the beach indicate that the tide is rising fast and that beach obstacles have still not been demolished. They ask request support from the demolition teams.

JUNO - 19th Field Regiments land and position their self-propelled guns for combat. The ever increasing number of troops and vehicles backing up on the beach are beginning to cause problems. Royal Corps of Engineers personnel open up breaches in the sea wall protecting the beach.

The two self-propelled artillery regiments employed on the 8th Brigade front, the 14th Field Regiment and the 19th Army Field Regiment, RCA, begin to land and have no real difficulty in getting off the beach.

0912:
914th Infantry Regiment: *"Many landing ships are now entering the Carentan Canal opposite WN 92 and 99. The landing has not yet begun. 5th and 6th Coy's 914th Infantry Regiment are engaged in combat against the paratroopers around Carentan Canal."*

0915:
JUNO - On "Mike Red" Beach, one exit is open across the dunes just west of Courseulles and the flooded area behind. A bridge is laid and a rough causeway built across an AVRE which had become submerged at a cratered culvert on the track which it had planned to use. Some tanks get across before the causeway fails and traffic has to be stopped until it is repaired.

General Omar Bradley is close to abandoning the continued landings at OMAHA because extra men can not get ashore as the beach and sea is full of casualties, the dead, wounded and dying.

Hitler wakes up, listens to the latest communiqués and then calls for Keitel and Jodl. He went to bed quite late the day before after listening to Wagner

916th Infantry Regiment: *"In front of WN 65, NE of St. Lawrence, sixty to seventy craft are landing troops at this moment. No report received from Pointe du Hoc. The situation is unchanged at Grandcamp. WN 65-68 and 70 are occupied by the enemy. Substantial new landings now taking place near WN 65 and 66."*

0917:
Communiqué no. 1 from the Supreme Headquarters Allied Expeditionary Forces is broadcast: *"Under the command of General Eisenhower, allied Naval forces supported by strong air forces, began landing allied armies, this morning, on the northern coast of France".*

Caption: Senior US officers watching operations from the bridge of USS Augusta (CA-31), off Normandy, 8 June 1944. They are (from left to right): Rear Admiral Alan G. Kirk, USN, Commander Western Naval Task Force; Lieutenant General Omar N. Bradley, US Army, Commanding General, US First Army; Rear Admiral Arthur D. Struble, USN, (with binoculars) Chief of Staff for RAdm. Kirk; and Major General Hugh Keen, US Army.

USNA 80-G-252940

0920:
ADMS (Assistant Director Medical Services) Royal Army Medical Corps visits the Main Dressing Station and proceeds up to the Caen Bridge with the CO under enemy machine gun fire and continuously sniped. Information is received that No. 2 Section, having established an Advanced Dressing Station at Bénouville, are cut off together with "A" Coy 7th Parachute Battalion. Several of No. 2 Section have not arrived at the rendezvous point. A Regimental Aid Post is established at the bridge site to collect casualties from 7th Para Battalion and "A" Company Ox and Bucks who are still holding the eastern bridge.

The ships in front of OMAHA Beach start firing on the German defences, as requested by General Huebner, who knows he risks firing at American troops. It lasts twenty-five minutes.

UTAH – USS *Fitch* stops to pick up more survivors from *Corry*

1st Division - 16th Regiment - 1st Battalion - "D" Company arrive on OMAHA Beach Easy Red and move in against a low bank while an exit is being cleared. The Mortar platoon and the 2nd platoon move into position along the beach and open fire on enemy positions approximately 75 yards away.

The German battery of Longues-sur-Mer ceases firing momentarily.

0921:
The 716th Infantry Division report that 30 enemy tanks are moving south toward Meuvaines.

0924:
GOLD – *Sycella*, wearing the flag of the Naval Commander, Eastern Task Force (NCETF) arrives. After giving support to the SWORD area she proceeds along the front keeping about two miles from the shore in order to judge the progress of the landings. Finding fighting on GOLD beach she fires 40 rounds at Arromanches at a range of about 8000 yards.

0925:
OMAHA - the 352nd Artillery Regiment report that 6 amphibious tanks are destroyed by mortars from the WN 35 strongpoint.

0928:
OMAHA - The 1st US Infantry Division is informed by the Ranger Commanding Officer that the enemy gun fire on exit D-G and an enemy battery behind Dog Green are hindering the landing.

0930:
SWORD Beach: the town of Hermanville is liberated by the South Lancashire Regiment with little opposition.

The Suffolks assemble near Hermanville and advance left into Colleville.

Les Roquettes is captured. By "C" Company Dorset Regiment.

General Gale is parachuted in North of Caen.

GOLD: Heavy German opposition halts the advance. With a fast incoming tide, the beach quickly becomes congested; the reserve brigades are held up. No 47 RM Commando land on Jig sector, Gold Beach and in doing so lose all but two of their LCA and much equipment including all their wireless sets. This does not deter them and they carry on with their objective to capture Port en Bessin. However, all contact is lost with them until the afternoon of the following day.

JUNO - A second exit is opened on Mike Green beach sector west of Courseulles.

16th Infantry Regiment, Company "L" calls the Battalion again and informs them that they are on the initial high ground. Almost immediately Sergeant Davis takes a patrol of three men to cut the road to Le Grand Hameau. He then adds one man to the patrol and moves up to the first building of Le Grand Hameau, looking for the flank of "J" Company. His mission also includes reconnaissance of a route by which "L" Company can advance. But while he was talking with a French civilian, a German came toward the patrol. They shot him.

At the same time machine guns start firing on the left and the patrol falls back toward the company. The troops claim that the Germans are drunk. Sergeant Davis could hear them laughing and giving commands in English in the hedgerows.

UTAH - Beach exits nos. 1, 2 and 3 are secured
OMAHA - General Omar Bradley receives an estimated loss report. 3,000 soldiers are out of the fight, while soldiers of the 16th Regiment of the 1st US Infantry Division are moving to Port-en-Bessin.

OMAHA - LCI 85 with the medical battalion on board makes two more attempts to land, a few men succeeding in getting ashore but several are cut down where they stand and others, still able to function are doing all they can for the injured. Fire is still raging in the hold and the ship continues to

Reloading on the beach at Hermanville
G Lugg personal collection.

Hellfire Crossroads - Hermanville
G Lugg, Personal Collection.

list. At this point a small landing boat comes alongside and about 30 men from the rear of the boat go aboard.

Sgt Len Lomell and S/Sgt Jack Kuhn of D Company Rangers discover 5 of the Pointe du Hoc relocated guns camouflaged in an orchard and trained upon UTAH beach with huge stockpiles of ammunition. Lommell and Kuhn render the guns unusable using thermite grenades, and escape before being detected. A message was sent back to Lt. Col. Rudder at Pointe du Hoc that the mission has been achieved

The top commanders are at sea, 11 miles from shore. The information that reaches them sounds like a complete disaster. General Omar Bradley, has to make a decision. Another assault by US troops, on UTAH has landed against little enemy opposition. Follow-up soldiers bound for OMAHA could be sent to UTAH beach instead. But troops could not be evacuated. Without reinforcements, and a break in the deadlock, all of the troops already on OMAHA would be killed or taken prisoner. It is a tough decision for General Bradley but he gives the order to press on. Something has to he done to help and Bradley calls in the big guns of the Navy.

After requisitioning a Sherman tank, the troops of French Commando Group under the command of Phillipe Kieffer (recently promoted to *Capitaine de Corvett*) seize the blockhouse and Riva Bella Casino at Ouistreham. His unit suffer 21 killed and 93 wounded; Kieffer himself is wounded almost immediately, having been hit by shrapnel in the leg, but refuses evacuation.

JUNO: The advance party of 176 Workshop and Park Company, Royal Engineers arrive on board the "*Clan Lamont*", a Cargo ship that has been quickly converted to a trooper with landing craft in the davits instead of lifeboats. Their mission is to land with the 3rd Canadians Infantry Division and recce for a site to receive and store bridging equipment for the Caen Canals and any other engineer equipment which will be landing later the next day by DUKW's. They are heading for Nan Red sector of the beach but the marker flag that greets them was Green, they were on Mike Green beach sector, right off target. This has happened as a result of the landing crafting veering suddenly to the right to avoid a "hedgehog" obstacle, part of the beach defences.

The sight that greets them on arrival is one of sheer devastation. An assault craft, broadside onto the beach, lay on its side, shattered; not a single Canadian soldier or the crew has made it. Two bodies are hanging from the side, where they have been blown by the force of the explosion. The clothing on the lower parts of their bodies, which are badly mutilated, are missing and large streaks of red ran down the side of the assault craft to the sea. Quite a number of damaged assault craft, some on fire, are beached. As the troops leave the craft and wade ashore there is an almighty sound behind them, the assault craft they have just left has been hit and is on fire, not all of the crew have survived.

A further LCI is heading for the beach but is ripped apart after hitting one of the shore defences, the troops jump out and have to push floating dead bodies aside to get to the beach. The smell of spilled diesel oil from all the damaged and abandoned vehicles filled the air. The beach master with his loud hailer is ordering troops off the beach to make way for the next wave.

"D" Company, Regina Rifles consisting of approximately 49 all ranks, is reorganised under the command of Lieutenant H.L. Jones. The company then sets out along the road to Reviers, two miles south, to seize the bridge over the Mue river. "C" Company, having accomplished its task in Courseulles, move on to join "D" Company at Reviers. There, both companies successfully attack a German HQ position, inflicting a number of casualties and taking more than 20 prisoners.

The town of Bernières is liberated by the men of the North Shore Regiment and the Queen's Own Rifles.

The German 352nd Artillery Regiment report that the WN 35 and 36 strongpoints are destroyed but the guns of the WN 40 destroyed 4 tanks and 3 landing crafts.

0931:
Scylla again fires on Arromanches before returning to anchor off SWORD.

0940:
SWORD - A dozen men of "X" Troop join up with 41 RM Commando and report that their Troop Commander Captain H.E. Stratford, M.C. has been wounded on landing and that they have also lost about 25 men killed and wounded on the beach.

"Y" Troop reports that the 2 i/c Major D.L. Barclay has been killed and that the Signal Officer Lieut. A.G. Aldis M.M. is a casualty. Lieut. Colonel Gray then decides to push on with the troops he has collected with "P" Troop followed by "Y" and "A". They start to move into Lion Sur Mer, followed by

"Sgt. Luckman reconnoitred a suitable place in which to grab a few hours sleep. The chosen house was large and in darkness as blackout conditions prevailed. It was locked and shuttered and when we broke in the inside doors were also locked. Even stranger, nearly every room was a bedroom, not long vacated it seemed for there was money on the bedside tables and some of the lamps were still alight. We looked at one another, some of us were pretty innocent - Sgt. Luckman laughed - of all the places he had chosen the local brothel!"

Mne. John B Wetjen, 47 Commando.

RM Museum Southsea ACQ 280/06

Cameron Highlanders of Ottawa having their breakfast in a farmyard that has suffered in the recent fighting.

© National Archives of Canada

three AVRE's to eliminate WN21 (Trout) and to attack the Chateau west of the town.

0945:
JUNO - 48 RM Commando regroups and pushes on to the Langrune strongpoint.

OMAHA - The second artillery barrage on the Beach comes to and end.

0950:
GOLD: Stiff resistance at Le Hamel. Commandos head for Port-en-Bessin to link with American forces.

OMAHA: Message to Division Commander aboard the USS *Ancon*, *"There are too many vehicles on the beach; send combat troops"*.

0955:
The 352nd German Infantry Division reports that all radio communications with the 916th Regiment have ceased.

10.00:
8th Parachute Battalion: Capt. Juckes Royal Engineers, reports to Battalion HQ that bridges were blown at 0915 and that he thinks Troarn bridge has also been blown. In addition he states that there is an Anti Tank gun, a Jeep and a glider plus 3 casualties in the river. An attempt was made to extract the Anti Tank gun but this was found to be impossible.

General Gale, Brigadier Poett and Brigadier Hugh Kindersley, Head of the 6th Airlanding Brigade head to Bénouville to assess the situation. They are walking across the bridge when two Kriegmarine boats set out aiming to get to Caen. Major Howard let them get to within 100 yards of the bridge before opening fire, the first boat is hit, goes out of control running into the east bank of the Orne with the crew surrendering. The second boat flees back to Ouistreham, it is later captured by No 4 Commando.

SWORD - After nearly three hours' fighting, La Brèche is captured. Its three guns and three heavy mortars, machine guns and rifle posts have done much damage to incoming and unloading craft during that time and have caused the attacking troops many casualties. Among those killed was the commanding officer of the South Lancashire, who lost, in all, five officers killed and six wounded with ninety-six other ranks killed or wounded. The East Yorkshires losses were equally heavy.

GOLD: The Green Howard's Battalion HQ and the majority of the Support Company are now firmly established ashore and proceeding as quickly as possible to the Battalion re-organising area at 904850 (East of Meuvaines) in the area of Pt52. The enemy are falling back quickly, but many snipers are left behind, hiding in the houses, woods and hedgerows to delay our advance. POW's are plentiful and these are being sent straight back to the beach.

OMAHA- 1st Division - 16th Infantry Regiment, establishes its Command Post (CP) just off the beach on the side of the hill East of St Laurent sue Mer. Battalions are moving forward, but are out of contact with Regimental CP. The beach and the entire territory are still under very heavy fire and companies are meeting heavy resistance. Several landing craft have received hits and troops still landing on the beach are receiving artillery fire, causing medium causalities. Things are becoming organized, however, and the situation is beginning to clear.

UTAH - Six battalions land including follow up troops – 12th and 22nd RCT's The La Madeleine strongpoint and the beach exits are captured.

OMAHA - Officers regroup their units and move among obstacles and minefields, searching for an exit out of what has become hell on earth. Thousands of dead and wounded are strewn upon the beach, mixed in with the drowning victims thrown up on the beach by the tide.

Incredibly, USS Texas closed to only 3,000 yds from the shoreline at OMAHA, almost grounding in an effort to give close support to the isolated groups which attempt to exit the beach and to bomb key points to the east of Moulins.

Men of the E/16th RCT seize WN64 situated to the east of Ruquet valley (Exit E1).

200 soldiers from 1st Battalion, 116th Regiment (29th US infantry division) have climbed the cliff and reach Vierville-sur-Mer.

German strong points inland are gradually overcome.

ROMMEL, unaware of the landings, calls his Chief of Staff, Lt. General Hans Speidel to get confirmation. He decides to drive immediately back to France and cancels his meeting with Hitler.

General Marcks takes the decision to counter-attack with the 21st Panzer Division.

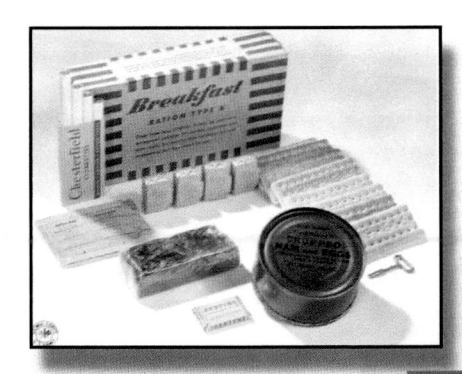

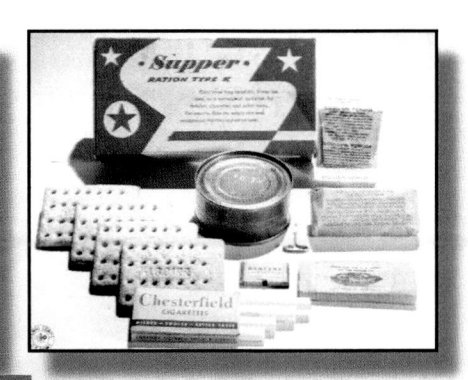

K Rations. USNA

R.A.M.C. attending to the wounded, note the cigarette in the injured mans hand.

R.A.M.C./PE/1/WALL/4

General Edgar Feuchtinger now receives the order to counter-attack with his tanks along the Orne river to deal with the paratroopers of the 6th British Airborne Division.

352nd Artillery Regiment: *"Information on the landings near WN 3 and 5, the enemy is on our left wing. Order to bombard the enemy with all canons available for the purpose of intercepting its supply lines. Report received from the 352nd Artillery Regiment: The status of ammunition IV/1352 AR is very worrying."*

1004:
JUNO - Advanced beach signal station "Nan" Red established

1010:
PT199 transfers a total of 61 *Corry* survivors, of which 12 were stretcher cases to USS *Bayfield*.

LA BRECHE: The LCI's carrying the 2nd Battalion KSLI (Kings Shropshire Light Infantry) touch down very much as planned at La Breche. It is NOT an easy landing with 4 to 5 ft of water and a sea running. The beach is still under Shell Fire. However with the aid of ropes carried ashore by the Navy the heavily laden men struggled ashore with few casualties and little loss of equipment. One LCI is hit by shell fire and sinks. All Companies then move forward to the Assembly Area as ordered whilst mopping up operations were still going on in houses adjacent to the beaches.

1012:
OMAHA - The command post of the German 726th Regiment of Grenadiers receive the following message from the WN 62 strongpoint: *" WN 62 is still firing with a machine gun, but the situation is critical. Elements of the 1st and 4th companies counter-attack"*.

Report received 726th Infantry Regiment: *Three auxiliary ships are sunk in the harbour of Port en Bessin direct hit by artillery.*

1015:
OMAHA - WN 62 strongpoint the two 76.5 mm guns are destroyed at the same time by the Naval artillery.

The German 916th Regiment reports that between 60 and 70 craft are landing soldiers in front of the WN 65 strongpoint at Saint-Laurent-sur-Mer. German troops of the Pointe du Hoc do not answer radio calls anymore.

1020:
SWORD - 48 RM Commando, B. Troop reports that Captain H. F. Morris Troop Commander is a casualty on the beach. Lieut. Colonel Gray then decides that since Force II had lost its commander, Major D.L. Barclay and both troop commanders he will take both forces under his own command and employ them as far as possible in their original role. "P" Troop then reports held up by LMG and sniper fire from the houses on either side of strong point.

1025:
OMAHA - three tanks are located by the German 916th west of the WN 38 strongpoint.

OMAHA - 115th Infantry land with the 1st and 2nd Battalions abreast on Fox Green beach, about 1000 yards east of that part of the beach on which it was intended to land. The 2nd Battalion on the right crossed the beach and start up the cliff, making slow progress due to mines. The progress of the 1st Battalion on the left was faster, it pushes inland to the South of St Laurent.

1030:
SWORD - On returning to the assembly area, 48 RM Commando CO orders them to move off according to plan. "B" Troop is to move straight to the beach defences immediately East of St Aubin ('Deathshead Section') while the remainder with "A" Troop as advance guard move on Langrune. Supporting LCG's (331 Flotilla Lt. Com. York) are asked over the radio link to lift fire from Deathshead Section at 1200 hrs. The advance is without incident; the vicinity of Langrune Church is found unoccupied.

West of UTAH Beach, American paratroopers of Dog Company (505th PIR) start fighting near the village of Neuville-au-Plain.

OMAHA - the two 75 mm guns of the Pointe de la Percee, the cause of widespread destruction, are taken out of action by the *McCook* destroyer.

OMAHA - 115th Infantry lands. WN 65 strongpoint, at the junction between the Easy Green and Easy Red beach sectors and protecting the E1 exit is now under control of the American troops.

Third platoon Company D of the 505th PIR (82nd Airborne), under orders of Lt. Turner Turnbull engages in combat at Neuville-au-Plain, outnumbered by the enemy 5 to 1. Thanks to their firepower and determination, the paratroopers hold off the enemy for 8 hours.

I shouted at the young mid-shipman to get the ramps down, and with a wave to the troops to follow I set off down it. I wasn't half way down before a big wave carried the boat off the obstacle we had apparently hit and somersaulted the ramp and me into the sea. I saw the great bows coming over me and the next thing I remember is finding myself walking up the beach, wet through of course, and with some of my equipment torn off, including my pistol, but was still clutching my stout ash walking stick.

Major D.J. Flunder, MC. VRD, 48 (RM) Cdo
RM Museum, Southsea 7/19/5

LCT 574 unloads on Juno beach 6th June 1944

Courtesy of Exbury Veterans Association and http://www.newforestww2.org/

OMAHA - H/116th blows a hole in the barbed wire with a Bangalore torpedo, heads down the beach about 200 yards and starts infiltrating through the gap. An enemy machine gun on the left kept up a continual fire which makes progress very slow. Their route is heavily mined, however, most of which are marked, and the engineers ware doing their best to take them out. After getting off the beach, they climb up a hill and cross another minefield before turning left and continuing on until they come to a road. The mortar platoon is set up in a position near some ruined buildings and a Command Post is also set up here. This position is approximately 600 yards from the beach. The machine gun platoons are in direct support of the rifle Companies. The 2nd Platoon can not be contacted and it is believed that they maybe captured

OMAHA -Two platoons of C/116th land on Easy Green beach from LCTs with bulldozers and about one ton of explosives each. Remnants of "B" and "C" Companies are then directed to exit D-1 and open it for traffic. It is necessary to wipe out several sniper positions before actual work could begin. Approximately 30 prisoners are taken in the ensuing action.

Two landing craft, LCT 30 and LCI(L) 44, steam full ahead through the obstacles off the Colleville beaches, firing all weapons at enemy strong points guarding the Colleville draw. The craft continue to fire after beaching. Not only did their action prove that the obstacles could be breached by ramming, but their fire, though failing to neutralize German positions in the Colleville draw, boosted the morale of the assault troops.

"At about 10.30 Jerry came over and bombed the beaches. What a row there was, then he started dive bombing us. Never will I forget that. There I was high on the bridge with no shelter and planes gliding down in the dark from all angles. We could not see them until they were on top of us. One dropped 3 bombs a few yards from us, he got such a warm welcome that he didn't come back. At 12 I went below to sleep, too tired to think of bombs, and slept like a log till 7.45." Signalman John Emrys Williams on-board HMS Diadem

Staffordshire Yeomanry touch down on White beach and have a dry landing. However, there is a terrible jam on the beach where no organization appears to be operating and no marked exits are to be seen. The majority of their tanks remain stationary for approx. 1 hour. In addition there is spasmodic shelling and a considerable amount of sniping. Traffic control seems nonexistent and even after leaving the beach vehicles remain head to tail for long periods on the only available routes. It is then decided not to proceed to the arranged Assembly Area and Sqns were ordered to rally in the area south of Hermanville. In order to save time CO 2 KSLI decided that his battalion should proceed on foot instead of riding on the tanks.

"C" Company. 1st Battalion Canadian Parachute Battalion takes an important pillbox that is giving them some trouble. The majority of "C" Company is dropped west of the River Dives, although some sticks are dropped a considerable distance away including one which landed west of the River Orne. Due to this confusion the company does not meet at the rendezvous as pre-arranged but goes into the assault on the Chateau and Varraville in separate parties. Major McLeod collects a Sgt. and seven OR's and proceeds towards Varaville. En route they are joined by a party under Lieut. Walker. One of the Sgts. is ordered to move his platoon to take up defensive positions around the bridge that the RE sections were preparing to blow. This is done and the bridge is successfully demolished.

Major McLeod and Lieut. Walker with the balance of the party then clear the Chateau and at the same time other personnel of "C" Company arrive from the DZ and clear the gatehouse of the chateau. The gatehouse then comes under heavy machine gun and mortar fire from the pill box situated in the grounds of the chateau. The pill-box also has a 75 mm A/Tk. Gun.

The whole position is surrounded by wire, mines and weapon pits. Major McLeod Lieut. Walker and five OR's climb to the top floor of the gatehouse to fire on the pillbox with a PIAT. The enemy 75mm A/Tk. gun returns fire and the shot detonates the PIAT ammunition. Lieut. Walker, Cpl. Oikle, Ptes. Jowlett and Nufield are killed instantly and Major McLeod and PTE. Bismuka fatally wounded. Ptes. Docker and Sylvester evacuate these casualties under heavy fire.

Captain Hanson, 2 i/c of "C" Company is slightly wounded and his batman killed while proceeding to report to the Brigade Commander who has arrived in the village from the area in which he dropped. "C" Company, together with elements of Brigade HQ and the RE's take up defensive positions around the village and a further party encircle the pill-box in order to contain the enemy. A further party of "C" Company under Lieut. McGowan who has been dropped some distance from the DZ arrive in Varaville in time to catch two German Infantry Sections who are attempting to enter the town. Lieut. McGowan's platoon open fire causing casualties and the remainder of the enemy

Nazi propaganda - the official caption that went with this photo reads:-

The "liberators" and the liberated.

Like a roll of destruction fall the bombers of the Anglo-Americans over the cities and villages of Normandy. In a few minutes they destroy what was built centuries ago. The number of peaceful French, who are buried under the rubble, is huge.

Bundesarchiv Bild 146/1983 077-23A

surrender. This platoon takes up firing positions firing on the enemy pill-box. "C" Company HQ which is located in the church yard pins an enemy section attempting to advance in a bomb crater killing at least three. The Chateau is evacuated and left as a dressing station. An enemy patrol re-enters the Chateau and captures the wounded including Capt. Brebner, the Unit MO and CSM Blair of "B" Company.

Heavy enemy Mortar Fire and sniping is brought to bear from the woods surrounding Varaville. During this time the local inhabitants are of great assistance, the women dressing wounds and the men offering assistance in any way. One Frenchman in particular, R Guenard, distinguished himself. Upon being given a red beret and a rifle he killed three German Snipers. This man subsequently guided the Brigade Commander and his party towards Le Mesnil. Although it is believed he is a casualty of the bombing attack that caught this party en route to Le Mesnil.

At approximately 1030 hours the enemy pill-box eventually surrendered.

General Feuchtinger is ordered to move his Panzer division to the west of the Orne Canal, and to the north of the Bayeux-Caen line.

1040:
SWORD - "P" Troop still held down. South Lancs at this time are drawing mortar and machine gun fire and are taking casualties.

J.P Royle, Major, No.1 Wing Glider Pilot Regiment reports *"Embarrassing but hearty reception from French females!"* In the Ranveille area.

Five beach exits have now been cleared from JUNO.

1045:
Ranville, a further attack by the enemy develops supported by self-propelled guns, which penetrate the village but are beaten off by 12th Parachute Battalion while 4th Air-landing Anti-Tank Battery accounted for three self-propelled guns and one tank.

UTAH fairly secure, reserve battalions coming ashore.

1050:
SWORD - Lieut. Colonel Gray orders "Y". Troop to prepare to back up the South Lancs and if possible to assault through them. 3 AVRE tanks arrive to assist when required. They were immediately put in support of "Y". Accordingly, the tanks moved up the road with "Y" Troop following. Within 100 yards of the strongpoint, an unidentified gun, which later proved to be a 50mm PAK, opens fire at very short range and knocks out the first tank. Within 5 minutes all 3 tanks are put out of action and enemy mortars have ranged on "Y" Troop which suffer casualties including Captain P.T.H. Dufton killed. The remainder of the Troop occupy the houses on each side of the road.

Reserve brigades begin to land on GOLD ; seven beach exits are secured. No 48 Commando have taken the Langrune coastal strip.

"Bombing by our medium bombers taking place. Battleships still sailing up and down beaches, firing all the time. Rocket firing craft now sailing backwards and forwards firing salvo after salvo at fortifications and inland. Noise beyond belief! We have now taken up position 3 miles from UTAH beach and have three destroyers and three spitfires for our protection. We are now controlling all Spitfires over beaches. Six RAF Air Sea Rescue Launches now fastened to 216." LAC Armitage

1055:
OMAHA - 1st and 2nd Battalions 16th Infantry Regiment get in contact with the Regimental Command Post and are moving forward slowly, hitting very heavy resistance.

1100:
ADMS recce several houses for Main Dressing Station for 195th Airlanding Field Ambulance.

The radio station of the Pointe de la Percee is attacked by USS *Thompson* who then lays in wait for the tell tale of sign of the flashes of the enemy guns revealing themselves.

18th Infantry begins to land at OMAHA.

UTAH - Germans intensify long range artillery fire on the beach and inflict some causalities, but have little effect in slowing up operations. Rear-Admiral Moon subsequently remarked *"Intelligence indicated extremely heavy defences against landing on "UTAH" beach. The 28 batteries defending the beach consisted of 111 guns heavy to medium calibre. Information obtained from air reconnaissance indicated that at least 75% of these guns were effective at the time of assault despite extensive pre D-Day bombing. Examination of captured batteries indicates that approximately 50% of the guns were still operational after capture. The neutralization of these formidable batteries by the bombardment group was so effective that these batteries offered*

US Navy pilots are briefed before flying a gunfire spotting mission over the Normandy beach heads, circa June-July 1944. Those present are (from left to right):
Wing Commander Robert J. Hardiman, RAF, Commanding Allied Spotter Pilots;
Ensign Robert J. Adams, USNR;
Major Noel East, British Army Intelligence;
Lieutenant Harris Hammersmith, Jr., USNR; and
Captain John Ruscoe, Royal Artillery, Gunnery Liaison Officer.
The US Navy officers are pilots of US Navy Cruiser Scouting Squadron Seven (VCS-7), which switched from their usual Curtiss SOC Seagull floatplanes to British Supermarine Spitfire fighters during the Normandy operation. VCS-7 was based at Royal Naval Air Station Lee-on-Solent, Hampshire (UK), and drew planes from a pool of Supermarine Spitfire or Seafire fighters. The squadron flew a total of 191 sorties between 6 and 25 June 1944, losing one aircraft to ground fire.

Official US Navy photograph 80-G-302115.

little opposition to either assault or follow up. As a result all landings of troops, equipment and supplies were accomplished with minor losses."

General Bradley receives the first encouraging reports of the day. One reads *"Men advancing up slope behind Easy Red. Men believed ours on skyline."*

SWORD - The 2nd Battalion KSLI, have assembled in the orchards immediately north of Hermanville as planned. Every officer and man has carried ashore a sandbag labelled with his name and in there is placed gas masks, cardigans and some other items of clothing and then dumped by Companies. This was well worth while and 95% were recovered the following day, the missing 5% destroyed by shelling. The Staffordshire Yeomanry (Sherman Tanks) were now landing and are supposed to advance on Caen, but make little progress forward, owing to congestion on the roads.

GOLD: The first wave of Durham Light Infantry hit the beaches, Private Geoffrey Moss, 151 Brigade, 9th Battalion was one of them. *"The noise around the beaches was like being in hell with 75 rockets being fired at once. Warships were circling around in groups of three waiting to go in. Battleship Warspite came broadside causing large waves and nearly turned our Landing Craft over. There were 6 American crew on the Landing Craft putting them ashore.*

"A lot of soldiers drowned trying to get off the landing craft and wading through the sea due to the weight of the equipment they were carrying. All equipment was strapped on very loosely in case we needed to take it off for fear of drowning, but this did not help a large number of them who did not make it onto the beach.

The equipment we had to carry included:
2 x ammunition pouches, containing bullets and hand grenades - one carried over each shoulder
Rifle
Pick
Shovel
Food pack
Emergency packs i.e. chocolate bar (only to be eaten in extreme hunger)
Airborne collapsible bike
2 cooking tins
French francs
'Housewife' - needle and threads
Boot polish
Each soldier was issued with a blanket and if you died you were buried in your blanket. The army charged the parents £1 for this.

My push bike probably saved my life when I bent down to undo the wing nuts to put the bike together, a bullet hit the bike and shot out a spoke on the wheel. The bikes were due to be used to get through the woods but had to be left behind, as all the trees were gone.

Once at Asnelles we got off the beach fairly quickly although there was a great loss of life from German fire. The noise was 'like hell on earth' with all the shelling, shooting and land mines going off all around them. Once over the dunes we went over high hedges, which we could not see what was on the other side, we then made our way down the tracks and through cornfields and onto Bayeux. During the march we saw lots of dead cows in fields who had died from shock, some were still standing up and some were on their backs with their feet in the air. Injured troops could be found in the cornfields as their rifle had been stood up in the ground in order for medics to find them easily. The cornfields were very high and we crawled on our hands and knees through them and the dust made us choke. The edge of the cornfields had been cut down for about 12 ft so when we came out of the fields, it was easy for us to be spotted by Germans before they entered the next one."

OMAHA - Message received by Commander Transport Three states that German defenders are leaving their posts and surrendering to US troops. Shortly followed by another message from a message of the V Corps staff embarked in a DUKW near the shore line stating that the troops were advancing up the western slope of the exit from Sector Easy.

Radio Message to Panzer Meyer: *What time will you start your attack? In what direction?*

1101:
Information from the 716th Infantry Division: *"On our right, off the bay opposite the mouth of the Orne, we can count thirty cruisers and a large number of landing craft. The enemy is able to penetrate on both sides of Château Vaux (Courseulles)".*

1110:
101st and 4th divisions' linkup on UTAH securing the first exit from the beach.

Report received III/726e Grenadier Regiment: *"Contrary to previous reports, WN 66 and 68 north of St. Lawrence, still holding firmly. At Pointe du Hoc, the enemy broke through with the two companies. Available reserves have been used to*

The US Coast Guard manned USS LST-21 unloads British Army tanks and trucks onto a "Rhino" barge during the early hours of the invasion on Gold Beach, 6 June 1944. Note the nickname "Virgin" on the "Sherman" tank.

USNA 26-G-2370

restore the situation. Observers say the enemy fired on the cliff with special shells containing rope ladders, with which you can easily climb the cliff".

1112:
JUNO - After heavy fighting, 7th Brigade secures the beach exit at Courseulles (Mike Red sector) and gets one exit fully working again.

914th Infantry Regiment: *"North of Pointe du Hoc, twenty large naval vessels are observed on the high seas, as well as two hundred to three hundred landing craft".*

1114:
726th Grenadier Regiment: *"At 11.10, the I/916e Infantry Regiment began to attack the enemy on the coast 22 km east of Asnelles. It seems that the enemy have now captured Asnelles. The situation on the left side is critical because the enemy has already reached the church of Colleville. WN 60 and 62 are able to defend themselves successfully".*

1115:
Rum ration just been issued and 'wakey-wakey' tablets to keep us going. – LAC Armitage

More reserve Brigades land on GOLD

JUNO - On the left sector, the North Shore Regiment find that the St. Aubin strongpoint appeared not to have been touched by the preparatory bombardment. "B" Company have the task of dealing with it, and this is done with the assistance of the tanks and later the AVREs, which use their petards with effect. The co-operation of infantry and tanks is excellent and the strongpoint is gradually reduced. The area was cleared four hours and five minutes after landing. It appears, however, that there is still sniping going on after this time.

OMAHA- CO 16th Infantry Regiment to Co 2nd Battalion Radio *"2nd Battalion is to hold up at point 38. Do not move further forward until you hear from us".*

1120:
Reply *"Hold up at 38. Right, and we have contact with 2nd Battalion. The 5th Company. is reported to be located at Surrain".*

OMAHA - Elements of the 5th Ranger Battalion reach the town of Surrain (South of Colleville-sur-Mer).

Banville and Ste Croix are reported captured by Canadian 8th Brigade.

1127:
OMAHA - the 916th Regiment of Grenadiers reports that the attackers hold the heights above the beach of Saint-Laurent-sur-Mer. The commander of the 352nd Infantry Division gives the following order *"Counter-attack the enemy to push it back to the sea".*

1130:
13th/18th Royal Hussars, Lieut Coker, with 5 tanks "B" Sqn begin to support 1st Special Service Brigade onto the Bridges at Bénouville over the Canal-de-Caen and the River Orne, which were taken over intact from 6th Airborne Div.

Two "B" Sqn Tanks are knocked out by 88mm South of Bénouville.

1st Dorsets now advancing across the open ground towards Buhot. On the right flank of the advance, "C" company cross the road from St Come de Fresné and press on towards their objective of the German strong point at Point 54. As they begin to climb the hill, they come under heavy fire from Point 54. Lieutenant Hamilton, leading them, is wounded. Corporal Carter takes command of the platoon and organised covering fire for 13 platoon, who make attempts to fight their way up the wooded track from Le Buhot to Point 54.

41 RM Commando, "B" Troop report that they have pushed ahead as far as the Cross Roads and that they have suffered casualties from mortar fire and from some unidentified mobile gun operating in the area and that (temporarily) without some support on the Chateau area they can not push on. The South Lancs have not been contacted. Since no support was available, their own 3" mortars having expended all their ammunition on the strongpoint, "B" Troop were told to remain where they were.

14th Army Field Regiment, R.C.A. now have 18 guns in action near Bernières

OMAHA - 16th Infantry, 1st Division. "F" Company runner returns from the Battalion with orders from Captain Finke to move all 2nd Battalion men to the right, where a breakthrough has been made about 500 yards down the beach. When the Company finally assemble at Battalion HQ, only the Company CO, 1st Sergeant, and 10 Privates are present. These Privates are used as local security for the Battalion CP. The 1st Sergeant by placing three men to the left flank of the CP is fired upon and pinned down temporarily by an enemy machine gun. One of the men manage to return to the CP immediately after he is fired upon and informed the Company CO that he believed the 1st Sergeant to be hit by the machine gun fire. Upon

> *"The order of the day, for all men was to get off the beach as quick as possible, do not stop, do not attempt to pick up survivors, there are others there to do that, just get off the beach."*

Aerial shot of US troops landing on Omaha beach.

USNA

receiving this information, Captain Finke, with one Private try to capture or kill the enemy machine gunner by working his way around the flank. He succeeds in getting to within 75 yards of the gun but both he and the Private are wounded by mortar fire and are evacuated to the aid station. This leaves the Company with no officers, a 1st Sergeant, and about 10 Privates.

"Our landing area was dictated by the presence of the beach obstacles. We had to land about 400 yards from the actual seawall. The men wading ashore were halted due to the shock of tremendous amount of fire on them and no place to go.

We had difficulty getting the men to move. There was great deal of enemy fire and they would take cover behind some of these obstacles that were there to catch assault craft. They were about the size of a ten or twelve foot telephone pole with a teller mine on the top of it. The whole area was just full of these obstacles. Any port in a storm. People would just try to take cover behind one of these poles. Well, it didn't provide any cover so you just had to force them to move no matter how you did it. It had so happened, I had sprained my ankle in the marshalling area and had to go ashore carrying a cane instead of a rifle. I used it to very good effect to just whack people until they moved. And it was not much fun obviously.

It was very rough getting up the beach because the sand was wet and deep and people would sink in. Everybody had a heck of a large load to carry so that the men were worn out when they got up there. Of course we lost quite a few on the way up. In fact, in that 400 yards I might have lost 25% of my command before we even got to the seawall. Of the 4 officers that were killed on the beach from my company, I think three of them were killed right almost right at the water's edge." Captain Finke

Information received by the 709th Infantry Division: *New landings are made across the width of the front. The enemy has managed to break through in many places.*

1133:
JUNO – Reserve Brigade Group arrive.

1135:
50th Division (British) is notified that 16th Infantry was in Colleville-sur-Mer and other units are progressing slowly and beaches are not yet cleared of fire. Commanding General instructs the LCG to fire on the church steeple in Vierville

1138:
Report received from the Luftwaffe in Caen: *"At 1121 fourteen large enemy ships were spotted off Grandcamp."*

1140:
OMAHA - 726th Grenadier Regiment: *"The South West exit at Colleville was captured by the enemy. More tanks are unloading in front of WN 62. Many tanks are stuck at the antitank ditch."*

1142:
914th Infantry Regiment: *"At sea, we now count twenty-two ships topped with balloons."*

1145:
OMAHA - The 1st Battalion, 18th Infantry Regiment (1st US ID) have landed.

1st Division - 16th Infantry Regiment to 1st Battalion, Radio. *"18th has landed. They will go in on your right. They will take your objective. You dig in and prepare for a counterattack. OK. "A" is on the right, "C" on the left, with "B" Co. following. We are still advancing slowly."*

16th Infantry Regiment to CO 2nd Battalion, Radio - *"I talked to Capt. Smith and told him about the 18th. How soon can you move the rear part of your CP here by us up forward? We have someone on the way back now to pick them up and guide them forward".*

1148:
Information received by the 709th Infantry Division on the left: *"We are no longer in contact with Carentan. The situation on the left is quiet."*

1150:
48 Commando "X "Troop is detached to tackle the next sector of beach defence (Dogfish One). "A" and "Z" Troops face South to prevent an enemy counter attack. "A" Troop send a patrol to the Bridge North of Luc sur Mer which is found unoccupied with orders to guard the bridge and make contact with 41 (RM) Commando. However, 41 Commando, are badly held up at Lion-sur-Mer and never reach the bridge.

The 6th Green Howards move on to Crepon.

"I sent them in I'm going to get them out". CSM Stan Hollis.

The 6th Green Howards are shelled on approach to Crepon. The shooting is coming from the village. D Company is ordered into the village to ascertain if the roads are passable. CSM Stan Hollis in the

Private Geoff Moss, Durham Light Infantry.

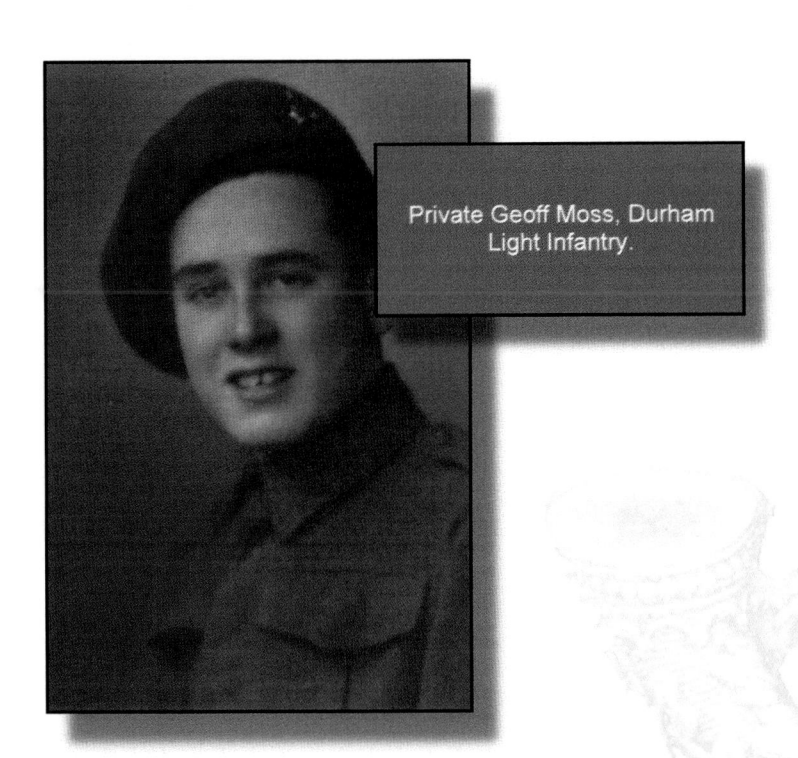

Durham Light Infantry advancing through a cornfield in Normandy.

Jim Tuckwell personal collection

meantime has taken command of no 16 Platoon after their officer had been killed. Hollis and his men enter the courtyard of the farm "du Pavillion" situated on the road out of the village to the west.

After searching the farm and only finding a young boy, Hollis searches the surroundings and the orchard behind the farm. Reaching the end of the wall a bullet whistles past his head. Hollis quickly takes cover and waits a few minutes before starting to crawl forward to start his observations again. He sees two dogs and a well camouflaged artillery gun behind a hedge 150m away. He returns with a small group of men and decides to attack with a PIAT.

Hollis and two men crawl through a field of rhubarb towards the gun, at the same time the rest of his men enter the orchard to cover Hollis. They are greeted by fire from men defending the battery and one short burst killed all eight men. Whilst this was happening Hollis and his two men have reached the other side of the rhubarb field and are now 50 meters away from the German position. Hollis loaded the PIAT and fires towards the target, it lands short, the battery was out of range. The Germans turn their gun and fire back almost immediately, in their haste to fire they have forgotten to lower the barrel and the shot goes over Hollis's head. Hollis shouted at his two men to follow him and he quickly crawls back across the field to join the rest of the battalion. At this point a deluge of fire rains down upon the orchard and it was then that Hollis realised that his two men have not retreated with him. He seizes a light machine gun and dashes towards the orchard. He finds his two men pinned down by enemy fire. He makes himself visible to the Germans to attract enemy fire and shouts at his two men to get back and then fires in the direction of the enemy. His magazine empty, he re-joins his two men under the shelter of the wall and together they make their way back to the company. For the second time that day CSM Hollis has come face to face with the enemy to save the life of his men. For his actions he is awarded the Victoria Cross, the only one awarded on D Day. His citation reads as follows…

In Normandy on 6 June 1944 Company Sergeant-Major Hollis went with his company commander to investigate two German pill-boxes which had been by-passed as the company moved inland from the beaches. "Hollis instantly rushed straight at the pillbox, firing his Sten gun into the first pill-box, He jumped on top of the pillbox, re-charged his magazine, threw a grenade in through the door and fired his Sten gun into it, killing two Germans and taking the remainder prisoners.

Later the same day… C.S.M. Hollis pushed right forward to engage the [field] gun with a PIAT from a house at 50 yards range… He later found that two of his men had stayed behind in the house in full view of, the enemy who were continually firing at him, he went forward alone distracting their attention from the other men. Under cover of his diversion, the two men were able to get back.

Wherever the fighting was heaviest he appeared, displaying the utmost gallantry… It was largely through his heroism and resource that the Company's objectives were gained and casualties were not heavier. …..he saved the lives of many of his men.

The Rev. T.H. Lovergrove, Padre for the 6th Battalion Green Howards, witnessed the event. "On the right D Coy were faced with a Pill Box at the end of a trench within 20 yards of where they had advanced and were immediately under fire from the Pill Box at which point CSM Stan Hollis rushed forward climbing on the top of it and managed to deal with it single handed. Lt. Colonel Robin Hastings commented " Hollis was personally dedicated to winning the war-one of the few men I ever met who felt like that"

JUNO – 9th Canadian Infantry arrive.

1158:
The 726th Regiment of Grenadiers report that three landing craft have sunk in Port-en-Bessin

1200:
Churchill speaks to the House of Commons. "…I have also to announce to the House that during the night and the early hours of this morning the first of the series of landings in force upon the European Continent has taken place. In this case the liberating assault fell upon the coast of France. An immense armada of upwards of 4,000 ships, together with several thousand smaller craft, crossed the Channel. Massed airborne landings have been successfully effected behind the enemy lines, and landings on the beaches are proceeding at various points at the present time. The fire of the shore batteries has been largely quelled. The obstacles that were constructed in the sea have not proved so difficult as was apprehended. The Anglo-American Allies are sustained by about 11,000 first line aircraft, which can be drawn upon as may be needed for the purposes of the battle. I cannot, of course, commit myself to any particular details. Reports are coming in in rapid succession. So far the Commanders who are engaged report that everything is proceeding according to plan. And what a plan! This vast operation is undoubtedly the most complicated and difficult that

Motorised patrols of Fallschirmjaeger

Bundesarchiv, Bild 101I-585-2182-31A / Zimmermann / CC BY-SA *has ever taken place. It involves tides, wind, waves, visibility, both from the air and the sea standpoint, and the combined employment of land, air and sea forces in the highest degree of intimacy and in contact with conditions which could not and cannot be fully foreseen.*

There are already hopes that actual tactical surprise has been attained and we hope to furnish the enemy with a succession of surprises during the course of the fighting. The battle that has now begun will grow constantly in scale and in intensity for many weeks to come, and I shall not attempt to speculate upon its course. This I may say, however. Complete unity prevails throughout the Allied Armies. There is a brotherhood in arms between us and our friends of the United States. There is complete confidence in the supreme commander, General Eisenhower, and his lieutenants, and also in the commander of the Expeditionary Force, General Montgomery. The ardour and spirit of the troops, as I saw myself, embarking in these last few days was splendid to witness. Nothing that equipment, science or forethought could do has been neglected, and the whole process of opening this great new front will be pursued with the utmost resolution both by the commanders and by the United States and British Governments whom they serve. I have been at the centres where the latest information is received, and I can state to the House that this operation is proceeding in a thoroughly satisfactory manner. Many dangers and difficulties which at this time last night appeared extremely formidable are behind us. The passage of the sea has been made with far less loss than we apprehended. The resistance of the batteries has been greatly weakened by the bombing of the Air Force, and the superior bombardment of our ships quickly reduced their fire to dimensions which did not affect the problem. The landings of the troops on a broad front, both British and American- -Allied troops, I will not give lists of all the different nationalities they represent-but the landings along the whole front have been effective, and our troops have penetrated, in some cases, several miles inland. Lodgments exist on a broad front.

The outstanding feature has been the landings of the airborne troops, which were on a scale far larger than anything that has been seen so far in the world. These landings took place with extremely little loss and with great accuracy. Particular anxiety attached to them, because the conditions of light prevailing in the very limited period of the dawn-just before the dawn-the conditions of visibility made all the difference. Indeed, there might have been something happening at the last minute which would have prevented airborne troops from playing their part.

A very great degree of risk had to be taken in respect of the weather.

But General Eisenhower's courage is equal to all the necessary decisions that have to be taken in these extremely difficult and uncontrollable matters. The airborne troops are well established, and the landings and the follow-ups are all proceeding with much less loss-very much less-than we expected. Fighting is in progress at various points. We captured various bridges which were of importance, and which were not blown up. There is even fighting proceeding in the town of Caen, inland. But all this, although a very valuable first step-a vital and essential first step-gives no indication of what may be the course of the battle in the next days and weeks, because the enemy will now probably endeavour to concentrate on this area, and in that event heavy fighting will soon begin and will continue without end, as we can push troops in and he can bring other troops up. It is, therefore, a most serious time that we enter upon. Thank God, we enter upon it with our great Allies all in good heart and all in good friendship." Churchill and King George VI dined together at Buckingham Palace and then drove to SHAEF HQ and then on to see ACM Sir Trafford Leigh Mallory at his HQ of the Allied air Forces to see first hand the reports coming in from the beach-heads.

Berlin also put out a statement: *The long expected attack by the British and Americans on the coast of northern France began last night.*

A few minutes after midnight the enemy landed airborne formations in the area of the Seine Bay, simultaneously making heavy bombing attacks. Shortly afterwards, numerous enemy landing boats, protected by heavy allied naval units, approached the coast on other sectors.

The German defenders were nowhere taken by surprise. They immediately took up the fight with the greatest energy. The parachute troops were partly engaged as they came down and the enemy ships were taken under effective fire while still on the high seas. Many parachute units were wiped out or taken prisoner; others were torn to pieces by exploding mines.

In spite of violent air attacks and heavy bombardment from the enemy ships, the guns of the Atlantic Wall immediately intervened in the fighting. They scored hits on battleships and on landing craft screened from view by smoke. The battle against the invasion troops is in full swing.

45 RM Commando reach Colleville-sur-Orne which is being heavily shelled.

R.A.M.C. assisting an injured soldier to a stretcher.

R.A.M.C./PE/1/WALL/4

UTAH – *"Our cooks are now carrying ammunition to guns, so no warm food. Corned beef sandwiches and hard American biscuits for lunch. Back on W/T watch once again until 1600 hours. Still very heavy seas running. German Air Force now waking up and bags of hostiles approaching. Still loads of trouble on the beaches."* LAC Armitage.

Commanding Officer, 2nd Battalion KSLI (Kings Shropshire Light Infantry), British 3rd Division reports to Brigade Command in Hermanville that only about one and a half Squadrons of Staffordshire Yeomanry are clear of the beaches and that a large minefield apparently covers the right flank of Hermanville across the axis of advance originally planned for the tanks. Brigade Command then orders the Battalion to advance on foot along main axis. The Staffordshire Yeomanry to marry up as soon as possible.

I.A. Murray. Lieut-Colonel, Commanding No.1 Wing The Glider Pilot Regiment visits 6th Airborne HQ and makes the following observations:
(1) The white stripes on gliders are of great value for picking out gliders already landed. If these markings are dispensed with in future something of the same nature on upper surfaces of wings is most desirable.
(2) The green hollophane lights were excellent but the red air sea rescue lights were not seen by all pilots.
(3) Differential brakes are essential when landing on L.Zs. which have posts erected.
From experience of this operation the following changes of equipment are suggested:-
(i) 2 trained snipers per section with snipers rifles fitted with telescopic sights.
(ii) Rucksacks in place of present web equipment.
(iii) Torches are not needed in operations as each glider has one as part of its equipment.
(iv) One jeep is required for Wing H.Q. if the Glider Pilot force is in more than one locality.
(v) In the place of T.S.M. guns it is suggested that each section should have two Mark V Sten guns. With the exception of the above, the equipment was most satisfactory. The morale of the men was very high, especially those forming part of gun crews.

8th Parachute Battalion - Royal Engineers return from Bures and it is decided to send a Royal Engineers party with a Jeep and explosives and one strong platoon into Troarn to blow the bridge or, if already blown, to widen the gap. Remainder of Battalion will move to the road junction. No word has been received of the patrol that has gone to recce northern approaches to Troarn. Force to blow bridge at Troarn is to move via Bures and then down axis of road south to Troarn.

224th Field Ambulance Main Dressing Station now set up in a farm near Le Mesnil, on instructions of Senior Officer in the Brigade. present (Lt.Col. A.S. Pearson D.S.O. M.C. 8 Battalion. The Parachute Regt). Number of casualties treated 5 officers & 47 O.Rs. (& 2 civilians). 10 operations performed by Capt. Gray.

6th Green Howard's report that they have successfully completed Phase 1 and are fast pushing on to Crepon.

UTAH - The four beach exits are now in the hands of the 101st Airborne paratroopers.

Pouppeville is captured; the link-up with the airborne forces is made. US troops gradually fan out to Beuzeville au Plain and Les Forges. German defences are penetrated in four places. US troops begin to move inland, although the beach is still under heavy fire. Sufficient space has been gained for the continuing smooth build-up.

Pointe du Hoc - The 6 last defenders of the observation post surrender to the American Rangers. Colonel Rudder transmits the following message *"Have reached the Pointe du Hoc. Completed. Need ammunition and reinforcements. Heavy losses"*.

After liberating Courseulles, three Regina Rifle Companies joins forces to march on Reviers.

Further landings at JUNO. Langrune is captured.

OMAHA - because of the lack of ammunition, the German Houtteville battery (4,500 meters from the beach, near Colleville-sur-Mer) refuses to fire salvos against the landing crafts approaching. 105 mm guns can only fire single shots.

1205:
OMAHA - US 1st Infantry Division to 16th Infantry Regiment, Commanding Officer - *"Can we get any tanks up to Colleville-sur-Mer?"*

A: *"No, none of them are up to here yet. They aren't off the beach. However, as soon as we can possibly get anything up, we will shoot it up to you. Keep yelling for it."*

914th Infantry Regiment: *"The shootout is conducted by the II / 1352nd Artillery Regiment at WN 3 and 5 to the left, where the enemy landed its entire companies. WN 1 is circled by the enemy."*

Artillery men of one the of Cannon Companies of the three 4th ID Infantry Regiments fire their 105mm howitzer at German positions.

USNA 111-SC-191933

Nazi propaganda photo with original text.

"This is their conception of the "liberation" of Europe! The city of St. Lo in Normandy, which was attacked by the Anglo-American air gangsters completely in ruins, this is the clearest evidence of the disposition of the aggressors against the French, who by this "liberation" have been killed in their hundreds."

Bundesarchiv, Bild 146-1994-035-17 / Vennemann / CC BY-SA

Lance-Corporal of the Royal Canadian Army Medical Corps attends to the wound on a young boys leg.

National Archives of Canada.

1210:
US 1st Infantry Division to 16th Infantry Regiment, Commanding Officer, Radio *"We must have some tanks or artillery up here soon. Will you see what you can do about it for us?"*

A. *"OK."*

1251:
Regina Rifles "C" Company reports that the bridge at Reviers had been secured.

1220:
Information received by the 709th Infantry Division: *The penetration of enemy tanks has already reached a depth of four kilometres. Before WN 3 and 5, one can observe twenty-two landing craft with barrage balloons. Counter measures in the form of tank reinforcements from the North and South-West are on their way.*

1223:
OMAHA - The 18th Infantry Regiment climbs the cliff and heads towards Colleville-sur-Mer.

1225:
General Gerow on USS *Ancon* was finally informed that American troops had been seen advancing up the slopes. East Red beach is now relatively safe, allowing reinforcements to land.

Germans report: *"Our troops in position at Pointe du Hoc are surrounded by two enemy companies. A counter attack is launched by elements of III/726e Grenadier Regiment."*

1230:
8th Parachute Battalion - War Diaries: O.C. "A" Company and Signals Officer reports to Battalion HQ. They have been dropped some 5 miles south of the Drop Zone. They bring one man with them. Major Wilson's patrol arrive back at the same time. Maj. Wilson states that he has met no opposition to the north of Troarn, but on moving further west down the railway line they run into a strong German position which pinned them down by fire. When they start to withdraw the Intelligence Officer moves off by a different route from the remainder of the party and has not been seen since.

SWORD, HMS *Ramilles*, *Warspite* and *Arethusa* start bombing coastal gun batteries.

177 French soldiers under Phillipe Kieffer link up with Airborne Division at Bénouville thus successfully completing their mission.

1235:
OMAHA - Division Commander is informed by Commander LCT Flotilla 19, *"LCT 623 reports Easy Red Beach closed by enemy fire"*. The Commander asked, *"Do you intend to shell or shall we continue to beach LCT's?"*. The Division intercepts a radio message to V Corps which states that enemy artillery was registering on Easy Red Beach and firing when craft arrived there; believed craft could be seen from church spire at Vierville.

Report received from the 726th Grenadier Regiment: *"Colleville is retaken. We are still in possession of WN 62 and 62b. However, 61 is still occupied by the enemy, including a tank."*

1240:
General Bradley receives a message from OMAHA Beach: *"Troops here blocked on the ground at Easy Red. Advancing through the cliffs overlooking Easy Green and Easy Red, reinforcements are arriving and the injured being evacuated."*

OMAHA - 726th Regiment of Grenadiers reports that the southern exit of Colleville-sur-Mer has been reached by the Americans and that many tanks were stopped by antitank ditches.

1243:
UTAH – USS *Barnet* completes unloading of vehicles and troops. A total of 114 casualties (10 dead on arrival, 10 died on board) were taken on board and 197 non-casualty survivors of the USS *Corry* (including the Commanding Officer) were received from USS *Fitch* whilst in the Transport Area.

1256:
OMAHA - The Assistant Division Commander reports to the USS *Ancon* that no identification of the beach defences is known; spasmodic artillery fire is falling in the area; advance elements Combat Team 115 have cleared the beach

1300:
SWORD: Company "B" of the 1st Suffolk Regiment seizes Morris battery at Colleville-sur-Orne. This battery contains 3 protected 105 mm guns. Sixty-seven artillerymen are captured. The advance then begins on Hillman. This fortification was the Regimental HQ for the coastal defences in the area and designated as WN 17, (The British code names was Hillman.) It covers an area of 600 x 400 meters and is surrounded by rows of barbed wire extending 600 meters out in every direction plus two rows of mines. This was Colonel Krug's Command Post and occupied 150 men of the 736th Grenadier Regiment in 12 underground concrete bunkers connected by tunnels and trenches.

The MO was worried about some casualties he could not get to in a Troop on one flank. I took one of our precious jeeps with a stretched frame on it and made two or three trips up and down the road said to be under enemy fire and brought them in. I doubt if we were fired at, although I heard one of the wounded men who had been up on the stretcher frame spinning a splendid yarn to one of the sick berth attendants of bullets cracking around him all the way back!

Major D.J. Flunder, MC. VRD, 48 (RM) Cdo
RM Museum Southsea - 7/19/5

Taking this important site is not going to be an easy task.

SWORD: 9th Brigade, 3rd Division reserve Brigade land on SWORD and immediately push towards Caen.

Ranville, the enemy attacks are increasing and the position of 12th and 13th Parachute Battalions is now critical, with the result that the leading commando of 1st Special Service Brigade is diverted to the area to assist the airborne troops and is -not released until the evening. This diversion, necessary and successful though it is, curtailed the offensive action of 1st Special Service Brigade and subsequently delay their penetration into Franceville Plage.

In the fighting at Ranville there were many gallant actions but one is outstanding. Lieutenant J. A. N. Sims, 12th Parachute Battalion, is in charge of a position held by a few men. German infantry attack, supported by two self-propelled guns, one of which Lieutenant Sims knocks out. The other gun kills his men one by one at point-blank range. However, the officer held his ground until the gun withdrew, leaving him with only three men.

6th Green Howard's are ordered to by pass any resistance on their way to Crepon unless absolutely unavoidable.

OMAHA - Troops begin to secure the beach. WN72 surrenders after an hour long Naval bombardment. This German strong point is situated in Dog Green sector protecting the Exit D-1 and gives access to the village of Vierville-sur-mer.
.OMAHA: Engineers build a makeshift road over the bluff at E-1 St Laurent-sur-Mer draw.

The city of Caen receives its first bombing of the day. 73 B-24 of the 2nd Bombardment Division drop 155.75 tons of bombs over the town. The neighbourhoods of Saint Jean, Saint Julien and the area around the castle are hit.

POINTE DU HOC: Colonel Rudder receives the answer to his message of 12:00: "*No reinforcements available. All the Rangers landed at OMAHA*".

OMAHA: US troops from G Company (*116th Regiment, 29th Division*) 1st Section are sent into the town of Colleville-sur-Mer, with the mission of clearing the town of the enemy, and to seize and hold it. The 5th and 2nd Sections are ordered to protect the right front of the Company. One section of 30 Calibre Heavy Machine Guns (HMG) of Company H, 16th Infantry are placed in position on the right flank. Unfortunately, only 13 men composed the 4th Section at this time, as the remainder were casualties of the landings. Another 30 Calibre HMG was put in position to cover the advance of the 1st Section into the town. The remaining elements of the 2nd Section were positioned on the left flank but became engaged in a fire fight in this vicinity and therefore could not render any covering fire or support to the 1st Section as it advanced into the town.

1302:
ORNE BRIDGE - Lord Lovat and his 1st Special Service Brigade complete with his personal piper Bill Millen arrive at the bridge.

1310:
JUNO - GOC 3rd Canadian Infantry Division land on "Nan" White.

41 RM Commando "A."Troop report that they have been mortared and fired upon from the houses on the left flank. Capt. C.N.P. Powell D.S.O. is a casualty. "B" Troop at almost the same time reports that the enemy are counter attacking about 60 strong on the left flank with mortars and an infantry gun in support. Lieut. Colonel Gray then decides that a counter attack on the Commando might become general and withdraws all Troops to the line of the lateral road running from the sea to the beach and up to the road junction which was an easier line to defend.

1315:
OMAHA - "G" Company reach the outskirts of Colleville sur Mer and occupy the church and a house due south of the church where they engage with the enemy at point-blank range. Although three men are killed almost immediately and two seriously wounded, these buildings are occupied and held. A heavy counterattack develops on all sides of the entire company at this time, but is beaten off successfully.

This engagement necessitates a consolidation of the company in an oval position as the enemy completely encircles them and no front can be fixed. In order to contain the ground that has been gained, no further effort is made to advance, and the company dug in and await the 18th Infantry to pass through and relieve the pressure. At this time the Company strength is 107 men and 6 officers, plus about 25 men from other organisations.

1317:
OMAHA - The Commanding General receives a message from Beachmaster Dog Green stating "*Beachmaster, 7th Beach Battalion, suggests 116th move inland; DG exit still blocked*".

Small calibre shells or mortars were constantly exploding in the water, and splinters were thumping on the sides of our craft. I watched the marine in his armoured box in front of me. From his activity, I judged that we were getting close. The thunderous noise drowned voices and the firing of individual weapons. The engines slowed and, suddenly, the craft bumped on the sand. We had arrived! Down went the ramp with a crash, and the armoured doors flew open.

Immediately, a burst of automatic fire crackled in, just over our heads. No one was hit.

With a yell, 2nd Loot White sprung to his feet and jumped out into the knee-deep water. To our surprise, he disappeared from sight! He had fallen into a shell hole, obscured by the water. Two stalwarts reached down, seized his shoulder straps and threw him up on to the beach, after which the centre row of men charged out.

"Follow me," I shouted. *"Do what I do, and run like hell! Don't stop for anything!"*

Brian Moss, Sergeant, 233 Field Company, Royal Engineers, attached to the 5 East Yorks

Tank cemetery, *"They were buried next to their tanks that served them so well."*

Capt. G. Lugg, personal collection.

The Division Headquarters receive information from an intercept that there is a general advance up the slop of Easy Red, and the advance continues on Fox Red with some men moving on ridge toward Port en Bassin.

Report received from the 716th Infantry Division: *"Our artillery reports the presence of forty tanks on their way to Ryes."*

1327:
JUNO - 48 Commando , "X " Troop reports objective "Dogfish One" clear, and as "Y" Troop is absent, are ordered to continue clearing Dogfish Two. Here almost at once, they come under Light Machine Gun fire from the area of the Cross Roads. The Troop Commander is unable to make progress down the Street and starts to work around to the right (inland flank). He then attempts to attack towards the sea but is unable to gain ground down this street either.

1330:
By this time 41 RM Commando "B" Troop and a section of "A" Troop have withdrawn to the line, 1 Section of "A" Troop is missing. "P" and "Y" Troops confirmed. "X" Troop, the smallest in numbers, was attached to "Y" Troop. The general understanding is that there is about 80 enemy in the strongpoint and 100 in the Chateau. By this time the majority of casualties have been evacuated to the Beach by the 6 Jeeps which landed at about 1000 hrs. The FOB's Jeep with the Bombardier and wireless set also arrive and contact is made with the destroyers. HQ moves from the Church to the Orchard

8th Parachute Battalion O.C. "C" Company arrives with 4 Officers and 51 Other Ranks on the Ranville DZ and gathers together 51 members of the Battalion. He sees in the distance the green verey lights being fired at the Battalion Rendezvous and decides to make straight for them. His route takes him through Herouvillette where they run into the enemy and have to fight their way through the village taking 6 causalities.

Lord Lovat and his men run across the Orne Bridge under fire which was bouncing off the metal sides. Col. Pine-Coffin CO of the 7th Parachute Battalion approaches them from across the road, holds his hand out to Lovat and said, *"We are very pleased to see you, old boy."* To which Lovat replied, *"I am afraid we are a few minutes later, Sir!"* They were in fact an hour and two minutes late. Contrary to popular belief - and Hollywood - Lovat's Piper Bill Millen did not pipe them across.

OMAHA - General Omar Bradley, on the warship *Augusta*, receives the following report: *"Troops previously stopped on Easy Red, Easy Green and Red Fox beaches, now are progressing on the hills behind the beaches."*

Message from the German 352nd Infantry-Division informs the 7th Army that the allied assault has been pushed back to the sea. Nothing could be further from the truth.

Naval Officer in charge of JUNO sets up advanced HQ.

Regina Rifles Battalion HQ followed by "B" Company, move from its position in Courseulles, leaving behind a number of civilians who have risked their lives to come out to welcome the Canadians with flowers and bottles of wine. The HQ joins "C" and "D" Companies at Reviers. The Battalion, including "A" Company, which have now moved inland, consolidate at Reviers. At this stage in the advance they have already captured 80 German prisoners.

1340:
OMAHA - Easy and Dog sector beaches are reported clear of opposition except for artillery and mortar fire.

1341:
OMAHA - The Navy inform the Division Commander, *"Beach Dog Green, White, and Red are entirely clear of opposition and ready to land troops; no opposition on beach. Easy Green and Red troops are ashore apparently waiting infantry reinforcements. All fire support ships are waiting for target assignment on shore."*

II/915e Infantry Regiment: *"The enemy infiltrates between WN 62a and 62b, our wing is thereby extended southward."*

OMAHA - the 726th Regiment of Grenadiers report that Germans are once again controlling Colleville-sur-Mer, the German resistance at Dog Green, Easy Green, Easy Red and White Red beach sectors has stopped.

1350:
The helmsman of LCI 538, then off Omaha Beach, sends a message to USS *Harding*: *"According to information received from observation teams on the ground we believe that the bell tower at Vierville is an observatory artillery and their are four machine guns in the tower. Can you destroy it?"*

> *"We heard a shout that Albert Lowson was down near the water's edge. Thorpe dashed off and, with assistance from Andy Thomas, dragged him up to us. Lowson had no obvious wound and yet appeared on the point of death. The lads raced back down into the bullet swept zone to pick up another lad, Mills, who had also also dropped at the tideline. Mills had taken a bullet through the chest. Two men picked him up between them and, as they did, Mills got another bullet through the chest, so they put him down again. I am certain my lads deserved a few decorations that morning but, as no officer was present to witness their efforts, they went unrecognised.*
>
> Brian Moss. Sergeant, 233 Field Company, Royal Engineers

Tank Cemetery at La Dilverande

Capt. G Lugg Personal Collection.

Permission is granted to fire on the church for 1 minute, indicating that they have already fired upon this church and that no more than 1 minute of ammunition was to be allocated. Harding opened fire at 3200 yards (2900m) and completely demolished the church in 40 shots.

It later appears that the information was completely false. It was obviously impossible to install four guns in the tower and the Americans controlled the centre of Vierville, and certainly did not ask for its destruction.

1358:
Report received the 352nd Artillery Regiment: *"The first group reports that Colleville is taken over by the enemy. Tanks at Asnelles have shifted to the East. The bridgehead here has expanded considerably."*

1400:
"C" Company Dorset Regiment are now in possession of Point 54, (WN 40A) after stiffer opposition than anticipated. 7 Germans are killed, and 2 officers and 15 ORs are taken prisoner. "C" Company takes up positions to support "D" Company's attack on Puits d'Herode. "D" Company pushing south through Buhot surprises and captures a Company of German pioneers with their transport.

Lieutenant Colonel Norie arrives at Point 54. He organises "C" Coy of the 1st Dorsets to provide covering fire for their colleagues from "D" Coy, who will move along the ridge towards Puits d'Herode. In order to undertake this manoeuvre, "D" company will need to capture a defended wood (marked as WN 40B on Allied intelligence maps) which lay between the two. This too proves to be well defended, and 18 Platoon, in the head of this attack, comes under heavy fire, and takes a number of casualties, including their platoon Commander and Sergeant.

Corporal Hawkins takes command of the troop and leads them to the relative safety of the tree line. He leaves them there whilst he scouts the enemy positions, before flanking the enemy and taking the position. For his actions Corporal Hawkins is awarded a Military Medal. The captured positions at WN 40B includes an 81 mm mortar position, a 'Spandau' position and an anti-tank gun position, complete with anti-tank gun.

225th Parachute Field Ambulance, RAMC, reports from Ranville that there is a considerable amount of sniping by enemy troops throughout the day, one of whom appears to be covering the main dressing station. Some mortar fire is experienced at intervals. Casualties flow in large numbers throughout the day. Surgical teams are working constantly from the time of opening. Capt Young RAMC is missing and Capt Tibbs reports the DZ is now cleared of casualties.

In a house near Crepon, a party of Germans were called upon by A Coy 6th Green Howard's to surrender. They refused, but when treated to a substantial does of Bren and Sten gun fire, they came out under the cover of a white flag.

OMAHA - Commanding Officer of the Engineer Special Brigade Group left the USS *Ancon* to set up headquarters on the beach.

POINTE DU HOC: The German defenders of the 84th Infantry Regiment abandon the western strongpoint.

UTAH - Major General Barton with the staff of the 4th US Division land and set up his headquarters on the shore.

OMAHA - 29th Signal Company Command Post was moved inland some three hundred yards under the shelter of a bluff overlooking the beach.

USS *Barnet* underway with Transport Division FIVE, less USS *Bayfield*, from the Transport Area heading for Portland, England with casualties.

Company "F", 3rd Battalion, 325th Glider Infantry Regiment, supporting Company C, 746th Tank Battalion land on UTAH Red Beach, de-waterproof vehicles and moved inland to make contact with the division.

JUNO - Banville. The Winnipeg Rifle Regiment's slow pace at this time is hampered by troop congestion on the beach rather than by the enemy. Troops from "A" and "C" Squadrons of the 1st Hussars are able to make their way forward and support "A" Company's advance southward. Ignoring the mines and anti-tank guns of the enemy the Shermans overpower these machine-gun screens, enabling "A" Company to move forward unhindered. By now prisoners are evacuated to the rear in small groups; many, as the War Diary records, *"we are a sorry lot."*

The remnants of "B" Company has reported that only Capt. Gower and 26 other ranks remained unscathed. They have taken and destroyed three casements and 12 machine-gun nests. About this time No. 15 platoon and No. 17 platoon which have supported the Canadian Scots and gapped the minefield rejoined their respective companies.

> "Some [German] *Tiger tanks had been spotted in front of the troops so we engaged them from about two miles, firing three 7·5″ shells at each of them. A 7·5″ shell makes a hell of a mess of a Tiger tank. The tank crews tried covering up their tanks with hay and straw but we still knocked out 27 tanks in an hour, some of the turrets spinning up in the air like yo-yo's."
>
> Royal Marine WCS Hiscock
> **PO/X112968 - HQ192 Squad. Onboard HMS Hawkins**

* Many allied soldiers and tankers saw or thought they saw Tigers, but in actual fact there were none of D Day. Most mistook the Panzer IV as a Tiger as it has similar profile

German soldiers on a camouflaged Panzer V "Panther" in town. These were not in action until the 7th June due to not being order ed to the front until the afternoon of the 6th June.

Bundesarchiv, Bild 101I-301-1955-22 / Kurth / CC-BY-SA

After consolidating its positions at Banville, the Regiment (now supported by tanks) is ready to renew the advance.

Meanwhile, In the prison courtyard at Caen, Nazi's begin shooting hostages and resistance fighters, without interrogation or trial. The massacre lasts an hour. The men and women hearing of the invasion and hopeful of an imminent release were executed one by one as a reprisal for the Allied Landings .To this day, the bodies of the hostages have never been found and there are no exact numbers as all records were destroyed but research shows that there was at least 85 and possibly an many as 100.

916th Infantry Regiment: *"The 5/916e Infantry Regiment initiated a counter-attack against the enemy between WN 62a, 62b, and 64, and will soon join the ongoing attack conducted by II/916e Infantry Regiment."*

1415:
1st Special Service Brigade - No. 45 RM Commando reach the bridge over the CAEN CANAL and contact the 6th Airborne. Snipers are proving themselves a nuisance in this area and while they are between the two bridges Lt. Col. Ries is shot by a sniper and wounded in the left leg. Major Gray takes Command.

All Canadian 3rd Division now ashore on Juno. Rapid advances start: troops link with those from Gold.

1425:
After heavy fighting, the town of Périers, south of SWORD Beach, is liberated by the Staffordshire Yeomanry tanks.

A rescue boat is sent by the USS *Barton* to pick up the wounded Rangers at Pointe du Hoc, but a barrage of German fire prevents its access.

1426:
OMAHA - Report received by II/915e Infantry Regiment: *"Our attack met an organized and tenacious resistance, causing heavy losses in our ranks. WN 62 still stands; WN 62c has no more ammunition for mortar. The enemy infiltrates south from the church and the castle of Colleville. A counter attack was ordered The enemy occupying the castle must be rejected regardless of the circumstances, WN 60 and 62 must absolutely remain in our hands."*.

1434:
Information received by the 716th Infantry Division: *"A very large dent was made by the enemy to the mouth of the Orne. Several WN west of the Orne are now encircled by the enemy. Landed units have met up with the parachute regiment behind the beaches. Near Ryes forty tanks of the heaviest type are it seems on their way to the Southwest."*

1445:
48 Commando "X" Troop moves back some 300 yds inland of the Railway and Naval Support requested. When the bombardment from the LCG's lift "B" and "X" Troops start to work their way down the street using the cover of houses and gardens. The line of the Railway is quickly gained but after that, both meet light machine gun fire down the street, and sniping and mortar fire from the gardens. "B" Troop continue to make ground although progress is slow owing to the substantial and frequent walls and fences that require to be breached.

JUNO - General Keller organizes a press conference in an orchard near Bernières.

1458:
OMAHA - The German 352nd Artillery Regiment reports that the village of Colleville-sur-Mer is once again under the control of the enemy.

1500:
1st Battalion Royal Ulster Rifles are airborne. All personnel taking part are provided with a fatless meal to prevent or reduce air sickness. Tea and water is provided in the gliders and all ranks are instructed to drink as much as possible before landing. Information received from Broadwell airfield that 9 Para Bn have been dropped on correct DZs and that landing strips for Gliders on LZs have been clearly visible.

ADMS attempts to reach area of 3 Parachute Brigade but was unsuccessful owing to enemy infiltration.

OMAHA - Elements of 29th Division Headquarters Company and attached units aboard LCI 414 land in the vicinity of Vierville-sur-Mer. The remaining elements of the Forward Echelon can get ashore at this time because of heavy machine gun and artillery fire falling on the beach. The command post originally scheduled to be set up at a chateau picked from a serial photograph can not be used because the advance elements of the assault troops have not reached their first objective. The elements of the advance group set up the first command post in a stone quarry one hundred

Fortified house at Lion-sur-mer, fired upon by landing craft during the afternoon of D Day and continued to reply until set afire in the evening.

G Lugg Personal Collection

With any luck the driver of this ambulance would have survived as being a British vehicle he was sitting on the right.

R.A.M.C./PE/1/WALL/4

yards from the beach on the road to Vierville-sur-Mer.

ROMMEL returns to headquarters at La-Roche-Guyon.

OMAHA - the 916th Regiment of Grenadiers counter-attacks the advanced American units between the WN 62a, WN 62b and WN 64 strongpoint.

1520:
6th Green Howard's are well South of Crepon and approaching Villers le Sec and are able to report back that Phase II had been completed.

1526:
OMAHA - Advanced elements of the First Division and 29th Division's staff are setting up Command Posts ashore near the beach exits from Sectors Easy and Dog respectively. St Laurent partially occupied plus the capture of Colleville.

OMAHA - The German counter-attack led by the 916th Regiment of Grenadiers in Colleville-sur-Mer fails.

1530:
COLLEVILLE-SUR-MER - Friendly Naval gun fire shells the town for 90 minutes with very heavy fire, causing seven casualties. Efforts were made to stop this fire by firing yellow smoke flares.

OMAHA - Hein Severloh, last defender of the WN 62 strongpoint, abandons his post after having fired 12,500 rounds. Situated in Easy Red sector, this strong point protected the beach exit E3 and gave access to the village of Colleville-sur-Mer and has been extremely troublesome.

1540:
OMAHA - USS *Oceanway I* is directed to close Fox Green Beach and discharge her 20 LCMs carrying M-4 tanks, these tanks are to be attached to the 16th RCT.

General Gunther Blumentritt calls Lt. General Speodel at Rommel's headquarters to announce that Hitler has finally agreed to send in troops from the 12. S.S. Hitlerjugend-Division based to the South of Rouen, and the Panzer Lehr based near Chartres.

1545:
Strongpoint Sole situated between Ouistreham and Colleville-sur-Orne falls to B Squadron 13/18th Hussars and the 2nd Battalion East Yorkshire. Forty Germans are captured

Report received from the 915th Infantry Regiment (Meyer's reserves): *"Contact made with I/916e Infantry Regiment, which is committed to our left. The general direction of our attack is Meuvaines-Asnelles. Assault guns joined the regiment".*

1555:
Queen's Own Rifles have taken the village of Magny and were advancing on Basly. Initially the Queen's Own had run into strong resistance at Bernières. The heaviest casualties have been taken by that battalion's "B" Company, which has landed with no tank support east of its assigned position. The company sustained 65 casualties in the first few minutes of its assault. Also the North Shore Regiment has been initially held up in its assault of St. Aubin by a German 50mm anti-tank gun emplacement.

1600: Air raid on the city of Caen. Bombing of the German battery at Mont Canisy by 37 Marauder bombers, which drop 61 tons of bombs on the site.

9th Brigade moves inland from SWORD Beach.

Staffordshire Yeomanry scouting ahead report enemy tanks advancing from Caen. The squadron with the Suffolks at Hillman strong-point is hastily moved to Biéville and is just taking up a position to the west when about forty enemy tanks, moving very fast, attack. Two are knocked out by the Yeomanry and two by the Shropshire anti-tank guns, the enemy retreat to the woods.

They are pursued by the Yeomanry and by field-gun fire, and when they show again more are destroyed. They swung off once more and are joined by others, and making a wide detour they head towards the Périers ridge. There, waiting for them, is a squadron of the Staffordshires posted at Point 61 for just such an occasion. Three more were knocked out and again they drew off. Thirteen have then been destroyed but they have already been persistently harassed by aircraft while they were south of Caen. On the western outskirts of the town eight Typhoons of the Second Tactical Air Force have dive-bombed tanks moving up to join the fight and have left two in flames and four others smoking.

Le Hamel is finally captured. 231st Brigade moves on to Arromanches. 69th Brigade encounters resistance in Villers le Sec/Bazenville area.

The Shropshire Regiment frees the town of Biéville South of SWORD Beach.

After carrying out their initial D-Day mission of capturing the La Fiere bridge on the Merderet river,

"*The fate of Germany and the fate of this conflict depend of the success of your attack*".

General Marcks ordering Colonel von Oppeln-Brokinoswski to counter-attack with the 21st Panzer division.

Two Fallschirmjaeger with handcarts loaded with equipment running through bushes.

Bundesarchiv, Bild 101I-587-2253-05 / Schneiders, Toni / CC-BY-SA the men from Company "A" of the 505th PIR prepare to meet the first German counterattack on the La-Fière causeway. After heavy artillery bombing, three tanks and 200 infantrymen make an advance on the road. The courage and determination of the men from Company "A" ensures that no other German will cross this bridge from the moment the bridge was taken on the morning of June 6th to the arrival of reinforcements two days later.

OMAHA - The first American Sherman tank reaches the road connecting the beach to Colleville through a small valley. It is then destroyed by an anti-tank gun.

General MARKS tells Colonel Hermann Von Oppeln-Brokinowski of the 22nd Tank Regiment: *"It's up to you to repel the invasion."*

Rommel has committed to frequent and furious counterattacks in an effort to push the allies back into the sea. Pointe du Hoc is especially targeted. The Rangers attempting to hold the position are seriously depleted having not got their reinforcements who have landed at OMAHA. The Germans who have the advantage of knowing the terrain and secret tunnels, are able to move about easier, firing upon the Rangers from various positions before moving to another and attacking from a different direction. The Rangers held on and beat back attacks from two different directions.

The 5th Rangers have now fought their way off OMAHA beach and are heading overland to Pointe du Hoc.

German counter-attack towards the bridge at La Fière, 3 km from Sainte-Mère-Eglise, defended by US paratroopers of Able Company, 505th PIR of the 82nd Airborne.

German counter-attack in the town of Périers, south of SWORD Beach.

Marshal von Rundstedt is authorized to engage his two armoured divisions

The 21st Panzer Division stationed near Caen have been waiting for more than three and a half hours while officers try to get the necessary authorization to attack. By the time the tanks were moving, the Allied bombardment has begun.

They have stopped and started, received orders and counter-orders and sent this way and that throughout the morning and early afternoon. By 1600, ninety German tanks and two infantry battalions of the 21st Panzer Division has assembled north of Caen. A general made a fiery speech. *"If you don't throw the British into the sea,"* he warned, *"the war will be lost!"*

1612:
OMAHA - Report received from the 726th Grenadier Regiment: WN 39 has been captured by the enemy. WN 38 is surrounded and WN 40 is also being attacked by six tanks and an infantry company. In addition, seven tanks are seen in front of WN 42, and several tanks face WN 44.

1617:
709th Infantry Division are getting very concerned about the high amount of landings taking place.

1630:
CAEN is bombed again. This time the targets are the bridges on the Orne river. Aircraft in groups of six drop their bombs at 3000 meters high. The bombing lasts for more than a quarter of an hour.

1634:
OMAHA - 916th Infantry Regiment: *"Between WN 62 and 64, the enemy cleared obstacles from the beaches with special tanks so as to widen the passage for its mechanized forces."*

1638:
GOLD - 726th Grenadier Regiment: *"Ryes (Due south of Arromanches) has fallen to the enemy."*

1650:
OMAHA - 352nd Artillery Regiment report: *"The IV. Group reports significant landings of tanks and trucks that are heading inland between WN 62 and 64."*

1658:
OMAHA, Saint-Laurent-sur-Mer- 352nd Artillery Regiment report: *"Urgent message. New landings of tanks and trucks between WN 67 and 73."*

1700:
OMAHA - The beach exit D1, controlled strategically by a house situated near fortification WN 73, is finally secured. All morning long, Company "C" of the 2nd Rangers fought alongside Company "B" of the 116th RCT in the German trenches at the top of the cliff in order to secure this strong point.

General Clarence Huebner lands on the Easy Red beach sector, the steeple of the Church of Saint-Laurent-sur-Mer, which covers German snipers, is destroyed by the American artillery.

PAGE 56   21 APRIL, 1944   TOP SECRET - BIGOT

TYPICAL STRONG POINT

ILLUSTRATED BY POSITION 668903 AT LES MOULINS, BEACH "OMAHA"

> *"Several major ships, Cruisers and Battleships, bombarded in line with armour piercing shells into the concrete fortifications that were holding up the landings. Large lumps of concrete, nearly as big as a house, were lifted out of the ground to make an opening for the breakout. It was a very long day."*
>
> **Royal Marine WCS Hiscock**
> **PO/X112968 - HQ192 Squad**

LEGEND

OBLIQUE VIEW OF PILLBOX (PLAN)

STRONG POINT

TOP SECRET - BIGOT

Machine gun past on Sword beach.

Capt. G Lugg Personal collection.

GRID NORTH

CTF 122

29th Signal Co Command Post was again moved inland to the outskirts of Saint-Laurent-sur-Mer, where communications are established to V Corps, 1st US Infantry Division, 116th Infantry Regiment, and the Engineer Shore Brigade. Communications are maintained through the night

8th Parachute Battalion - Lt. Brown returns from Troarn. He states that they have met a little opposition in Troarn which has been dealt with and the Royan Engineer's have increased the gap in the bridge to 40 feet. 7 prisoners are brought back from a Machine Gun post which is attacked. They are identified as 21 Panzer Division.

Telephone cable to Paris cut by 249 Field Company, Royal Engineers.

100 enemy tanks are on the move West of Caen. Meanwhile the RAF continue to to bomb and strafe the enemy on all sectors of the beachhead.

1710:
The German 916th informs the 352nd ID H.Q. that the village of Saint-Laurent-sur-Mer is now controlled by the enemy.

1715:
HMS *Hilary* and other ships and craft shift inshore and take up berths in accordance with the prearranged berthing plan. At the same time, the Naval Commander, Eastern Task Force – who has been touring the beaches in a US coastguard cutter during the afternoon – arrives in the *Scylla* and anchors in "JUNO" area in order to be centrally placed for a meeting of Flag Officers and Commodores.

OMAHA - Commanding General, 1st Division and his staff leave the USS *Ancon* to establish their H.Q. on the beach.

1730:
OMAHA - Hostile action against the beach has ceased except for the sniping and the recurring artillery and mortar fire. The work of organising the beaches for further unloading is progressing in an orderly fashion.

The Queen's Own Rifles of Canada reach its D Day objective, Anguerny Heights, and dig in. The most forward position is the village of Anisy which has been taken by "D" Company after a sharp brush with the enemy.

General de Gaulle speech ("*The ultimate battle is engaged!*") is broadcast on the BBC.

Squadron "C" of the Staffordshires, fighting with 6-pound antitank guns and Sherman tanks, open fire on the German armoured vehicles at Biéville.

Report of the 915th Infantry Regiment (Meyer's reserves): "*By the time we arrived at the assembly area, the enemy infantry and tanks occupied Villiers-le-Sec and the coast south of the village. Faced with a higher opponent number, Reconnaissance Battalion (on our right wing) is forced to retreat to St. Gabriel as we are unable to fight the mass of enemy tanks. We are no longer in contact with the I/915 Grenadier Regiment near Bazenville on our left. The detachment commander, Lieutenant-Colonel Meyer was apparently seriously wounded.*"

1740:
8th Parachute Battalion. Attack made on "B" Company position by 5 Armoured Fighting Vehicles. Attack beaten off and one enemy 6-ton truck full of stores captured.

1743:
726th Regiment report that the enemy has broken through in Sainte-Honorine and heading south towards Russy.

1750:
916th Regiment report that the enemy is constantly being reinforced and has entered Vierville Asnières and Louvières. The SW edge of Ryes is occupied by an enemy company of sappers.

1800:
Meeting of Flag Officers and Commodores.

UTAH: "*Corned beef once again for supper – oh for a change! Aircraft controlled by our ship have confirmed shooting down two raiding JU 88s. Everybody happy. ASR launches gone out to look for German pilots reports no sign of them.*" **LAC Armitage.**

Strategic point Daimler, consisting of 4 x 155mm artillery guns situated near the entrance to Ouistreham, falls to the men of the 2nd Battalion East Yorkshire. Seventy Germans are captured.

8th Parachute Battalion report strength of Battalion:
Approx 17 Officers,
300 O.Rs.
Weapons Battalion very short of Light Machine Guns (L.M.Gs.) 2 x 3" mortars and one captured German.
3 Medium Machine Guns (M.M.Gs.)
6 P.I.A.Ts.
Signals 2 x 68 sets.

The beach was covered in casualties, some Canadian, some ours. The surf was an incredible sight with beached and half sunken landing craft wallowing in each successive wave. Just offshore other craft were stuck on obstacles or sinking and some of which had been hit were burning.

Threading through them other craft were still coming in. Some tanks struggled ashore from a bad beaching and some bogged down in the shingle. They had their turret lids closed, and those that were moving were heading for a large group of the wounded. I was sickened to see one run over two wounded men and it was heading for our good *Padre, John Armstrong, badly wounded in the thigh, to whom I had spoken to on my way up the beach (typically he had been vehement that I should not stop by him exposed to enemy fire), and furious I ran back down the beach and hammered on the turret to try to get somebody to poke his head out. This had no effect at all, so I stuck and anti-tank grenade in its track and threw myself flat while it went off. That stopped it.

Major D.J. Flunder, MC. VRD, 48 (RM) Cdo
RM Museum Southsea, 7/19/5

* Padre John Armstrong was rescued and went on to become the Bishop of Bermuda

5th East Yorkshires (3rd Mechanised division) under fire. Note that some are wearing the "Turtle" helmet which was issued to British and Canadian troops for the first time for D Day.

National Archives of Canada.

4 x 18 sets which allowed communication with Companies.

Capt Perry (OC 48 Commando "B" Troop) is in the houses about 50 yds from the cross roads. From an attic light he could see the Germans and that they appear to be in a bad way, he is ready to assault.

Before he could move, Capt Perry was killed by a sniper and although the Troop continues slowly to make their way forward, no proper assault is made. Eventually 2/Lt Rubinstein (now OC '"B" Troop) reports that he is held up on the edge of the cleared area some 20 yds short of the Cross Roads.

UTAH – by 1800 21,328 troops 1,742 vehicles and 1695 tons of stores have landed in UTAH area at the loss of PC 1261, three LCT and one LCF, all probably mined.

JUNO - Surrender of the German garrison sheltered in the bunkers in Nan Red sector at St.-Aubin-sur-mer. Elements of the 3rd Canadian Div, North Nova Scotia Highlanders reach five kilometers inland. 1st Hussar tanks cross the Caen-Bayeux railway, fifteen kilometres inland. Canadian 9th Brigade link up with the 50th Division at Creully. Snipers and small groups have maintained the sole resistance during the advance on this village. Lt. Mitchell of D Company with a section of riflemen silence an enemy machine-gun nest along the bridge near Creully. Throughout the day the No. 22 W/T Set with its unwieldy carriage is bogged down continuously. The Headquarters signal section is under constant mortar fire. Lt. Robson, a liaison officer with the Brigade, is wounded; but he has the honour of being luxuriously evacuated — driven by Sgt. Jorgenson in a German staff car which took him safely to the rear.

With evening fast approaching, the Battalion sets about digging in just south of Creully. Five officers and 78 OR's arrive from the reinforcement unit that evening — all were posted to "B" Company.

"B" and "C" Company of the Regina Rifles, accompanied by B Squadron, are ordered to move forward to Fontaine-Henry. "C" Company is instructed to by-pass Fontaine-Henry, and go forward to Le Fresne-Camilly, the Battalion's intermediate objective.

The Free French warship *Georges-Leygues* opens fire on the battery of Longues-sur-Mer, west of GOLD Beach (which had attacked some allied ships).

1810:
OMAHA - the German 915th Regiment report that it has moved behind the enemy lines at the castle of Colleville-sur-Mer and that the wounded cannot be evacuated.

1820:
On returning to 48 Commando HQ which had now been established in a Farm ,the CO finds two Centaur tanks of the 2nd RMAS Regt which have been sent to assist. After some delay, one was sent down each road with improvised means of communication with the infantry. The presence of these AFV's help the infantry forward a little on "B" Troops front.

North Nova Scotias and the 27th Armoured Regiment (The Sherbrooke Fusiliers Regiment), acting as the Brigade's advanced guard, move off from the assembly area to pass through the Queen's Own and the Chaudière and carry the advance southward. Three companies of the Highlanders ride on the Sherbrooks' tanks.

1825:
POINTE DU HOC: General Dietrich Kraiss, commander of the 352nd Infantry Division, reports to the officer in charge of the 916th Regiment of Grenadiers: *"The 1st company of the 914th Regiment must counter-attack at the Pointe du Hoc to solve the situation. Detachments from Le Guay strongpoint must also attack from the east".*

1828:
726th Regiment: *"Enemy tanks are trying to force their way from Sommervieux to Magny. In order to counter this threat, six or seven assault guns are sent to the Regiment."*

1830:
OMAHA - The 26th Infantry Regiment (1st US Infantry Division) lands.

JUNO - 46 RM Commando arrive off ST. Aubin-sue-Mer and proceed one hour later to anchor off SWORD to report to Flag Officer, Force S.

1840:
The Division at 32. Flak Battalion: *"A heavy battery should be positioned in each East and West entrance to Bayeux to protect the approaches against enemy tanks."*

1900:
OMAHA - 1st Division Commander, Lt. General Huebner in charge of 1st Infantry Division, lands at Easy Red and sets up command post on OMAHA.

A British Supermarine Spitfire fighter receives maintenance from mechanics of U.S. Navy Cruiser Scouting Squadron Seven (VCS-7), which used these planes to spot Naval gunfire during the June 1944 Normandy invasion. Men present are (from left to right): James J. O'Connor; C.N. Pfanenstiel; Chief Aviation Machinist's Mate V.G. Disa; Aviation Machinist's Mate Third Class R.P. Theirauld; and Edmund Pachgio.

VCS-7 switched from their usual Curtiss SOC Seagull floatplanes to British Supermarine Spitfire fighters - given the paper designation "FS-1" by the U.S. Navy - during the Normandy operation. VCS-7 was based at Royal Naval Air Station Lee-on-Solent, Hampshire (UK), and drew planes from a pool of Supermarine Spitfire of Seafire fighters. The squadron flew a total of 191 sorties between 6 and 25 June 1944, losing one aircraft to ground fire. The "kill" marking below the cockpit was applied by a previous user.

Official U.S. Navy photograph 80-G-302108

Heavy fighting taking place at Colleville-sur-Mer between the US troops and the German defenders.

1925:
POINTE DU HOC- the Germans, supported by elements from Le Guay, launch an offensive at the east of the small American beachhead.

1930:
Lieut. Stevens reports to HQ that he and the missing section of RM 41 Commando, "A" Troop have returned having been cut off. On the way back he knocks out a German armoured car with a grenade. Except for sniping and light machine gun fire from the houses where Germans have been left behind, all was quiet during the rest of the night. Casualties for 41 Commando are approximately 140 killed, wounded and missing.

C Company Regina Rifles report they have reached Fresne-Camilly and have cleared it.

1935:
OMAHA - 1st Engineer Battalion is informed that if there were any DD tanks located, the battalion was to give them to anyone needing them.

1940:
OMAHA - German fire barrage on the beach in the area of Colleville-sur-Mer, where the landing operations are continuing. Some losses among US Troops.

POINTE DU HOC - General Kraiss is informed of the German advance, "The 9th Company of the 726th Regiment of Grenadiers is surrounded by the enemy from the east and the south".

He then reports: "The defensive line sector held by the 916th Infantry Regiment extends from the eastern edge of Colleville through the WN 69c, 69 to 71c. From WN No. 74 to the west, everything is in order. The enemy engaged at Pointe du Hoc is contained in the South and West by the 9th Coy 726th Grenadier Regiment."

1945:
POINTE DU HOC - the 916th Regiment of Grenadiers reports the dropping of paratroopers near Le Guay strongpoint.

1950:
6th Green Howard's ordered to halt their advance towards St Gabriel as the enemy infantry and anti tank opposition in front is too much.

2000:
As far as the eye can see aircraft and gliders are heading in. The gliders are being set free and the bombers continuing inland to their targets.

The men of 4 Commando Group arrive at the village of Hauger. They spend the evening establishing strong defences.

OMAHA - The anti-tank entrenchment of Les-Moulins, situated near beach exit D3, is filled with troops.

The French Commandos of the 1st BFM (Battalion Fusilier Marine) reach the town of Le Hauger.

Bénouville is captured. St Laurent and Colleville are also finally captured.

Canadians from Juno Beach reach Villons les Buissons, seven miles inland.

Attack by 21st Panzers reach coast between Sword and Juno at Luc-sur-Mer.

Six Germans manage to infiltrate the British lines after the battle at Périers-sur-le-Dan point. They reach the coast near Lion-sur-mer to observe the landing operations before turning back.

2005:
SWORD beach area. Hundreds of parachutes fill the sky as the 6th Airborne jump from their troop carrying aircraft. One aircraft has an engine on fire as it was hit whilst turning to return to the UK.

SWORD Elements of the 21st Panzerdivision manage to slip between the Canadian and British forces between SWORD and JUNO beaches and reach Luc and Lion sur Mer, However re-enforcement's failed to arrive, with the paratroopers arriving and at the risk of being surrounded General Marks Panzers made a tactical withdrawal.

2010:
"C" Company North Shore Regiment which was to seize the inland village of Tailleville, meets no opposition until it reaches the actual outskirts of that Hamlet. Here the enemy, well dug in, fought long and hard; in spite of early optimistic reports, it was "nearing evening" before the company, with tank support, finally clear the place, taking over 60 prisoners.

2015:
HILLMAN - After sustained artillery bombardment the 1st Battalion Suffolk Regiment with more tanks

"An amusing incident occurred (though I was more concerned that it might attract the attention of some sharp eyed Jerry). A small piece of phosphorus had landed on the helmet of the man ahead of me, causing his camouflage to smoulder. Understandably, I was keen to extinguish the potential hazard, but equally keen to avoid the phosphorus whose presence precluded the use of bare hands. I, therefore, resorted to the rifle butt, an act which did not meet with the whole hearted approval of the unwilling torch bearer."

Mne. John B Wetjen, 47 Commando.

RM Museum Southsea ACQ 280/06

Canadian troops arriving on Juno Beach

Courtesy of Exbury Veterans Association
and http://www.newforestww2.org/

in support from C Sqn 13th/18th Hussars plus A Sqn Staffordshire Yeomanry, 2 batteries of 33 and 76 Field Regiments Royal Artillery, a detachment of 245 Field Coy Royal Engineers and a machine gun platoon on 2nd Battalion The Middlesex Regiment make a second attack on Hillman and overcame any further resistance from the Germans who stayed in the bunker overnight before surrendering in the morning.

2030:
56th and 151st Brigades reach the outskirts of Bayeux and the Caen-Bayeux road.

6th Durham Light Infantry have advanced to the Bayeux-Caen road and are ordered to dig in for the night at Esquay-sur-Seulles where they are joined by The Northumberland Hussars. As night fell 6th Durhams had remarkably suffered no fatalities on their first day on French soil

Green Howard's ordered to continue their advance to St. Gabriel.

2100:
Brig B.W. Leicester (Commander 4 Special Service Brigade) called in at 48 Commando HQ stating that a counter attack might be expected at dawn and ordered the Commando to consolidate Langrune against attack. Light is now failing, and the CO decides that as the Commando is much reduced in numbers, he would hold the ground gained with the smallest possible force and concentrate the remainder around Commando HQ to cover the approaches from the South and East. Beginning of Operation "Mallard". An armada of 249 aircraft arrives on the coast at Ouistreham. The aircraft of the 38th and 46th Groups bring in 219 Horsa gliders and 30 Hamilcar gliders, which serve as reinforcement for the 6th British Airborne Division. Two landing zones are set aside for these aircraft. LZ (Landing Zone) "N" is situated to the north of Ranville in the same area as DZ "N", and LZ "W" is situated between the villages of Bénouville and St-Aubin-d'Arquenay. 256 gliders are scheduled for the operation but only 249 of them arrive over the French coast. The planes towing the gliders cut them loose over Ouistreham and the gliders finish their descent alone, a few minutes later, huge amounts of equipment are parachuted onto the landing strips. As soon as the first gliders land at LZ "W", the Germans open fire. Regardless, the 6th Airborne landing Brigade's losses are minor, and the operation is deemed a success.

HMS Largs reports a lull in the firing. As far as the eye can see there is one continual flow of aircraft. From one horizon to the other airborne troops are arriving. All eyes are looking towards the heavens and seeing such a spectacle that no one ever thought possible. Aircraft towing gliders and tremendous fighter cover, thousands of aircraft filled the sky. Two Lancasters are shot down.

6th Airborne Divisional Postal until arrives by glider to set up the Field Post Office.

Troops under Major MacDonald of 8 Field Ambulance start to clear casualties from Bénouville Bridge to Field Dressing Station in beach area. Some 50-60 casualties were evacuated in this way.

Green Howard's now occupy area to the West of St. Gabriel under cover of heavy barrage laid down by 86 Fd Regt RA and a MMG concentration laid by B Coy 2 Ches.

Mission "Keokuck": Thirty-two Horsa gliders of the 434th Troop Carrier Group, towed by C47's, land on the LZ "E" north of Hiesville. They bring in 165 men from headquarters and medical corps, 40 jeeps, 6 motorcycles, 6 x 57mm artillery guns, and 19 tons of material destined for the 101st t Airborne.

POINTE DU HOC - 24 Rangers of "A" company, 5th Battalion, who landed on OMAHA Beach reach Pointe du Hoc and provide much needed and very welcome reinforcements.

As the gliders fill the sky the the German armour on the coast retreats and runs straight into the Canadians. There are many confusing skirmishes as tanks, armoured half tracks, and infantry try to find a weak spot in the line. In one encounter, an entire platoon of Le Régiment de la Chaudière are wiped out. In another, the Winnipegs take 19 German prisoners. Despite being bone-tired and facing an enemy who knows the terrain, the Canadian line can not be broken.

100 82nd Airborne Gliders land with artillery, engineers and special troops.

307th Airborne Medical Company lands and immediately begins assembly, recovering by use of life rafts much equipment from gliders that had landed in shallow water near the banks of the Merderet River. A clearing station is set up at the crossroads north of Blosville.

OMAHA - 26th RCT, Rifle Regiment are now all ashore.

Major General Feuchtinger Commander of the 21st Panzer Division, spots from his vantage point at

"The sea was quite lumpy, with waves running about four feet high. One moment you could see a ship, and the next moment it disappeared from sight. Very soon, vomit bags were in heavy use. Festung Europa, here we come, covered in vomit!"

Brian Moss, Sergeant, 233 Field Company, Royal Engineers

Landing ships putting cargo ashore on Omaha Beach. "A panoramic view of the Omaha beachhead after it was secured, sometime around mid-June 1944, at low tide". The Coast Guard-manned LST-262 is the third beached LST from the right, one of 10 Coast Guard-manned LSTs that participated in the Normandy landings. Among identifiable ships present are LST-532 (in the center of the view); USS LST-262 (3rd LST from right); USS LST-310 (2nd LST from right); USS LST-533 (partially visible at far right); and USS LST-524. Note barrage balloons overhead and Army "half-track" convoy forming up on the beach. The LST-262 was one of 10 Coast Guard-manned LSTs that participated in the invasion of Normandy.

USNA 26-G-2517

Lebisey the gliders of Operation Mallard landing at St-Aubin-d'Arquenay. He cancels his plans to advance towards the coast, and instead sends only 3 Companies in that direction. The attack is ambushed by the Canadians. Survivors are forced to retreat toward Caen.

2115:

The 2nd Battalion, Royal Warwickshire Regiment of the 185th Infantry Brigade arrive from SWORD Beach and begin taking over the Bénouville and Ranville bridges' defences.

"On the beach I obtained another Schmeisser to replace my Sten, a Luger, and a BSA 500 motorcycle. I also liberated an Opel car, although the enemy had ripped out the dashboard, leaving a mass of wires. One of my men experimented with joining various wires and eventually got the engine running.

We marched on. Actually, I puttered along at walking pace on my motorcycle. The track we took was dusty and led away from Ver sur Mer towards Crepon. As the village of Crepon came in sight, we heard shots. Someone in the church tower was shooting at us. Our infantry set up a 6-pounder and, in no time at all, some of the church tower came down and the shooting stopped. Just beyond the village was Verdun Ferme, a typical French farm with high walls around all the buildings. We stayed the night at the farm. I slept in a slit trench I had dug outside the wall. Brian Moss

The GOC sends out his orders for the night by liaison officer:
The Canadian 7th Brigade on the right is to occupy the area Le Fresne - Camilly - Cainet.
The 8th is to hold the area Colomby-sur-Thaon - Anguerny and to contain La Délivrande and Douvres-la-Délivrande with a view to clearing them both at first light in the morning.
The 9th Brigade is to occupy the area Villons-les-Buissons - Le Vey.
The 10th Armoured Regiment, and the 6th less one squadron, are to revert to the command of the 2nd Armoured Brigade and harbour in the area Beny-sur-Mer - Basly. (In fact, the whole of the 6th Armoured Regiment harboured at Pierrepont in the 7th Brigade area.)

Division orders active patrolling and "utmost preparation" to meet a counter-attack at first light.

2130: General Montgomery embarks from Portsmouth aboard the Destroyer HMS *Faulkner* to enter Normandy and take command of his troops.

"The beach was filled with men and machines by the time we arrived, I admired the beach masters, the medics and the padres – because they stayed on the beach all the time, If the man you were landing with was shot, you weren't allowed to stop and help him. The beach master would be there saying, 'you carry on up the beach, we'll look after him.'" Albert Williams TAC H.Q. Unit

Marshal Rommel arrives at his command post by car after a journey of around 800 km.

2145:
OMAHA - Artillery barrages firing from the south-east of the area of Maisy are reported.

2200:

On Périers ridge, a woman named Marie-Louise Omont leaves her shelter and is surrounded by farm animals killed by artillery and two German soldiers cautiously moving along the pasture wall. They looked, the French woman wrote, "*lost, disoriented, sad.*" She told them they must still have friends where the guns were firing. As they left, she wondered, "*What will be their fate? How many more of them are still in the area, hiding and watching?*"

Nearby, British soldiers carry the bodies of three men to a meadow. They are placed beside other dead soldiers from the Signal Corps and Artillery Regiments.

Grave registration units would identify and bury them where they lay. Telegrams of condolence and appreciation for the ultimate sacrifice in war would be sent to the families. Later, the soldiers would be disinterred and laid to rest in one of seventeen British cemeteries in Normandy.

JUNO – *Scylla* returns to SWORD area for the night.

2215:

6th Airborne Division - 6th Airlanding Brigade - 2nd Battalion begin to move forward to cross the bridges. At this time four glider loads have failed to land. A few people have been hurt in crash landings including the Commanding Officer who manages to carry on and the Loading Officer who has to be evacuated. Major Howard commanding the Bridge Assault Force reports to the Commanding Officer and says that the route to the concentration area is clear. Despite the darkness

> We had numerous targets and were told that our gunnery was good and effective. At times we were close enough to see the men ashore through glasses. One Marine came to me on the Keyboard saying that he had been looking at the beach through glasses watching a German soldier running along the beach in between shell bursts, backwards and forwards until his luck ran out. The first two waves of troops were virtually wiped out but after a massive softening up by bombardment, the third wave got through.
>
> Royal Marine WCS Hiscock
> PO/X112968 - HQ192 Squad.
> On board HMS Hawkins

S.S. Panzer Grenadiers

Bundesarchiv, image 146-1994-025-11 / Mielke / CC BY-SA

of the night the Regiment moves quickly into the concentration area and a temporary HQ is set up.

2230:
CAEN is bombed for a third time. The area near the port is heavily damaged.

ARROMANCHES is liberated by the men of 1st Battalion, Royal Hampshire. The allies reach the outskirts of Bayeux.

HMS *Largs* reports being bombed by enemy aircraft, they can not fire back due to allied fighters in the vicinity.

2300:
SWORD: German air raid awakens those that have tried to get a few minutes sleep. Rocket carrying landing craft with 1000 rockets on each one fire at the aircraft. Tons of flak going up force the men on the ships to take cover. Two bombs fall close to Warspite but no damage done.

OMAHA Beach: Major Tegtmeyer reports by radio to Colonel Ficchy that nothing has been done to evacuate the wounded and something needs to be sorted out asap.

Colonel Thomas J.B. Shanley (2/508th) decides to abandon the attack planned for the Douve Bridge at Pont-l'Abbé, and directs his men to the regiment's gathering point, an elevation known as Hill 30. Once arrived, the group organises strategic defences for the zone.

HQ and HQ Battery of the 82nd Airborne, the 319th Glider Field Artillery Battalion and the 320th Glider Field Artillery Battalion fly silently into Normandy and encounter severe enemy small arms and mortar fire. Reorganisation commences immediately but is handicapped by the intense enemy fire. The section of the 456th Parachute Field Artillery Battalion attached to the 505th PIR jumps with the 3rd Battalion but is only able to assemble one of the two 75 mm Howitzers which have been dropped.

POINTE DU HOC: Counter-attack led by 40 German soldiers from the 1/914th against the US Rangers.

2320:
OMAHA - The predicted air attack is now being delivered. There are no radar warnings of the approach of the hostile planes and the first information of the impending attack is the sight and sound of an enemy plane which passes over the flagship at low altitude. Only a few more planes go over of which three were shot down. Several bombs are dropped in the transport area but cause no damage.

Commander of the Army Corps, General Marcks: "*Tomorrow, as today, the division will be able to offer strong resistance to our archenemy. However, due to the significant losses we have suffered, reinforcements should be assigned the day after tomorrow. The losses in men and material are considerable. Many artillery positions are buried under the debris from artillery and aerial bombardment. The garrisons nests of resistance (WN's) provide a valiant defence. WN 74-91 are at full defensive ability despite the loss. All available reserves are incurred. Every inch of ground must be defended until new reinforcements can be sent to you*".

2330:
Much of the initial fighting may have finished, but Albert Williams got little sleep beneath the canvas of his lorry, as he passed through the night into D Day+1 at the top of the beach. He wasn't the only one who felt nervous in the war-echoing night. "*I remember an American came over and asked if I could take a look at a problem he was having with his Jeep. I went over to the car, and he pointed at the fluorescent speedometer. He was worried that it would be seen by enemy fighter planes. That's how nervous we all were at the time. He said he couldn't work out how to turn the light off. I laughed and told him he wouldn't, as it wasn't a light, it was fluorescent paint. I fixed the problem by putting a paper bag over it, and he went off greatly relieved.*"

At around midnight Major John Howard handed over command of the bridges to the Warwickshire Regiment and his company left to join the rest of their battalion at Ranville

224th Parachute Field Ambulance, RAMS, reports Lieut. Philo with Cpl. Cummings & a captured German medical orderly went to Breville & capture 63 German ORs. 5 wagons, 1 m/g & approximately 30 blankets. In the late afternoon and evening the MDS which is together with Bde. HQ & HQ 1 Canadian Parachute Bn. is constantly sniped but the Field Ambulance suffered no casualties. Approximately two thirds of the Unit are still unaccounted for.

2359:
Enemy aircraft which were not seen during the day have now appeared over the beachhead and many bombs were heard to fall.

Pointe du Hoc: General Kraiss reports to the General Marcks that "*The attack against the 1st*

> *Dear Mother,*
>
> *Well here I am, safe and sound in France, sorry I have not written before but I have been a bit busy the last few days…*
>
> *Anon*

Forward 14"/45 guns of USS Nevada (BB-36) fire on positions ashore, during the landings on "Utah" Beach, 6 June 1944 Source:

US Navy Photo #: 80-G-252412

Company of the 914th Regiment of Grenadiers is still ongoing".

JUNO: Crossing between command posts, Lieutenant James Doohan is hit by six rounds of friendly fire, four in his leg, one in the chest, and one through his right middle finger. The bullet to his chest was stopped by a silver cigarette case and without doubt would have killed him. His right middle finger has to be amputated, something he concealed throughout his acting career.

By evening the 3rd Division has linked up with the British 50th Division from GOLD Beach to the west, but to the east the Canadians are unable to make contact with the British 3rd Division from SWORD Beach—leaving a gap of 3 km (2 miles) into which elements of the German 21st Panzer Division counterattacked.

Along with the Canadians was a French resistance soldier named R. Guenard who fought and died with them and who had no known relatives, he is buried with Canadian soldiers in Beny-sur-mer.

The overall situation at Midnight:

SWORD Beach, 29,000 troops landed, with fewer than 1,000 casualties. The troops had reached six miles inland.

GOLD Beach 25,000 troops had been landed on GOLD, with fewer than 1,000 casualties

OMAHA – A tiny, precarious beachhead has been established. There are pockets of US forces over an area approximately five miles wide by 1.5 miles deep.

The troops who landed on UTAH have reached about four miles inland. An almost textbook landing; by midnight, 23,250 troops were ashore, with under 200 casualties. The US airborne divisions suffered 2,499 casualties, including 338 killed.

JUNO, 21,400 troops landed, with under 1,000 casualties. The original aim of capturing the airfield was not achieved. No link-up had yet been made with SWORD beach to the east.

The Royal Winnipeg Rifles War Diary's final entry on that day emphasizes: *"NOT ONE MAN flinched from his task, no matter how tough it was — not one officer failed to display courage and energy and a degree of gallantry. It is thought that the Little Black Devils, by this day's success, managed to maintain the tradition set by former members. Casualties for the day exceeded 130."*

About 170,000 men are now fighting in Normandy. Allied Command is optimistic. Reinforcements continue to arrive.

A large bridgehead has been established, six miles wide and deep, linking up with Canadians at JUNO Beach. No. 47 Royal Marine Commando are ready to take Port-en-Bessin on following day.

With the drive towards Caen temporarily stalled, the 3rd Division make ready to resume the advance the next day…

"I often hear the phrase, 'When the Americans liberated us,' in conversation. No. The Americans were with the British, the French and the Canadians, during the landings and it was, after all, Britain that suffered the crux of the struggle for several years."

Louis Mexandeau, a former war veterans minister on how some overlook the contribution made by other Allied Nations.

In amongst a sea of Canadian graves lies R. Guenard, buried with the men he fought with.

SITUATION 2400 HRS 6 JUNE 1944
HQ. FUSAG

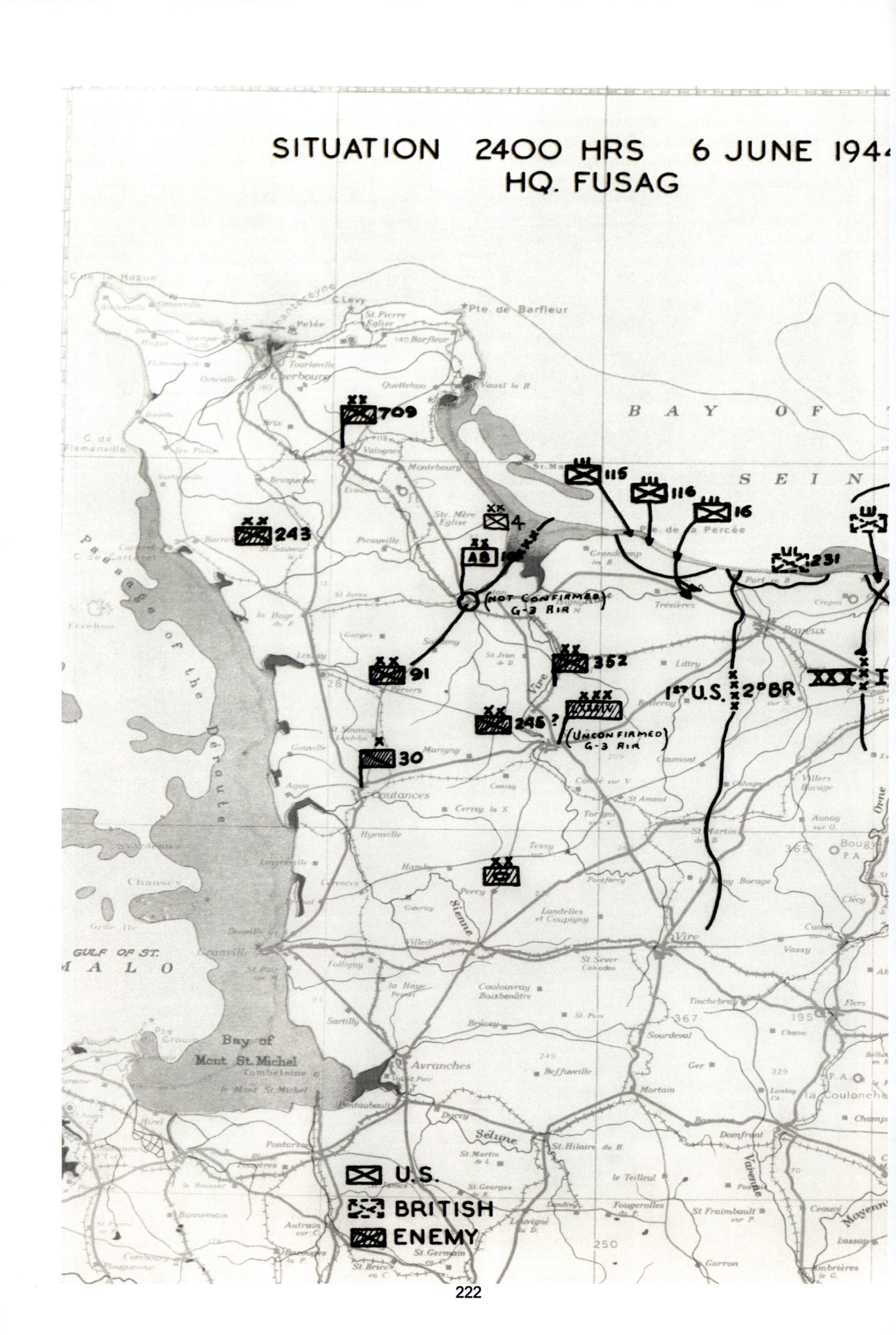

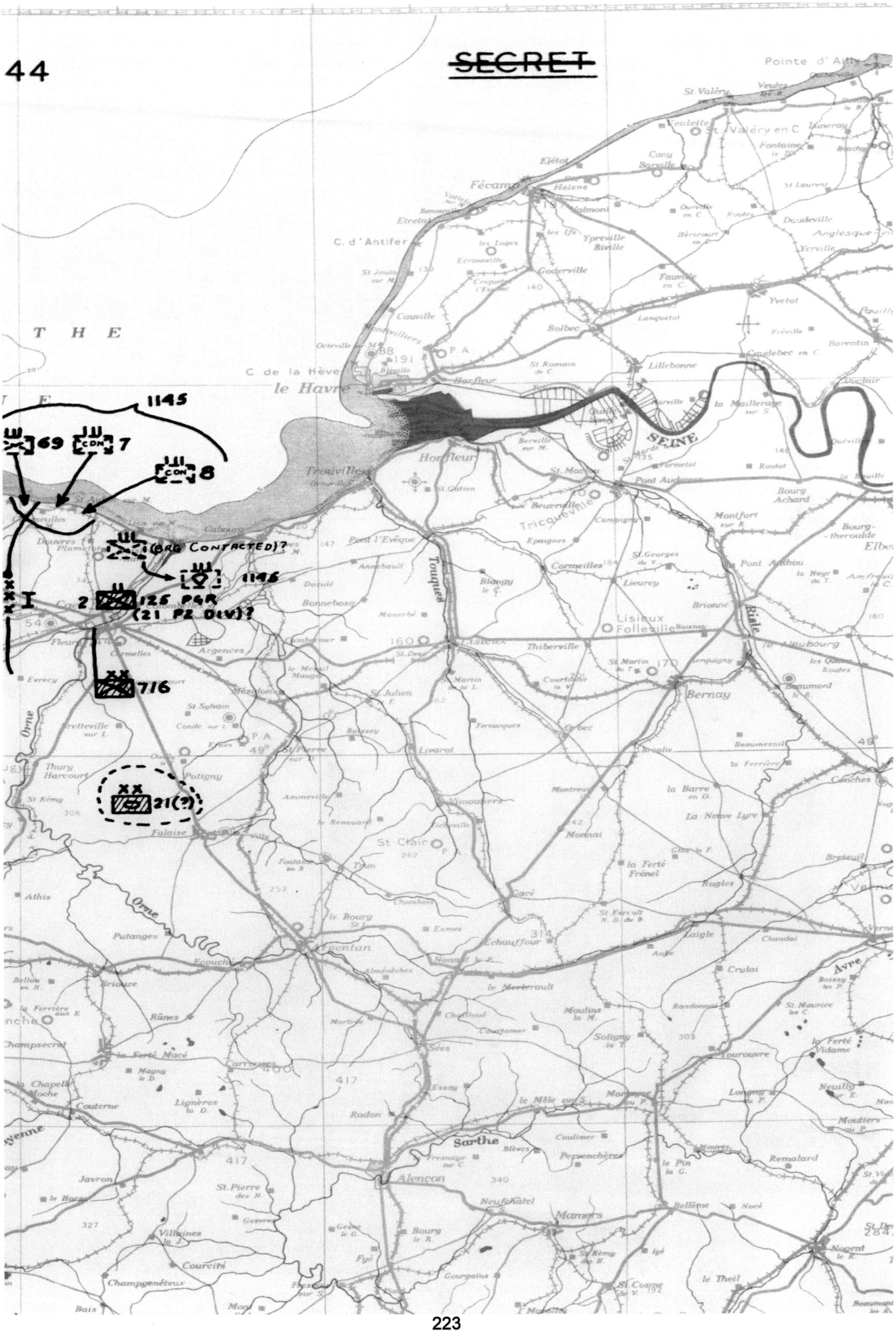
44
SECRET
1145
69
CDN 7
CDN 8
(BRG CONTACTED)?
1146
I
2
125 PGR
(21 PZ DIV)?
716
21(?)
THE
le Havre
C. de la Hève
Harfleur
Honfleur
Trouville
Cabourg
SEINE
Fécamp
Etretat
C. d'Antifer
Goderville
Bolbec
Lillebonne
Yvetot
St. Valéry en C.
Pointe d'Ailly
Pont Audemer
Pont l'Evêque
Cormeilles
Lisieux
Bernay
Caen
Falaise
Argentan
Orne
Touques
Risle
Vimoutiers
Livarot
Orbec
Thury Harcourt
Potigny
Evrecy
Gacé
Laigle
Sées
Alençon
Sarthe
Mamers
Bellême
Nogent le R.
Mortagne
Echauffour
la Ferté Macé
Carrouges
Conches
Rugles
Verneuil
Avre
Montfort sur R.
Bourg Achard
Brionne
le Neubourg
Beaumont le R.
Thiberville
Dozulé
Bonnebosq
Honfleur
Putanges
Briouze
Rânes
Couterne
Lignières
Javron
Villaines la J.
Courcité
Fresnay sur S.
Neufchâtel
le Mêle sur S.
Moulins la M.
Courtomer
Montreuil
Monnai
la Ferté Frênel
la Barre en O.
la Neuve Lyre
Breteuil

"On the way down the high street we were met by a six foot, eighteen stone Gendarme, who stood in the road waving his arms in the air. We stopped to find out what the trouble was, but there was no trouble, we has blind drunk and singing. We stopped to have a bit of light relief, and we were glad we did, for he produced a bottle of Calvados and insisted we all share with his ecstatic happiness of liberation. Never having drunk Calvados we all did the same and took a big gulp and a couple of swallows. Then, bang, it hit us. The clear watery liquid turned to red hot fire in our throats, leaving us gasping for breathe!"

Mne. Norman G. Marshall. 7/9/15 RM Museum, Southsea

Troops returning to the UK

Capt G. Lugg private collection

WHAT?
FACTS, FIGURES AND FORGOTTEN HEROES.

Have you forgotten yet?...
Look up, and swear by the green of the spring that you'll never forget.

Siegfried Sassoon

Facts and Figures

D-Day and Operation Neptune was the biggest seaborne invasion and the greatest military campaign the world had ever seen, the likes of which will probably never be seen again.

Below are some facts and figures that give some indication of the sheer numbers of people and equipment needed for such an ambitious assault.

Allied troops landed in Normandy - 156,115
American (OMAHA & UTAH beaches + airborne) - 73,000
British (GOLD & SWORD beaches + airborne) - 61,715
Canadian (JUNO Beach) - 21,400
Airborne troops (included in figures above) 2 - 3,400
Aircraft supporting the landings - 11,590
Sorties flown by allied aircraft - 14,674
Aircraft lost -127
Personnel in Operation Neptune - 195,700
American - 52,889
British - 112,824
Other allied - 4988

2,727 Ships
1,213 Warships
832 Landing craft
300 Minesweepers
286 Destroyers
22 Cruisers

As well as the troops who landed in Normandy on D-Day, and those in supporting roles at sea and in the air, millions more men and women in the Allied countries were involved in the preparations for D-Day. They played thousands of different roles, both in the Armed Forces and as civilians.

The Forgotten Heroes'

There were many people involved in the Normandy landings that often get forgotten. I have selected two, a female nurse and an Army Chaplain that are representative of hundreds of others.

Women

We forget that there were many women involved in D Day. Members of the Queen Alexandra's Imperial Military Nursing Service (QAIMNS) and many of the Navy nurses of the QARNNS were there at the frontline to care for Allied casualties and injured Prisoners of War.

With thanks to QARANC below are extracts from the war diaries of Nursing Sister Margaret Eva Price describing her experiences with the QAs as part of the WW2 British Liberation Army.

She was called up at age 50 as a QA reservist. She was born 24 February 1894 and left Barts as a qualified SRN in November 1920. She then returned to Barts for a six week duty as a Sister 2 in 1923. Much of her training period involved nursing WW1 soldiers in the surgical wards, which her family think may explain her interest in army nursing.

These war diary extracts have been kindly provided by her family, who knew her as Aunt Madge. After the war Sister Price became Matron of a Sussex nursing home and entertained Princess Alexandra when she came to open a new wing. She wore her QA medallion. Sister Price died in 1983.

It has always been the tradition of the Q.A.I.M.N.S. to serve wherever they are needed. In peacetime this may mean anywhere in the British Empire, in wartime in all theatres of war in places as far apart as Iceland or Singapore, Scotland or Mesopotamia, and in the present stage of the war, on the Continent or in Burma. We are now at what we know is the final phase of the war, and since June last year a very large proportion of the Service is with the British Liberation Army – having followed the troops across the Channel, camped in Normandy orchards and trekked across North France and Flanders into the countryside of Belgium and the villages of Holland near to the Western borders of Germany.

In order to be of use to the Army, it is as well to know how they live, just as those who have experienced illness can tell far better than those who have never been ill, what it feels like. We are all apt to be slightly un-imaginative about something which troubles us personally not at all, but when we have lived it for ourselves, it means something and that knowledge can be translated into practical efficiency.

Like the men, our units mobilised in U.K. and when the time came, proceeded to a marshalling area, ready for embarkation. This meant living in a transit camp until we left England. These camps are remarkably well run and we lived in great comfort. The food was excellent, there were hot and cold showers, and even organised entertainment in the form of a cinema. The only drawback was that we now had to break off communication with the outside world, owing to security being such a vital matter. We felt rather like disembodied spirits, as though still at home, no news could be given to one's family.

Nursing Sister Margaret Eva Price

QARANC

However, the period was a busy enough time for most units as there was less than 24 hours to wait and our minds were on personal equipment and how to compress all necessities into the most portable form. Throughout the hours in camp, a business-like voice could be heard issuing instructions over a loudspeaker to those who were due to depart. Our turn came at the reasonable hour of 6.30a.m. Breakfast was at 7 a.m. and departure was timed for 8 a.m. for the nearest port. Here again, all was rapid and well-organised – no more than time for a cup of tea before we went up the gangway onto a Hospital Carrier. We were the first members of the Service to be transported on that particular Carrier and the staff on board were somewhat tickled to see their colleagues laden like pack-horses struggling up the gangway. Tin helmets, water bottles, gas masks, haversacks, were all carried slung like those of the men. The crossing was quiet and uneventful and again we had every facility for washing, much appreciated as we always expected each time to be the last. We slept in our clothes that night, anchored off the French coast, and although there was a certain amount of air activity overhead it was easy enough to pass right out in the rather drugged atmosphere of a rigid black-out.

We were ashore next morning by 9 a.m. and it was a good feeling to know that we were following up those who had stormed the beaches on D-Day. Everyone left behind in England after June 6th knows how empty the country seemed when all the troops had left. How quiet London appeared, how different the journey in a train where one could get a compartment to oneself instead of standing in a corridor lined with the British Army. Well, it was our turn to be among them now "over there" and our privilege to live under the same conditions. We came to it feeling lucky to be in it and although there are times when this feeling wears thin, because it is no longer a novelty, I doubt if anyone would want to be without the experience.

The next few weeks must be sketched quickly because we were not working. General impressions stand out, the dusty ride from the beach over bad roads to our destination in Normandy. The welcome given us by the men who caught sight of us passing, and seemed glad to know we were with them. Journey's end for that day was another transit camp attached to a large hospital, and there we stayed for ten days, adapting ourselves to being under canvas. When the weather was good it seemed like a summer holiday in rather peculiar surroundings. When bad, we tried to adjust ourselves, rather painfully, to walking across two sodden, muddy fields to breakfast wearing the invaluable army boots, tin hats and gas capes for protection.

Off again after ten days to stake out a claim on our own field with our own board outside showing that we counted at last among the "also rans" in Harley Street – so called because the road was lined with the Medical profession. This field seemed particularly wet and the tents had a nauseating habit of falling down when the gales started. We often felt we were qualified for the rum ration at that time, especially the night when the Post Office collapsed and our sodden letters were brought back the next day to be re-written. However, we developed some sort of routine and in between the business of lighting the stoves to get ourselves and our clothes clean, we found time to lorry-hop into the nearest town for the odd spot of entertainment at the E.N.S.A. Theatre

The Army Chaplain.

It can not be over emphasised how important the role of the Army Chaplain was and still is. in the services. There role was so much more than providing a church service or burying the dead. They were of great comfort to the troops who would often go out of their way to ensure the Padres did not get injured. They were moral boosters, comforters, tea makers and often stretcher bearers. They worked very closely with the Medical Corps as they were closely linked, being volunteers and did not carry arms.

These are the words of The Rev. T.H. Lovegrove, who was the Padre attached to the 6th Battalion of the Green Howards and landed with them on Gold Beach on the 6th June 1944. His story is representative of so many others and is re-produced with the kind permission of The Museum of Army Chaplaincy, Amport House. Lovegrove Papers.

Extracts from "A D-DAY LANDING"
The Reverend T H Lovegrove MC.

"It was my privilege to serve as Padre with the 6th Battalion of the Green Howards, part of the 50th Tyne & Tees Territorial Division. Many had served with the Regiment in France including Dunkirk. They were subsequently posted to the Middle East and became part of the 8th Army Desert Force. They were at Alamein; described by Churchill as the " end of the beginning". They came home via Sicily and were eventually to learn they were to be part of Operation Overlord for which Churchill also had a word "The Beginning of the End". So we came to Gold Beach, Normandy.

We were fortunate to have a substantial number in our Ranks who could rightly be called Veterans'; men who had become experienced in battle conditions, and who in a wonderful way absorbed reinforcements in a manner which ensured the efficiency and high morale of the 6th & 7th Battalions being maintained. In this the CSMs (Company Sergeant Major) played a vital role and many a young subaltern owed much to their influence and example.

What is the Padre's role in such an undertaking? Both in the preparation period and the actual action he is perhaps the one person with time to be a confidant, a Counsellor; time to share the family concerns, the hopes and fears of all involved. The emphasis is upon SERVICE rather than Services, though at least I had an opportunity to conduct a Service from the bridge of our destroyer on the Sunday before D Day the following Tuesday.
My course to D-Day began when I was flown from North Africa to Sicily to join the 50th Northumbrian Division (TT) attached to the 6th Battalion The Green Howards as a replace-ment for a fellow Baptist Chaplain who with the doctor had been killed by a direct hit on their First Aid Post. At the end of the campaign the Division was brought back to England and it was not long before we knew we were to be one of the Assault Divisions for the 2nd Front, for which we went into intensive training, which included Assault exercises on Loch Fyne and for which on the Day I was mighty glad we had been so prepared.

To show how a Padre can make a psychological blunder about a month previous we had a full scale exercise off Hayling Island with, and on, the craft we should be with on the day. I conducted a Service on board our ship which included the: Brigade Headquarters our supporting arms and my own Battalion. The Captain of the ship read the lesson and I preached for 10 minutes on the text 'The Hour is now come'; and discovered I had created an air of deep depression. "After all the Padre would be in the know; here were we thinking this was a practice and its the real thing and so things we would not have brought on the actual day and what we would have included on the day we had not got! Fortunately I had an opportunity to repair the damage a month later when I again conducted a Service with a different text from Psalm 24. After which the Captain asked me to go down to his cabin not for a drink or a social word but with a request 'Padre would you pray for me; you know what is happening tomorrow and how important it is we succeed in our task, Padre I'm not big enough I want some help!'. There in his cabin I commended him and those aboard to God to strengthen and support our endeavour.

Of D-Day itself — delayed to the Tuesday because of the weather. At first light I recall vividly how the sea was full of ships of all kinds and overhead the planes were bombing and the naval bombardment was in progress, We were due to land on Gold Beach; the first wave of infantry would follow the Tank Landing craft and the men got into the small LCIs which were on the davits where normally would be the life boats, and were lowered into what was quite a rough sea. With the doctor and others we awaited the return of the LCT and to board we had to go down the scrambling nets and choosing the right moment to jump into these boats — no easy task with full kit, and then about 100 yards from the Beach transfer into the small assault craft who had disembarked the assault companies. Nearing the Beach our orders were, no matter where we were, the moment the ramp went down out we went; I was lucky only getting my feet wet but we lost some men who landed in shell holes, though some we managed to hang on to. My first reaction on getting on the Beach was how narrow it was and I was glad that my job was to keep with the Battalion under orders to push on; as we lay waiting for the clearance of the minefield in front of us I recognised a number of our Battalion who were casualties, and saw something of the action which won D- D Coy CSM Stan Hollis the only Normandy VC. As we pushed in land I became very much involved with the Doctor and we had plenty of work to do. By the end of the day I was trying to meet needs in the various Companies by keeping in touch with the 500 cc Norton Bike, issued to the RSM Dixon who very reluctantly handed it over.

There were considerable Casualties on the first day, but these were cared for by the Beach Groups who were magnificent; our task to push forward as soon as able. There was one encounter on the Beach with a young Lieutenant who was obviously feeling the strain who said to me "Padre its alright for you, you've got faith, but many of us have nothing and its Hell."

After the first day, small patrols were sent out to seek enemy positions. My practice was to see the Patrol away, often with a silent prayer if requested, but always a silent one and I would wait at the departure point until their return. I was often the main link link between the wounded and the RAP and the MO. and would mobilise assistance when necessary.

I must mention one incident that lives with me. I had witnessed something of the heroic action of CSM Hollis, for which he was awarded the V.C. After the debacle of Point 101 when, in the complexity of the Bocage landscape men were being whittled away by sniper fire. Stan Hollis came into the RAP with a couple of his lads who were wounded and he broke down bitterly on my shoulder at this killing of what he called 'his men' by an unseen enemy. I have never forgotten his tears as a token of his concern for his company especially for those who had been at Dunkirk and come through the Desert fighting unscathed. A strong man in tears!! Thus you can realise how appropriate the 2nd Army Prayer was to us in the Normandy undertaking.

"O Lord God, when Thou givest to Thy servants to undertake any great matter; grant them also to know that it is not the beginning; but the continuing of the same, until it be thoroughly finished, which yieldeth the true glory: through him, that for the finishing of Thy work laid down His "Life, our Redeemer, Jesus Christ. Amen."

Yet for me Normandy may have begun with D Day but it did not end there, much was to follow particularly as we got bogged down in the Bocage country, high corn, and hedges and every day more and more of the men being killed or wounded by the unseen enemy.

Take the Sunday after D-Day, we were to move to point 102 and then attack point 101; the first part would be a peaceful routine march, so we were told but it did not happen that way and by the end of the day we had lost 2 Company Commanders-- one of them I had presented for Confirmation at Winchester Cathedral, in the absence of the Anglican Padre — 6 other Officers, 20 NC0s, and a large number of other ranks.

The position became untenable, and the possibility of being captured made a withdrawal inevitable and my own feeling? so irrational — here was I going to be taken prisoner and I was improperly dressed; my battle dress top was on a stretcher to cover a corporal with a massive abdominal wound, and another casualty had my water bottle.

During that period until breakfast, we had five different COs, 3 in one week, and more than half the Battalion had been killed or wounded, and that included CSM Hollis who I was able to bring out, though the shell which caused his wound smashed the windscreen of my jeep, punctured a tyre and when I returned to the dressing station and was on my way back and was prevented, as Ronnie Lofthouse pointed out by a Teller mine over which I had passed on two occasions, but which because of the narrow lane I had not touched. The next day looking for some of the men who had been killed in that Point 101 attack, I had an anti-personnel mine all to myself but managed to get back to the doctor. When I rejoined the Division they were between Nimegen and Arnhem trying to get some of the boys out.

Rev. Lovegrove was decorated with an MC Ribbon Award, for action in the early days of the Normandy Landings. His citation reads as follows.

On the 19th July 1944, 6th Green Howards carried out an advance on Lion Vert - Les Landes sector. At about 1500 hrs.

The leading Coy came under fire from enemy spandaus and rifles and several men were wounded. Padre Lovegrove immediately went forward in his jeep and whilst still under accurate and sustained fire assisted in the evacuation of all the casualties.

On returning from the RAP he stopped near a Reserve Coy HQ just at the moment it came under heavy mortar fire wounding 2 Officers and 6 OR's. At the same time his jeep was hit by a large bomb fragment. Padre Lovegrove immediately turned the vehicle and while bombs were still falling proceeded at once to Coy HQ where once again he was largely responsible for supervising the evacuation on all casualties.

During these two incidents, this officer showed a complete disregard for his own safety which was earned the admiration of all ranks of the Bn. His prompt action and fearless conduct undoubtedly contributed in saving life from severe loss of blood.

He was himself wounded on the 21st July whilst acting in the same fearless manner."

20/7/44.

Headquarters
50 (Northumbrian) Division
B.L.A.

My dear Mrs Lovegrove,

Henry has asked me to write you a little note to let you know he has been slightly wounded, and to assure you there is nothing to be anxious about. So I promised him I would do so tonight so that when you receive the official War Office notification you should not be anxious as to the extent of his injuries.

He was wounded this afternoon when a mine blew up quite near him. He sent me a message and I went down at once to see him at the C.C.S., where wounded are taken before going on to the General Hospital. He was very cheerful when I saw him and we chatted and laughed together for some time, for apart from a little stiffness he seemed to be free from pain. He has a few bits of shrapnel spread over his person and as soon as they are removed should be well and about again. But no doubt he will be writing you himself, telling you how he is, in a day or so.

I am awfully sorry he has been wounded for he has been doing a grand job of work, which has been much appreciated by Officers and Men alike, and we other Chaplains will be sorry to lose him — temporarily I hope — from our team. He has done extremely well. I hope you are well and that the mail will get through to you quickly so as to avoid any suspense on your part.

With every good wish, and God bless you.

Yours very sincerely, Geoffrey Lawes
Senior Chaplain

Letter sent to Rev. Lovegroves wife from The Senior Chaplain Geoffrey Lawes, informing her that her husband had been injured. The writing doing his best to assure her that his injuries were minor and she had nothing to worry about.

The letter is dated the 20th July but Rev. Lovegrove was not injured until the 21st July. © The Museum of Army Chaplaincy, Amport House. Lovegrove Papers.

END NOTE

Whilst writing this book a couple of people told me about family connections with D Day which I felt needed to be included.

In passing a friend mentioned that his wife's great uncle was at Pegasus Bridge and was killed shortly after. I asked if she could possibly find out some more and with a little research we managed to piece together some details.

He was just a regular guy, not much more than a boy doing his bit for his country and is representative of so many other young men just like him. It is to them that we owe a huge debt of gratitude.

Dictated by his niece Margaret Patricia Shaw nee Davies, this is reproduced in her own words.

Elwyn George William Davies. Born 1st Nov 1924, died of wounds 16th June 1944.

One mystery that I've got no answer for is that his surname is Davis but on his headstone it's written Davies. I don't know whether he changed the spelling on enlisting in the army or if it was an error. Another possible reason could be that my grandfather (his father) died in 1926, my mother (his sister) was 9 years older than him, she and my father married in 1937, Elwyn was very close to both of them and my father being 15 years older than him became a father figure to him and my father's surname was Davies.

I was 5 when he died but I can remember him, seeing him in uniform especially one leave when he wouldn't come near me as I had chickenpox, and he didn't want to catch it and miss whatever was going on at camp. The next time he came home he brought me a puppy and called it 'Friday' as obviously Friday was the day he gave it to me..

The last time we saw him was when he came home around about the time of his grandmother's birthday - May 21st. If he had leave between then and D-Day, he may well have gone to see his fiancée in Manchester - that was his second engagement! He was quite a lad I think but lovely with it, we found so many girls' addresses later but the only girl's photo he had with him was of me aged 4-5 and the back of that had girls' addresses over it.

I was told by mother that she used to get very cross with him as he used to use her teddy bears as a parachutist, tying hankies to them and dropping them out of the bedroom window, so it's no surprise he ended up jumping out of planes.

He tried to join up when he was underage and did go off somewhere but the family got him home though as soon as he was of age he was back in the army - he was born at Elliot Street, New Tredegar, Mon, South Wales, his father was George Davis and his mother Elizabeth. He went to Cwmsyviog Infant and Junior School, then New Tredegar Central School and finally New Tredegar Technical College. I remember going there with my mother to the unveiling of a plaque with his name and about 9 others I think were all killed in the war.

I remember going to Brecon to see him and can remember sitting by the river and I think he was then in Royal Welsh Fusiliers. I know it wasn't the South Wales Borderers, after that he probably volunteered for Paras and I'm sure there is a regiment stated on his headstone as it would have been part of the 6th Airborne Division. He absolutely loved it and then he was nicknamed 'Dizzy' Apparently they had to do so many jumps to qualify but he told me he would do jumps for other lads who didn't feel like doing it. In fact my grandmother acquired a dog at this time and it was named 'Dizzy' - quite aptly as it jumped through the kitchen window at least twice because he saw a cat on the windowsill.

I'm sure he did some training at Ringway Manchester and I also think he was at Salisbury.

One of his officers who he talked about a lot was Richard Todd (the actor) who he called 'Sweeney Todd'. I remember a photograph he brought home - long narrow one - possibly the official photo of the regiment and both he and R Todd are on it (my uncle was a private) it looked like hundreds of men to me and afterwards we were told that so few came home.

Another photo I remember is of a group of them (possibly 20) and a woman (prob WRAF or ATS) and she was the one I believe who packed their parachutes, they liked the same person to do that each time.

I also remember that he would never let any of the family go to the bus top or station to see him off and I think that the last time he was home, the adults sensed something was about to happen and my mother spoke years after of hearing so many, many planes going over on the night of 5th /6th June and feeling certain that Elwyn was going.

He also had a notebook in which he kept girls' addresses (again) train times, money or no mon-

ey. One afternoon he wrote they'd been having a lecture on recognising German tanks and I think afterwards he said he went to the pictures!

D-Day, he was at Pegasus Bridge - whether he jumped or went in the glider I don't know. I like to think and really hope that he jumped as that was what life was about for him, what happened after, I don't know. One of his friends who was with him right up until 16th June came to see us, but I was never told any of that warfare. I do know that we were told by Len, his friend, that Elwyn had both legs blown off - again I don't know by what- and he was taken to a field hospital where he died without regaining consciousness. BUT what was so awful for the family was the telegram came telling us he was wounded in action, and in the weeks following, we heard no more. My father wrote to all the hospitals admitting casualties, even put notices in the paper asking if anyone had news of him, and then August Bank Holiday (it was then at the beginning of August) another telegram came telling us that Elwyn had died of his wounds on June 16th.

It was when Len came home (he lived in the next village) and came to visit that he told us what had happened, how long after D-Day that was I don't know…

After a little research we were able to fill in the gaps for Margaret about her Uncle Elwyn.

The 7th (Light Infantry) Parachute Battalion was formed from the 10th Battalion The Somerset Light Infantry in November 1942. It initially belonged to the 3rd Parachute Brigade but was transferred to the 5th Parachute Brigade as the 6th Airborne Division was formed in 1943.

The Battalion jumped into Normandy on D-Day the 6th June 1944 and relieved the glider-borne coup de main that had captured the bridges across the Orne River and Canal. It participated in the defensive battles around Breville and the eventual break-out to the Seine, before being withdrawn back to the UK in August.

This is the 7th Para War diary for the 1st to 16th June with a few memories and private diary entries added. From this we can determine that he died between 0425 and 0850 in Herouvillette during heavy shelling, he was 19 years old…..

7th Para. Commanding Officer : Lt. Col. R.G. Pine-Coffin

1st June 1944. Place: Tilshead

1000 - CO briefs Battalion for operation Overlord in a cinema in Tilshead.

1500 - Escape cards issued. (Maps printed onto playing cards and sandwiched together which would come apart when soaked in water.)

2nd June 1944. Place: Tilshead

Company Briefing - 1800 hrs Conference at Brigade HQ Harwell.

3rd June 1944. Place: Tilshead

Company Briefing - 1800 hrs Conference at Brigade HQ Harwell

2100 - Co-ordinating conference with Major HOWARD "D" Company 2 Ox & Bucks.

4th June 1944. Place: Tilshead

Visit to Fairford Airfield to fit parachutes and meet aircrew and then returned to Tilshead.
1800 hrs Conference at Brigade HQ Harwell.

5th June 1944. Place: Tilshead

Battalion moves to rest camp in Fairford Park. The journey was broken when the Battalion formed up at a disused Transit Camp for Padre Rev. E.M. Parry to conduct his last open air service as the next day, attending the wounded at Benouville he was killed. As they went through the villages they threw their loose change to the village children who were at the roadside cheering them on their way.

1900 hrs Battalion moves to airfield they were introduced to the air crew, offloaded their weapons and equipment and were informed they would board their aircraft at 2200. They checked their equipment one last time and blackened their faces.

2320 hrs Battalion takes off.

6th June 1944.

The 7th Parachute Battalion landed in Normandy. Many men of the battalion were scattered or landed on the wrong drop zone.

0100 - Ranville

Battalion completed the drop but went into action with Companies at half normal strength due to some plane loads being dropped in wrong places and one load not dropping at all.

0300 - Lieutenant-Colonel Pine-Coffin in command had only around forty percent of the battalion at the forming up point, although men continued to

"This ended a great day for the 7th Parachute Battalion. They fulfilled their task. They had held the West bridgehead and had twenty one hours continuous and hard fighting. The men were tired but well satisfied and proud of their achievements. Casualties had amounted to sixty killed and wounded."

General R.N. Gale Commander of 6th Airborne Division

Elwyn George Davies

appear throughout the day. Relatively few of their supply containers had been found, meaning that they possessed few heavy weapons or radio sets.

0325 - Battalion occupied objective and held it against various counter-attacks "A" and "B" Company being heavily engaged. Casualties: killed 3 Officers, Capt Parry (Padre), Lt Bowyer and Lt Hill, and 16 Other Ranks. Wounded: 4 Officers, Major Taylor, Capt Webber, Lt Hunter & Lt Tenple & 38 Other Ranks. Missing: 170 Other Ranks did not rendezvous after the drop.

0500 to 0700 - First German assault on the bridges which consisted of isolated and often uncoordinated attacks by tanks, armoured cars and infantry, which grew in intensity throughout the day. The Luftwaffe attempted to destroy the Caen bridge with a 1,000 lb (450 kg) bomb, which failed to detonate, and two German Navy coastal craft, which attempted to attack the bridge, were also repelled.

1325 - Battalion of Commandos passed through Battalion positions – Lord Lovats Special Service Brigade with his piper Bill Millen.

1900 - Leading elements of the British 3rd Infantry Division arrived and began to relieve the battalion.

2200 - Stick from aircraft which failed to drop arrived by glider - included Major Tullis and Lt Theobald and R.M.O. Capt Young..

2230 - Royal Warwickshire Battalion arrived and put in an attack on Benouville.

By midnight, the Battalion was being held in reserve behind the 12th Parachute Battalion occupying Le Bas de Ranville and the 13th Parachute Battalion holding Ranville

7th June 1944. Place: Le Port & Benouville

0015 - Battalion relieved by Royal Warwicks.

0045 - Battalion arrived in Brigade res and rest area at 105734. Odd parties of men re-joined the Battalion at various times during the day.

Place: Le Hom

1330 - Battalion moved out and took up a defensive position in area 112735 (Div res).

8th June 1944. Place: Le Hom

Battalion positions shelled and mortared at various times during the day, sometimes heavily.

2100 - Battalion seaborne party arrived.

9th June 1944. Place: Le Hom

1111 - Shell burst in area of Battalion HQ. 3 Other Ranks killed - 8 Other Ranks wounded.

1340 - L/C Spendlove (missing at time of drop) reported fighting with Special Service Commandos.

1450 - Shell burst over "B" Company area. 4 Other Ranks wounded.

2140 - Enemy aircraft bombed Battalion area.

2150 - Enemy aircraft strafed "B" Company area - 1 man wounded.

10th June 1944. Place: Le Hom

0500 - "B" Company area shelled for 30 minutes - 2 Other Ranks killed, 1 Other Rank wounded.

1025 - Party of enemy at 119740 reported believed destroyed by Battalion mortar and MG fire.

Place: Le Mesnil

1535 to 1809 - Battalion completed successful attack on enemy in woods between Battalion position and LE MESNIL taking up final position in LE MESNIL. Cas - wounded 1 officer Major NEAL, and 10 Other Ranks. Estimated 30 enemy killed - 90 take prisoner.

11th June 1944. Place: Le Mesnil

0630 - 2 prisoners captured.

1500 - "B" Company area shelled and mortared.

1530 - Battalion visited by BBC representatives.

2330 - Lt Thomas (B Company) shot and wounded by Company sentry.

12th June 1944. Place: Le Mesnil

1502 - Shelling and fire from North, Battalion stands to for an hour and "A" Company moves to 138726 to support 1 Canadian Battalion.

2155 - Unknown missile lands in "B" Company area. 6 Other Ranks wounded.

13th June 1944. Place: Herouvillette

1030 - Battalion moves to and takes up position in Herouvillette

1225 - A and C Company re-join Battalion.

1245 - Slight shelling of "B" Company area.

1530 - Slight shelling of "C" Company area.

1940 - Battalion area attacked by 4 or 5 Typhoon aircraft and swept by cannon fire. No casualties.

2335 to 2350 - Bombing around Battalion area.

14th June 1944. Place: Herouvillette

0415 to 0430 - Bombing around Battalion area.

2245 - Bombs (mortar) landed in "C" Company area. One NCO killed, 3 Other Ranks wounded.

15th June 1944. Place: Herouvillette

1640 - Enemy shelling near "B" Company area.

1650 - Two enemy maps found at 122722. One marked.

16th June 1944. Place: Herouvillette

0145 - 2 bombs fell 300 yards from Battalion HQ.

0425 to 0850 - Battalion area heavily shelled and mortared. 4 Tanks observed 600 yards SW of "C" Company.

Casualties: 2 Other Ranks killed and 4 Other Ranks wounded. Battalion mortars return fire of enemy in wood to E of "B" Company area.

0910 to 1030 - A Company move to clear wood. Caualties 1 Officer wounded (Lt McDonald) 3 Other Ranks wounded. 10 enemy killed, 11 POW taken (5 wounded) Armoured Cars moved to support "B" Company during "A" Company attack.

1700 – Commanding Officer attends Brigade Commander's conference and receives orders for change over with 8 Para Battalion. Company Commanders given orders on return.

2030 - Advance Party of 8 Battalion arrived and own advance party departs.

7th Para. Total Casualties 452, Killed 90.

General Montgomery boards a warship to attend a meeting of the Chiefs of Staff somewhere off the coast of Normandy
June 8, 1944
USNA

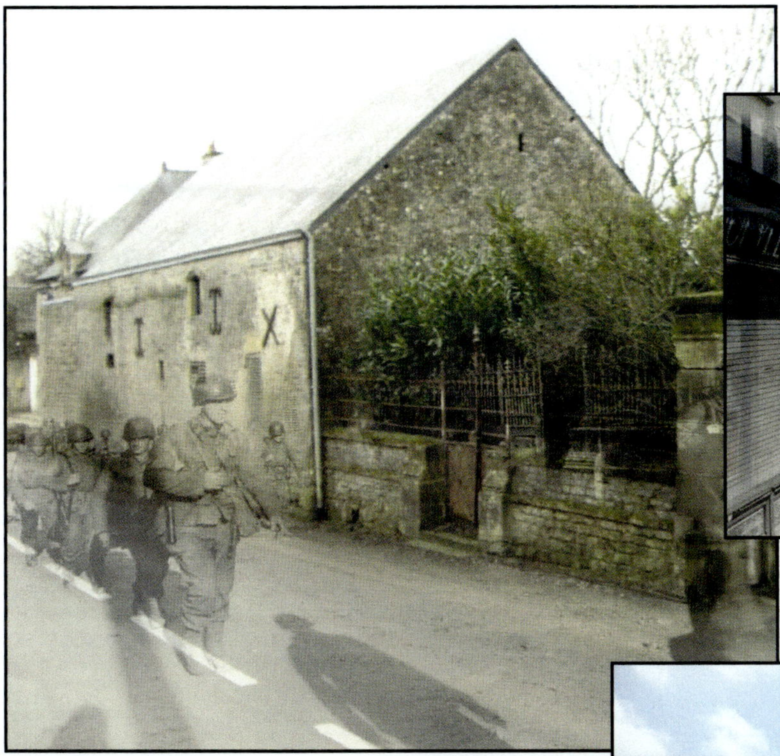

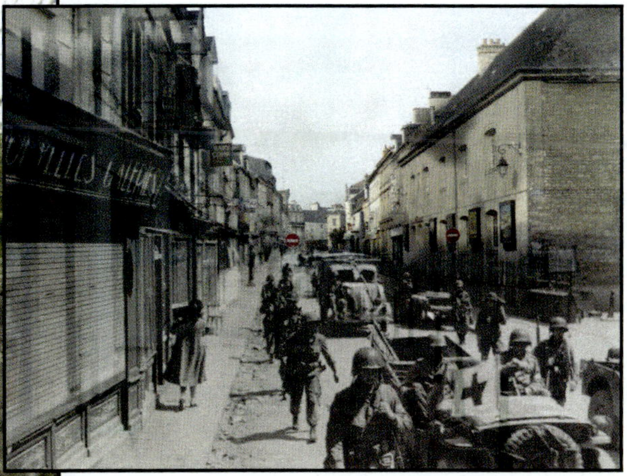

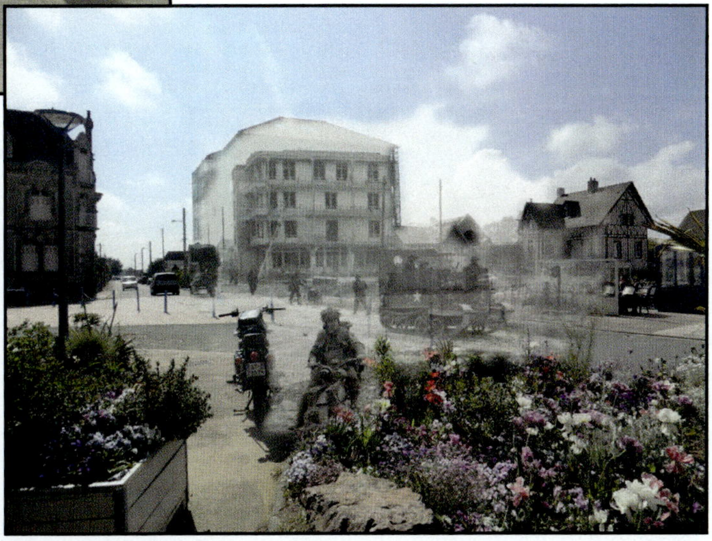

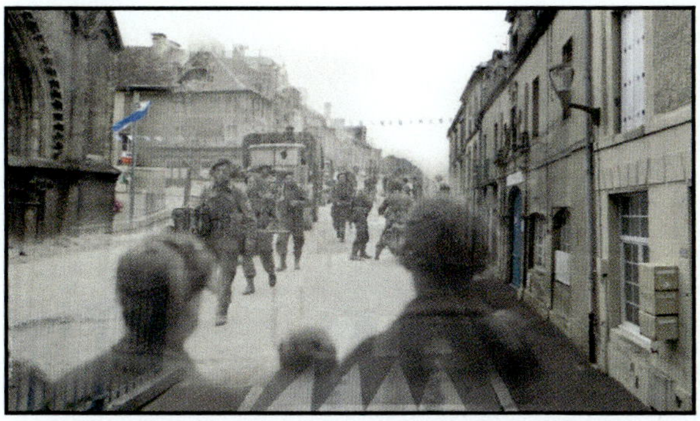

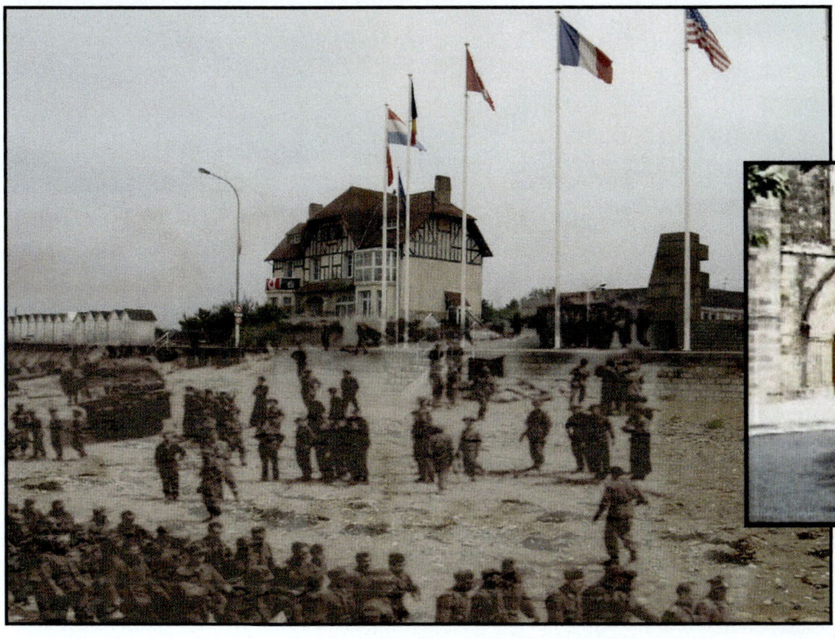

Ghosts - then and now

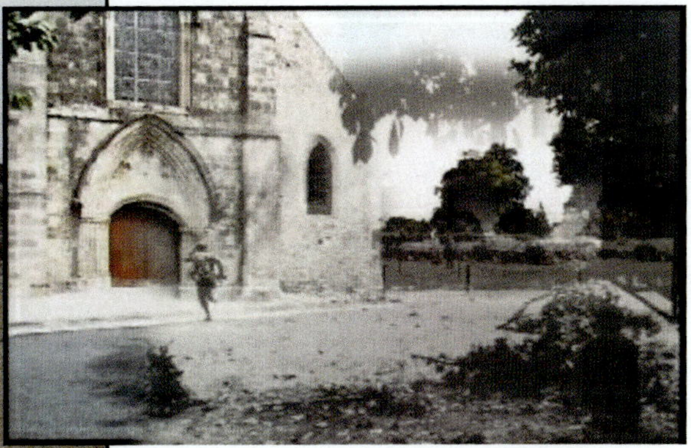

The following short story does not directly relate to D Day but more of the mopping up afterwards, but is worthy of mention for obvious reasons.

Reg Martin - My father.

Reg Martin served in 4th Battalion Grenadier Guards and drove a Churchill tank. His division landed in Normandy, then followed the advancing troops through Belgium, France and Holland and into Germany.

During one of their manoeuvres - 'Operation Bluecoat' - his division was joined by a large intake of Scots Guards. Most were very young and in order to give these frightened lads confidence, it was deemed by the commanding Officers that during the advance all the tank commanders should have their heads above the turret hatch.

On the opening day, 30th July 1944, his unit advanced on the left flank from the Caumont l'Evente - Briquessard road with the 3rd Scots Guards on their right. They moved towards Lutain Wood ...
These are my Dad's words ...

'Gerry had a field day. All the tank commanders were easy targets for German snipers. Captain Grey, our commander, was shot in the head shortly after we began the advance. We radio'd back to base and were ordered to retreat immediately which we did. The tank was full of his blood.

When we arrived back at base we brewed up a cup of tea while we dug his grave ... and buried him there.'

As both the family of the officer and the inhabitants of Le Repas were emphatic in their desire for Captain Grey's body to stay in the village, it was decided that it should remain there. The grave is marked by a private memorial.

Known as the Livry Isolated Grave, it is a rare example as most were brought into military cemeteries post 1945.

I am so very proud of my Dad.

Lynne Barker

Reg Martin marrying his childhood sweetheart Ruby. April 18th 1942

George Grey was born 2nd December 1918, and became a Member of Parliament for Berwick-upon-Tweed in August 1941, aged only 22 - quite an achievement. He was one of the youngest members of the House of Commons in the twentieth century.

The memorial on the grave takes the form of cross, surrounded by a small stone wall with a gate. The stone with which the memorial is made was brought specially from the Houses of Parliament - a fitting tribute to this young MP.

Left: The Livry Isolated Grave
Right: Captain George Grey of the 4th Bn Grenadier Guards, 6th Guards Tank Brigade, this photos was given to each of the tank crew by Captain Grey's family to thank them for what they had done.
Below: Reg Martin (left) and his tank crew

Photos courtesy of Reg Martin's daughter Lynne Barker.

Five years before he died, General Eisenhower went back to Colleville-sur-Mer. It was the first, and only, time he made that journey after the war. Looking over OMAHA Beach, he spoke from his heart:

. . . these men came here - British and our allies, and Americans - to storm these beaches for one purpose only, not to gain anything for ourselves, not to fulfil any ambitions that America had for conquest, but just to preserve freedom. . . . Many thousands of men have died for such ideals as these. . . but these young boys. . . were cut off in their prime. . . I devoutly hope that we will never again have to see such scenes as these. I think and hope, and pray, that humanity will have learned . . . we must find some way . . . to gain an eternal peace for this world.

70 years after D-Day, even though the world is no closer to finding "some way to gain an eternal peace" we can at least agree that those who fought, and died to free Europe, altered the course of history, and it is them that we remember today.

They went with songs to the battle, they were young.
Straight of limb, true of eyes, steady and aglow.
They were staunch to the end against odds uncounted,
They fell with their faces to the foe.

They shall grow not old, as we that are left grow old:
Age shall not weary them, nor the years condemn.
At the going down of the sun and in the morning,
We will remember them.

LEST WE FORGET

General Dwight (Ike) D. Eisenhower.

Commander Supreme Headquarter Allied Expeditionary Force

If I should die, think only this of me:
That there's some corner of a foreign field that is forever England.
There shall be in that rich earth a richer dust concealed;
a dust whom England bore, shaped, made aware,
gave, once, her flowers to love, her ways to roam;
a body of England's breathing English air,
washed by the rivers, blest by suns of home.
And think, this heart, all evil shed away,
a pulse in the eternal mind,
no less gives back somewhere the thoughts by England given;
her sights and sounds; dreams happy as her day;
and laughter, learnt of friends; and gentleness,
in hearts at peace, under an English heaven.

Rupert Brook
(1887-1915)

The grave of Private Thomas Patterson Tullock. He is now with his comrades in the Bayeux Cemetery in Normandy.

© The Museum of Army Chaplaincy, Amport House. The Lovegrove Papers

…some corner of a foreign field…

Glossary

a/r - Acting Rank
AAA – Anti-Aircraft Artillery
AAC - Army Air Corps (UK);
A&E - ammunition and explosives
AAMG - antiaircraft machine gun
A/B - Airborne
A/C - Aircraft;
A/Cdre - Air Commodore
ACM - Air Chief Marshal
Adj - Adjutant
ADM – Admiral, four star naval flag officer
ADMS – Assistant Director of Medical Services
ADS - Advanced Dressing Station
AEAF - Allied Expeditionary Air Forces
AEV - Armoured Engineer Vehicle
AFV - Armoured Fighting Vehicle
AIFV - Armoured Infantry Fighting Vehicle
ALG - Advance Landing Ground
AM - Air Marshal
Amb - Ambulance
Amn - Ammunition
APC - Armoured Personnel Carrier
AR – Automatic Rifle
ARMD - Armoured, Armour Corps
Arty - Artillery
ATR - Anti Tank Rifle
AVRE - Armoured Vehicle Royal Engineers
AVGP - Armoured Vehicle General Purpose
AVM - Air Vice Marshal
Battalion - An infantry unit containing between 500-800 men, and commanded by a Lieutenant-Colonel.
Bde – Brigade. A formation of two or more Battalions acting together under the overall command of a Brigadier
BDST - British Double Summer Time
BG - Battle Group
BGen - Brigadier General
BGHQ – Battle Group Headquarters
BOG —Beach Operations Group
Bren gun - A Light Machine Gun, carried by every British and Canadian platoon.
Brig - Brigadier (rank)
Brig. Gen. - Brigadier General (rank)
BSM - Battery Sergeant Major
Btn - Battalion
Bty – Battery
CAMC - Canadian Army Medical Corps
Capt. - Captain (rank)
CAS - Casualty
CCS – Casualty Clearing Station
Cdr - Commander (Naval rank)
CDS - Chief of the Defence Staff
CF - Canadian Forces
CG-4A Waco - The standard glider of the US Army. It was cheap and the design was easy to mass produce, however it was not as robust as the British Horsa and was prone to structural failure.
CL - Casualty List
CLH – Canadian Light Horse
Cmd - Command
Corps - A formation of two or more Divisions acting together as a self-contained unit under the overall command of a Lieutenant-General.
Coup de main - Literally translated as cut of hand, but in a military terms refers to a sudden surprise attack
Coy - Company A subdivision of a Battalion, commanded by a Major and consisting of approximately 120 men
CP - Command Post
CPO – Chief Petty Officer
CRE – Commander Royal Engineers
CSM - Company Sergeant Major
CWO - Chief Warrant Officer
DADMS - Deputy Assistant Director Medical Services
DD Tank - Duplex Drive Tank, designed to "swim" ashore.
DDF – Defensive Fire
DDMS - Deputy Director Medical Services
Division - A formation of two or more Brigades
DO - Duty Officer
D of W – Died of Wounds
DCM – Distinguished Conduct Medal
Det – Detachment
DFC – Distinguished Flying Cross
DFM – Distinguished Flying Medal
DSC – Distinguished Service Cross
DSM – Distinguished Service Medal
DSO – Distinguished Service Order
DUKW - an amphibious truck. The designation of DUKW is not a military acronym; the name comes from the model naming terminology used by GMC
"D" indicated a vehicle designed in 1942,
"U" meant "utility",
"K" indicated driven front wheels,
"W" indicated two powered rear axles.
Dvr – Driver
DZ - Drop Zone
ELG - Emergency Landing Ground
En – Enemy
Engr – Engineer
ETA - Estimated Time of Arrival
FAP - First Aid Post Fd - Field
FDS - Field Dressing Station
Fj - Fallschirmjäger - Paratrooper
F/L - Flight Lieutenant
FLAK - Anti-aircraft gun
Flt - Flight
FMP - Field Message Pad
F/O - Flying Officer
Fuh. - Fuehrer - Leader
FUP – Forming Up Point (or Position)
Fw. - Feldwebel - Sergeant
FW - Focke Wulfe
G/C - Group Captain
Gefr. - Gefreiter - Private soldier rank
Gen - General

Genlt - Generalleutnant - Lieutenant General
GenMaj - Generalmajor - Major General
GFM - Generalfeldmarschall - Field Marshall
Gnd - ground
Gnr - Gunner (private in artillery)
GOC - General Officer Commanding
Gp - Group
GP - General Purpose
GPR – Glider Pilot Regiment
GSW – Gunshot Wound
Hamilcar - The largest of the British gliders
HM – Her/His Majesty
HMCS - Her Majesty's Canadian Ship
HMG - Heavy Machine Gun
HMS - His/Her Majesty's Ship (UK)
Horsa - British glider
HptFw. - Hauptfeldwebel
Hptm. - Hauptmann - Captain
HQ - Headquarters
i/c - In charge
Int – Intelligence;
I/O - Intelligence Officer
JFHQ - Joint Force Headquarters
JG - Jagdgeschwader - Fighter wing
Kdo. - Kommando - Commando
Kdore. - Kommodore - Commodore
Kdr - Kommandeur - Commander
KG - Kampfgeschwader - Bomber wing
KIA - Killed In Action
KKptn. - Korvettenkapitan - Corvette Captain (Lieutenant-Commander)
Kptn.z.S - Kapitän zur See - Senior Naval Captain - Ger.
KSLI - Kings Shropshire Light Infantry
KwK - Kampfwagenkanone - armoured vehicle gun
KZ - Konzentrazionslager - Concentration Camp
Lb - Pound (weight)
LCA - landing craft, assault
LCI - landing craft, infantry
LCdr - Lieutenant Commander (Naval Rank), **LCol** - Lieutenant Colonel - US.
LCP - landing craft, personnel
LCpl – Lance Corporal
LCT - landing craft, tank
LCU - landing craft, utility
LCVP - landing craft, vehicle and personnel
Lee Enfield - Standard Rifle used by British Infantry
LeFH - Leichte FeldHaubitze - light field howitzer
LGen - Lieutenant General
LHS - left hand side
LMB – Light Mortar Battery
LMG - Light Machine Gun
LO - Liaison Officer
L of C - Lines of Communication
LR - Long Range
LS - Leading Seaman
LSMR - landing ship, Multiple rocket
LST - Landing Ship, Tank
Lt – Lieutenant - Leutnant
Lt. Gen. - Lieutenant General
Lt. Col. - Lieutenant Colonel (rank)

Lt (N) - Lieutenant (Navy),
Lw - Luftwaffe - Air Force
LZ - Landing Zone
Mallard - The codename to bring the Second Lift of the 6th Airborne to Normandy on the evening of the 6th June.
Maj - Major (rank)
Maj. Gen. - Major General (rank)
MBT – Main Battle Tank
MC - Military Cross
MDA - Main Defensive Area
MDS - Main Dressing Station
MFH - Military Field Hospital
MGen - Major General
MIA - Missing in Action
MO - Medical Officer (doctor)
MoD - Ministry of Defence - UK.
MP - Military Police
MTRU - Motor Transport Repair Unit
N/A - not applicable
NAAFI - Navy, Army, Air Force Institute
NCO – Non-Commissioned Officer (ranks other than officer ranks above private)
NOIC - Naval Officer In Command
NOK - Next of Kin
NYK – Not Yet Known
NTR – Nothing To Report
Obgfr. - Obergefreiter
Oblt. - Oberleutnant
Obs - Observation (USAAF)
OC - Officer Commanding (usually of company sized unit
OIC - Officer in Charge
OKW - Oberkommando der Wehrmacht - High command of German armed forces.
OOB - Order of Battle
OP - Observation Post
Op – Operation;
OR - Other Ranks, not Officers
OS - Ordinary Seaman (Basic)
PaK - Panzer Abwehr Kanone - Anti Tank Gun
PakSh. - PaK Schutze - AT gun (shooter)
PFF - Pathfinder Force
PIAT - Projector, Infantry, Anti Tank
PIR - Parachute Infantry Regiment
PIU - Photographic Intelligence Unit
Pl - Platoon.
P/O - Pilot Officer
PO - Petty Officer (Naval Rank equal to Warrant Officer)
POW - Prisoner of War
PR - Photographic Reconnaissance
Pte - Private
PzJgr - Panzer Jaeger - Tank Hunter (Tank Destroyer)
PzKpfw - Panzerkampfwagen - armoured fighting vehicle (usually tank)
QARANC - Queen Alexandra's Royal Army Nursing Corps
QM - Quartermaster

QMG - Quartermaster General
QMS - Quartermaster Sergeant
QOR - Queen's Own Rifles of Canada
RA - Royal Artillery (UK)
RAP - Regimental Aid Post
RAdm/RADM - Rear-Admiral (naval rank)
RAF - Royal Air Force (UK)
RAMC - Royal Army Medical Corps
RASC - Royal Army Service Corps
Recce - Reconnaissance
RCT - Regimental Combat Team
RHQ - **Regimental Headquarters**
RM - Royal Marine (UK)
RRR - Royal Regina Rifles
RSM - Regimental Sergeant Major
R/T - Radio Telephony
RTB - Return To Base
RTC – Returned To Corps
Rttm. - Rittmeister - Cavalry Captain
RTU - Return To Unit
RV – Rendezvous, Radio vehicle
S-Boot - Schnellboot - Fast Torpedo/gunboat
Sdkfz - sonderkraftwagen - special purpose vehicle (used for almost all military vehicles)
SHAEF - Supreme Headquarters Allied Expeditionary Force
Sig – Signalman; Signal
Sigs - Signals
SLt - Sub-Lieutenant
SNCO - Senior Non Commissioned Officer (Sergeant and above)
SP - Staging Post;
Spr – Sapper
Sq/Sqn/Sqd - Squadron
S/S - Staff Sergeant
S/Sgt. - Staff Sergeant
SS - Schutz Staffeln - Protection Detachments, armed wing of Nazi Party
Sten -Sub-machine gun, usually carried by British officers and NCO's.
StFw. - Stabsfeldwebel - Staff Sergeant - Ger.
StGefr. - Stabsgefreiter - Staff Corporal
Stick - The collective term used to describe a group of parachutists in a single aircraft.
Stn - Station
Sttrfuh - Stosstruppfuhrer
Stubafuh - Sturmbannfuhrer
StuG - Sturmgeschütz - Assault Gun (self-propelled)
SU - Support Unit; or Servicing Unit
Svc - Service
Tk – Tank
Tn - Transport
T/O - Take Off
Tonga - The codename given to the airlift on first night of the 6th Airborne Division's landing.
Tp – Troop
Tpr - Trooper (Private rank equivalent - cavalry and some police)
Tps - Troops
T/R - Transmitter/Receiver

U-Boot - Unterseeboot - Submarine
Uffz. - UnterOffizier - Under Officer
Universal Carrier - A tracked and lightly armoured vehicle used by the British for a number of duties
U/S – Unserviceable
US - United States
Ustfuh - Untersturmfuhrer
UXB - Unexploded Bomb
UXO - Unexploded Ordnance
VC – Victoria Cross
VCAS - Vice Chief of the Air Staff
VCDS – Vice Chief of the Defence Staff
VCP – Vehicle Check Point
Veh – Vehicle
WAAC - Women's Army Auxiliary Corps (UK)
WAAF - Women's Auxiliary Air Force
Wehrmacht - German army forces, not including the SS.
Wg - Wing
WIA - Wounded In Action
WN - Widerstandsnest, German strong point
WO - Warrant Officer; or War Office (UK)
WO1 - Warrant Officer First Class
WO2 - Warrant Officer Second Class
W/Op - Wireless Operator
W/T - Wireless Telegraphy (morse code communicatons)

Acknowledgements

My thanks to everybody who was happily helped and donated stories and photos to this project.

Geoffrey Slee of www.combinedops.com for his help and generosity is passing on stories and memories.

Paul Cheall for extracts from "Bill Cheall's memoir, Fighting Through from Dunkirk to Hamburg, is available in hardback through Pen and SWORD and at most book stores priced at £19.95. To read the first chapter and more, go to http://www.fightingthrough.co.uk/." Also for his help in supplying other memories and stories.

Richard Shilvock for spending so much time on the WN Spreadsheet.

Manny Trainor and Steve Shaw for proofreading.

Gareth Morlais for extracts from his Grandfathers diary. Signalman John Emrys on HMS Diadem.

Wilf Shaws family

Chris Buswell at www.qaranc.co.uk

Brian Moss for his memories

The Airborne Museum Pegasus Bridge, Normandy

Utah Beach Museum, Normandy

Museum de Debarquement, Arromanches, Normandy

Anna and William Able

Lyn Barker

Caitlin Firth

Lyn Barker for memories of her father.

D Day Museum, Portsmouth, www.ddaymuseum.co.uk

Green Howards Museum, Richmond, North Yorkshire

The Royal Marines Museum, Southsea, Hampshire, PO4 9PX.
www.royalmarinesmuseum.co.uk

Airborne Assault Museum - Duxford.

Dorsetshire Regiment Museum. Dorchester.

Canadian War Memorial
Merville Batterie Museum, Normandy

Maisey Batterie, Normandy

Juno Beach Centre, Normandy

Overlord Museum, Normandy,

Omaha Beach Museum, Normandy

Musee Airborne, St Mere Église, Normandy.

Commando Museum, Ouistreham, Normandy

The US National Archives and Records Administration (NARA)

The Army Medical Services Museum - Aldershot

The Museum of Army Chaplaincy, Amport House.

Jim Tuckwell.
http://durhamlightinfantry.webs.com/

Geoff Moss - Durham Light Infantry and his family

Bunderarchiv. Koblenz

The Eisenhower Museum for permission to reproduce documents.
http://www.eisenhower.archives.gov/

The New Forest Remembers Project.
http://www.newforestww2.org/

Mrs L Carrie (my mother) for her support

Bob Searl. www.pbase.com/rhssr

Mr E. Coffey (my husband) for his unending support, encouragement and cooking dinner when I ran out of time and for the huge amount of books purchased to help with my research.

The Project 70 Team

Baz Firth
Mike Crutch
Steven Shaw
Steve Darling
Jon Whitworth
Jamie Chestnutt
Manny Trainor

Biblography

Operation Neptune, Landings in Normandy, June 1944. Battle Summary No 39 (1947)

D Day Fortifications in Normandy - Steven J Zagola, Osprey

D Day Gold and Juno Beaches by Ken Ford - Osprey

D Day Omaha beach by Steven J Zaloga - Osprey

D Day Sword Beach and the British Airborne landings by Ken Ford - Osprey Publishing

D Day Utah Beach by Steven J Zaloga - Osprey

Normandy 6th June 1944 by Georges Bernage - Heimdal

D Day by Warren Tute, John Costello, Terry Hughes - Pan

Parnells History of the Second World War.

Commandos and Rangers, D Day Operations by Tim Saunders - Pen and Sword

Operation Tiger - The American Exercises at Slapton Sands

D Day and Normandy 60 years on - The History Channel

Pegasus Bridge by Stephen E. Ambrose

D Day by Stephen E. Ambrose

The German Battery at Longues sur Mer by Remy Desquesnes

Red Devils in Normandy by Georges Bernarge - Heimdal

D Day Operations manual - Haynes

10 Days to D Day by David Stafford - Abacus

Dawn of D Day by David Howarth - Collins

Various Regimental War and Personal Diaries

D-Day, Then and Now, after the battle series, volumes 1 and 2.

Gold, Juno, Sword, George Bernarge, Heimdal

Utah Beach, George Bernage, Dominique Francois, Heimdal.

Omaha Beach< Georges Bernage, Heimdal.

Battleground Europe:
- Sword Beach, Tim Kilvert-Jones
- Juno Beach, Tim Saunders
- Gold Beach -Jig, Tim Saunders
- Omaha Beach, Tim Kilvert-Jones
- Utah Beach, Carl Shilleto.
- Merville Battery and the Dives Bridges, Carl Shilleto

Normandy 1944, Niklas Zetterling, JJ Fedorowicz Publishing Inc.

The Manner of Men, 9 Para's heroic D Day Mission. by Stuart Tootal

Aboard a Coast Guard-manned LST bound from the French coast to England, German prisoners give a US Coast Guardsman the lowdown on how they happened to be captured. The prisoner with his finger pointing upward is translating his German colleague's remarks about Allied air power.
USNA

BOULEVARD COMMANDANT KIEFFER

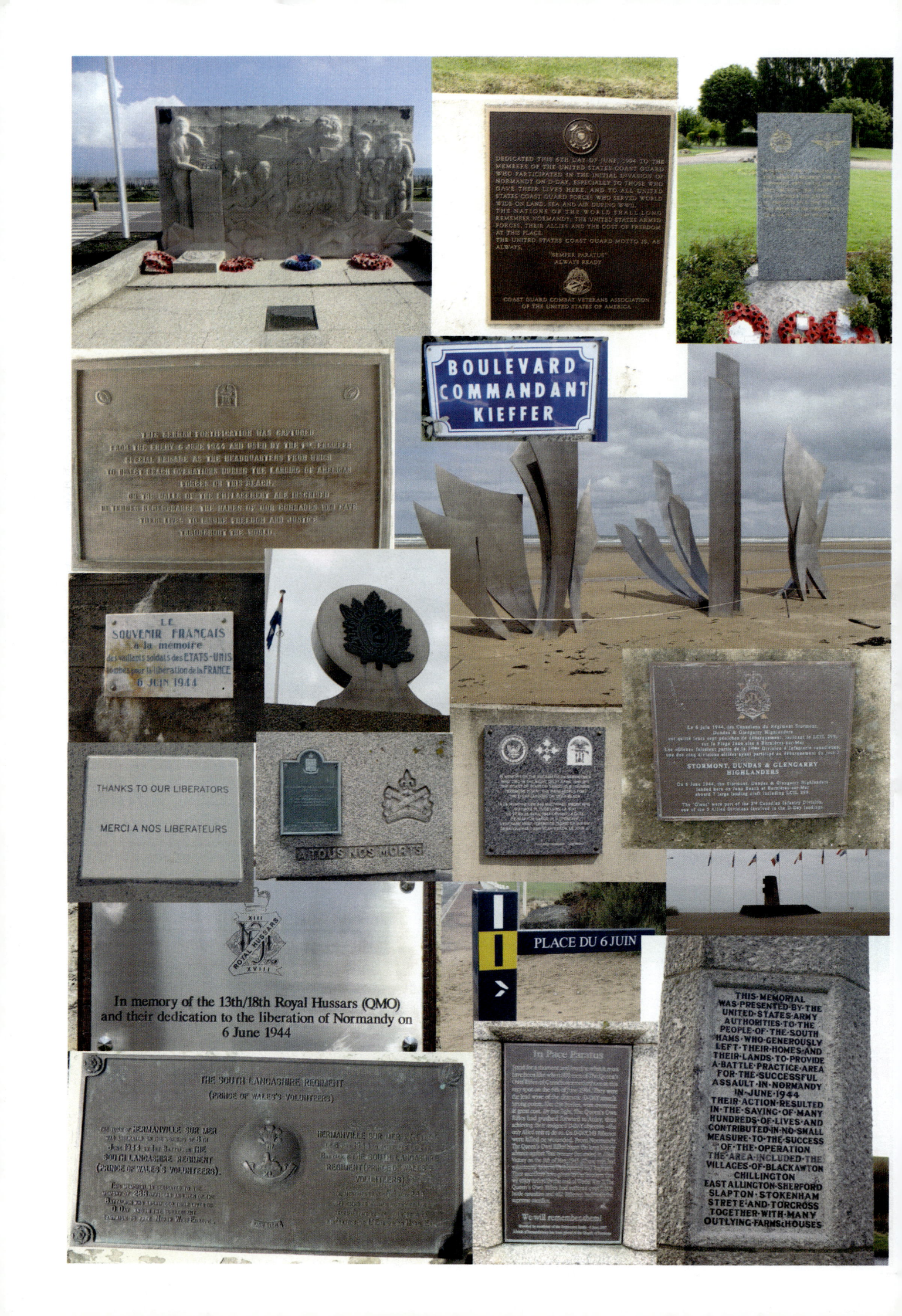

LE SOUVENIR FRANÇAIS
à la mémoire
des vaillants soldats des ETATS-UNIS
tombés pour la libération de la FRANCE
6 JUIN 1944

THANKS TO OUR LIBERATORS

MERCI A NOS LIBERATEURS

STORMONT, DUNDAS & GLENGARRY HIGHLANDERS

In memory of the 13th/18th Royal Hussars (QMO) and their dedication to the liberation of Normandy on 6 June 1944

PLACE DU 6 JUIN

THIS MEMORIAL WAS PRESENTED BY THE UNITED STATES ARMY AUTHORITIES TO THE PEOPLE OF THE SOUTH HAMS WHO GENEROUSLY LEFT THEIR HOMES AND THEIR LANDS TO PROVIDE A BATTLE PRACTICE AREA FOR THE SUCCESSFUL ASSAULT IN NORMANDY IN JUNE 1944 THEIR ACTION RESULTED IN THE SAVING OF MANY HUNDREDS OF LIVES AND CONTRIBUTED IN NO SMALL MEASURE TO THE SUCCESS OF THE OPERATION THE AREA INCLUDED THE VILLAGES OF BLACKAWTON CHILLINGTON EAST ALLINGTON SHERFORD SLAPTON STOKENHAM STRETE AND TORCROSS TOGETHER WITH MANY OUTLYING FARMS & HOUSES

THE SOUTH LANCASHIRE REGIMENT
(PRINCE OF WALES'S VOLUNTEERS)

BOULEVARD WINSTON CHURCHILL

A 300 METRES A L'EST
SE TROUVAIT L'AERODROME
B 11 DE LONGUES SUR MER
OPERATIONNEL DU 21 JUIN 1944
AU 4 SEPTEMBRE 1944 AU COURS
DE CETTE PERIODE J. AUBERTIN
P. CLOSTERMANN ET J. REMLINGER
HEROS DES F.A.F.L SE TROUVAIENT
EN CE LIEU AU SEIN DU
SQUADRON 602 · CITY OF GLASGOW
UNITES EGALEMENT PRESENTES
SQUADRON 132 · CITY OF BOMBAY
SQUADRON 453 RAAF
SQUADRON 441 RCAF

BERNIERES-SUR-MER
A SES VICTIMES
DU DEBARQUEMENT
JUIN 1944

IN PROUD MEMORY
OF OUR DEAD
1ST ENGINEER
SPECIAL BRIGADE
H-HOUR 0630
D DAY 6 JUNE 1944

6 JUIN 1944
A NOS LIBERATEURS
LA COMMUNE DE
SAINTE MARIE DU MONT
RECONNAISSANTE

ON JUNE 7TH 1944, THE SOLDIERS OF
N°3 COMMANDO FOUGHT ON THIS SITE
ICI LE 7 JUIN 1944 ONT COMBATTU
LES SOLDATS DU N°3 COMMANDO

ROYAL ENGINEERS